MW01195910

The Jailhouse Lawyer

The
Jailhouse
Lawyer

CALVIN DUNCAN

AND SOPHIE CULL

PENGUIN PRESS   NEW YORK   2025

PENGUIN PRESS
An imprint of Penguin Random House LLC
1745 Broadway, New York, NY 10019
penguinrandomhouse.com

Copyright © 2025 by Calvin Duncan and Sophie Cull

Penguin Random House values and supports copyright. Copyright fuels creativity, encourages diverse voices, promotes free speech, and creates a vibrant culture. Thank you for buying an authorized edition of this book and for complying with copyright laws by not reproducing, scanning, or distributing any part of it in any form without permission. You are supporting writers and allowing Penguin Random House to continue to publish books for every reader. Please note that no part of this book may be used or reproduced in any manner for the purpose of training artificial intelligence technologies or systems.

PP colophon is a registered trademark of Penguin Random House LLC.

What A Wonderful World
Words and Music by George David Weiss and Bob Thiele
Copyright © 1967 Range Road Music Inc., Quartet Music and Abilene Music
Copyright Renewed
All Rights for Range Road Music Inc. Administered by Round Hill Carlin, LLC
All Rights for Quartet Music Administered by BMG Rights Management (US) LLC
All Rights for Abilene Music Administered by Concord Sounds
   c/o Concord Music Publishing
All Rights Reserved Used by Permission
Reprinted by Permission of Hal Leonard LLC

Book design by Daniel Lagin

LIBRARY OF CONGRESS CATALOGING-IN-PUBLICATION DATA
Names: Duncan, Calvin, author. | Cull, Sophie, author.
Title: The jailhouse lawyer / Calvin Duncan, Sophie Cull.
Description: New York: Penguin Press, 2025. | Includes bibliographical references and index.
Identifiers: LCCN 2024043986 (print) | LCCN 2024043987 (ebook) |
   ISBN 9780593834305 (hardcover) | ISBN 9780593834312 (ebook)
Subjects: LCSH: Duncan, Calvin. | Jailhouse lawyers—Louisiana—Biography. |
   Lawyers—United States—Biography. | Legal assistance to prisoners—United States. |
   Law—Study and teaching—United States. | Criminal justice, Administration of—
   Corrupt practices—United States. | Judicial error—United States.
Classification: LCC KF373.D83 C85 2025 (print) | LCC KF373.D83 (ebook) |
   DDC 340.092 [B]—dc23/eng/20240918
LC record available at https://lccn.loc.gov/2024043986
LC ebook record available at https://lccn.loc.gov/2024043987

Printed in the United States of America
1st Printing

Some names and identifying characteristics have been changed to protect
the privacy of the individuals involved.

The authorized representative in the EU for product safety and compliance is
Penguin Random House Ireland, Morrison Chambers, 32 Nassau Street,
Dublin D02 YH68, Ireland, https://eu-contact.penguin.ie.

For Mamie

Contents

Part 3

Part 4

Part 5

The Jailhouse Lawyer

Prologue

W hether I shall turn out to be the hero of my own life, or whether that station will be held by anybody else, these pages must show."

For twenty-three years, I served as an inmate counsel, or jail-house lawyer, at Angola prison in Louisiana. I was incarcerated there for a murder I did not commit; I learned the law in its shadow.

For many of those years I taught a law class, and of all the literature I recited to my students from the front of the room, this line from Dickens was the one I quoted most.

I learned it not from reading *David Copperfield*, but John Irving's *The Cider House Rules*, a novel about an orphan named Homer Wells who, like me, grew up without any memory of his mother. Like Homer, my and my sister's efforts to belong in somebody else's home were largely a failure. From the ages of six and seven, we knew we were on our own, and no help was coming.

As a teenager, it became apparent that my circumstances weren't going to improve, only my ability to take things I was lacking. I protected my younger sister by stealing food and clothing for her, and getting into fights with boys who paid her too much attention. I stole televisions to make sure I had enough cash to pay my own bond if I got arrested, so I wouldn't have to call on my aunts. Being a man didn't mean escaping the streets, only surviving them.

In prison, the notion of being a man narrowed even further. In that environment, the whole goal is to rob you of your concept of self. To the guards, we were children. To the lawyers, we were a means to an end. To the institution, we were a source of job creation. To each other, we were a conquest. Being willing to kill to protect my body from interference—that was being a man.

I was lucky enough to survive that chapter of prison life. At Angola, in the Main Prison, I saw some of the older guys reading books, and I started to wonder if perhaps a man is someone who liberates his mind by reading. So I read Martin Luther King Jr., Dante, and Harper Lee. I spent my time with guys who were focused on helping themselves and helping others. I became friends with Woodfox, Hooks and King, Mwalimu, Gary, Norris, Checo, and Wilbert.

None of us had any realistic chance of getting out of prison at that time. Good conduct wasn't going to help us. Getting a certificate wasn't, either. Our fates were sealed. We were all serving life sentences.

But that didn't stop us from asking the question: What makes a man?

We had come to understand how ludicrous it was that our identities as Black men were reduced to our behinds. No one asked: "What do you stand for?" Or "Are there any rights you have that are worth fighting to protect?" Nobody expected us to live honorable lives, but we weren't willing to succumb to that view.

So we helped each other get our education. We taught each other the law. We drafted bills for the legislature and organized our families to support their passage. We invited judges and lawmakers to meet with us at the prison. We published investigative journalism. We led reentry programs. We sent money home to each other's children. And when miracles happened and some of us started getting out of Angola, we made sure we never forgot the men we'd left behind.

When I finally made it out of prison, I learned not to talk about it. You realize people don't want to hear it. Even those of us who were inside together will only mention certain things. We can't share too openly about our experiences, because we're still maintaining the version of ourselves that we crafted inside.

A few days after my release, I met a young Australian woman named Sophie, who worked with me at a law office in New Orleans. We were taking trips to Shreveport, Louisiana, to campaign alongside churches and civil rights organizations for the removal of a Confederate flag from the local courthouse lawn. On these car rides, I finally found a place where I could talk honestly about my experiences. Sophie asked me about my life in prison and listened to my stories with openness. Having the opportunity to share without being judged helped me take stock of my life. Instead of being Calvin the inmate lawyer, or Calvin the innocent man, or Calvin the orphan, or Calvin the returning citizen, I started to see myself as a man in full. When we decided to work on a book together, we went about it the truest way we knew: my personal account, shared with my friend, who had a deep appreciation of the forces I was up against. If my journey has taught me one thing, it's that God puts unexpected people in our lives at the moment we need them the most.

We as a society don't get to hear stories of Black men helping each other. Perhaps if people were allowed to tell, and to hear, such stories, then we would be more inclined to ask why our country devalues Black children the way we do. Why we make a point to figure out if the whales are coming too close to the shore, or if the eagles aren't hatching enough of their young, or if the bees are dying off, but when it comes to the conditions experienced by Black boys in our neighborhoods, we already seem to know all we need to know.

I want the world to know that a group of Black men, in the darkest place in America—the incarceration capital of the world—rose above our situation to help each other.

May these pages show that it's the people from whom we expect the least who, in the face of impossible odds, do extraordinary things.

Calvin Duncan

Part 1

Well, then, Homer, I expect you to be of use.

DR. LARCH,

THE CIDER HOUSE RULES

1982

Calvin had a sixth sense for being watched.

He calmly folded the jeans he'd been holding against his waist and scanned the workwear supply store.

The other students from the Job Corps campus rummaged through piles of flannel and cotton, still giddy at being chosen to come down the mountain. They were allowed to spend their clothing vouchers only once every few months.

Calvin met his supervisor's eye and noticed the same feeling of foreboding that had woken him that morning, an old warning from childhood that signaled the approach of danger.

The doorbell chimed, and a customer walked in. The cool draft sliced through his unease. This wasn't New Orleans, he reminded himself. He shouldn't always expect the worst.

"Calvin." His supervisor gestured him over. "We need to get back to campus."

"What's happening?" he asked.

"You've got visitors."

YEARS LATER, WHEN CERTAINTY WAS SLIPPING AWAY FROM HIM, CAL-vin would think back to his time on Mount Hood and be sure of only three things:

First, the lake. Not Timber Lake, the official name of the Job Corps campus where he studied, but the crescent of water at the campus's middle, too small to have a name. He passed it each morning on his way to the welding workshop, still and iridescent—a map to find his way home.

Second was the quiet. Or rather, the sounds of quiet: pebbles scraping under his boots and snowdrifts gathering on the dormitory roof—moments of solitude that taught him what peace felt like. A lesson he tucked beneath his ribs for safekeeping.

And third, those three words: "You've got visitors." The ending of the story he had worked so hard for, where he made it out of New Orleans to seize a future of his own making, and the beginning of this story, the one he couldn't seem to escape, when they came looking for him on the mountain.

THE STUDENTS GRUMBLED THEIR WAY ONTO THE MINIBUS. CALVIN found an empty row and sank low in his seat, hoping the other boys wouldn't suspect he was the reason for their early return.

As the bus pulled onto the road, he sat quietly, listening to his classmates joke and harass each other.

Who would come all the way to Oregon to see him? Not his family. Not even Mamie would make a trip like that.

His mind hurtled back to a phone call with his aunt Brunetta months earlier. He'd only called home twice since leaving New Orleans in January. Mamie, his sister, was the reason he bothered at all.

"I saw your face on the news." Brunetta's fearful tone had caught him by surprise. "A white boy got shot near the Quarter, and now the police are looking for you."

"I wasn't near any shooting, Aunty," he protested.

But she wouldn't let it go. "You think I don't know the face of my own child? That was your photo. You keep your head down, you heard me?"

He had pushed the call out of his mind, sure the police would realize their mistake and move on.

But what if they didn't?

As Portland's suburbs receded into farmland, a snowcapped peak rose in the center of the bus's windshield. Normally, the sight filled Calvin with awe, but today it left him unsettled.

Oregon had never been part of his plan. Six months earlier, he wouldn't have known where to find the state on a map. He never imagined a world of towering mountain ranges, ferns as large as palm trees, pristine river water he could drink from a canteen. Yet at the first sight of Mount Hood, he knew he'd escaped New Orleans just to find it. As though it had been in his sights all along.

A product of President Johnson's "Great Society," the Job Corps trained young people in vocational skills while giving them a place to live. Students were usually referred there by school counselors or juvenile courts, but Calvin had sought out the opportunity on his own, aware of the program from an earlier stint at a campus in Texas when he was sixteen.

Though unfamiliar at first, the mountain's beauty quickly pulled Calvin in—the bird chatter at dawn, morning frosts, the smell of leaf litter on his path to the welding workshop.

While he felt somewhat distant from the other students, it didn't take long for him to find his place. Most boys at Timber Lake were from rural towns in Oregon, with a few kids from California; only Calvin came from the South. Early on, he befriended a boy from Oakland who confided in him about a debt he owed to an older kid over unpaid weed. Calvin offered to settle it with a fight, and they had remained allies since.

The students began their days with classes to prepare for their GED exams, then spent their afternoons learning a trade. At night, they played basketball in the gym or snuck into the woods behind the dormitories to shoot dice and box; on weekends, they explored a three-mile stretch of beach on the Columbia River called Rooster Rock. When summer brought berry season, Calvin delighted in the fruit at nearby farms, the purple juice staining his fingers for days. Beyond the lush scenery, however, it was the quiet that captivated him most. Much later, he would remember Timber Lake as the first place he felt safe.

As the bus began its ascent, gears groaning at the winding road, Calvin felt a sense of calm. The trees outside his window rose like a fortress.

Twenty minutes later, they turned down a dirt road, and the campus came into view. On one side, the dormitory buildings dotted a gentle rise. On the other, old-growth pines gave way to a narrow lake the color of the sky.

In the quiet of early mornings, before the campus was fully

awake, Calvin would sit alone by the lake, thinking of his sister. He imagined her passing by the old-timers on her way to school—the ones who perched with their lines on the flats of the Mississippi, waiting for a tired catfish to give up the ghost.

He wished Mamie could have experienced Mount Hood with him. If only people from New Orleans could see this place.

When the bus pulled to a stop, he noticed Bob Hartsuyker, the campus head counselor, standing at the entrance to the administration building.

Another sign something was wrong.

The boys clambered out in single file, one playfully punching Calvin's arm on the way past. Calvin waited a beat, then walked over to Hartsuyker.

"Two detectives from the local sheriff's office are inside." The counselor's usually cheerful expression was drawn.

Calvin crossed his arms, fighting his fear. Perhaps sitting down with the detectives would help. If the Oregon authorities realized he had no connection to the crime, the New Orleans police would continue their investigation elsewhere.

He followed Hartsuyker into the building. Mack Ferrick, the campus director, met them at his office.

Inside, two men were waiting: one lanky and stone-faced, the other round with small, watchful eyes. The round one directed Calvin to sit across from him at the long conference table, while the tall one posted himself by the door.

Calvin maintained an outward calm, but their presence unsettled his resolve. It wasn't the prospect of being questioned that bothered him—he'd had more than a few brushes with the law. It was the intrusion. New Orleans wasn't supposed to follow him here.

When they were six and seven years old, Mamie and Calvin had unexpectedly lost their mother. Though their father was living, they knew the world as orphans. They spent years being shuttled between aunts, sleeping on floors in crowded apartments and squirreling meals from neighbors' houses. At ten, Calvin began shoplifting food from corner stores; at sixteen, burglarizing houses. He didn't mind his stints in juvenile detention—he saw friends and received three meals a day—but he hated leaving Mamie alone. Each was all the other had in a city that seemed bent on destroying them.

Earlier that year, Calvin seized a chance to leave New Orleans, no small feat for a teen in his position. After hitching a ride to Los Angeles, he stayed with his cousin until the Job Corps sent him to Oregon. Leaving Mamie behind wasn't easy, but she was the reason he was compelled to go. Once he could send money home, she could plan her own escape.

His other motivation was his daughter, Ayana, born shortly after he arrived at Timber Lake. Ayana's mother, Earline, was Calvin's high school sweetheart, and though they were no longer together, she still relied on him for support.

Ayana's birth had sharpened Calvin's ambition. He had earned his welding certificates and was on the path to a high school diploma. By the end of the year, he wanted to graduate from the Job Corps and enlist in the military. Seeing the Pacific Northwest inspired him to do what most of his peers couldn't imagine: travel the world, survive his twenty-first birthday, make a life for his family.

Yet New Orleans had a way of ruining things, which is what worried him about sitting down with these men.

"I'm Lieutenant Reed and this is Detective Peterson. We're from the Clackamas County Sheriff's Office," said the round deputy. "Here to ask you a few questions."

Calvin nodded.

"I understand that you're known here as Calvin Jones. Are you, in fact, Calvin Duncan?"

He hesitated, unsure if he wanted to answer their questions. "Uh-huh."

Three years earlier, he'd been expelled from the Job Corps in Texas for fighting. When he decided to rejoin the program out West, he forged his cousin's birth certificate and used his surname.

Neither Hartsuyker nor Ferrick blinked at the deputy's question, already aware that Calvin went by Duncan. Many students used more than one name.

"How long have you been here?"

"About four months."

"Did you ever reside in Louisiana?"

"Yeah."

"We're here about a murder in New Orleans. We need to ask you some questions about the night it happened."

Calvin studied the deputy doing the talking, the one named Reed. His cheeks were the color of a ripe tomato.

He sensed Hartsuyker surveying the officer in his periphery and recalled their first conversation, where Hartsuyker offered an orientation of the campus. The counselor advised Calvin to avoid the small towns at the mountain base, especially after dark. Clackamas County was a rural area in a state that, for much of its early history, had forbidden Black people from living there. That threat had felt distant from within the campus confines—until now. He swallowed, suddenly understanding the danger.

"I don't know anything about any murder," he told Reed.

"We have information from the New Orleans police suggesting you and your friend were involved in a robbery on August 7, 1981. Do you wish to make a statement?"

"No. Like I said, I don't know nothing."

The deputy's eyes narrowed. "The police from New Orleans say you do. Why don't you make it easier on all of us and tell the truth?"

Calvin shrugged. "'Cause I don't know what you're talking about."

"Did you have any knowledge that you were wanted by the police?"

"Yeah, my aunty told me it was in the news."

Reed glanced at his partner, who scribbled on a notepad. "An eyewitness identified you as the perpetrator that night."

"Who?"

"A woman. She was with the person that you and your friend killed. She says there was a scuffle for the gun, that you fired. Who's the other person that was with you?"

Calvin recognized the officer's move. He turned to Hartsuyker, who shot him a regretful look.

"I don't have nothing more to say," he told the deputy firmly.

Reed's nose and mouth curled like he smelled something rotting. "Why did you leave Louisiana in the first place? Because the police were looking for you?"

"I came here for the Job Corps, to learn welding. I'm signing up for in the military."

"That's a good story. I think you needed money. I think you robbed this man, and when he resisted, you panicked and shot him."

"Wherever you're getting that from, it's wrong." Calvin's intuition urged him to flee the office, though he dared not run.

Mercifully, Ferrick interjected. "He's told you everything he knows. I think that's enough."

Reed pushed back his chair. "We'll have to finish this down at the jail, then."

"I didn't have nothin' to do with it," Calvin protested. "You have the wrong guy."

"It doesn't look that way to the New Orleans police, I'm afraid. Calvin Duncan, aka Calvin Jones, I am placing you under arrest—"

Calvin turned to Ferrick. "Mr. Mack, they have the wrong guy!"

Ferrick looked shaken. "You'll have to go with them for now, Calvin, but we'll get this sorted out."

A mix of fear and embarrassment rose in Calvin's chest.

"Please, don't handcuff me here," he pleaded with Reed. "I don't want the others to see."

The deputies led him out of the rear of the building to shield him from the walkway to the dormitories, but by the time they reached the patrol car, Calvin could feel the stares of his classmates at his back.

Ferrick and Hartsuyker stood by while the lanky officer opened the rear passenger door and motioned for Calvin to get in.

Calvin stopped short at the sight of the dark cabin. The smell of the worn vinyl seats made him want to vomit.

He lifted his gaze to the lake, clinging to the image of the still blue water until the officer pushed him down into the back seat.

This is a mistake, he told himself. I'll come right back.

CALVIN CRANED HIS NECK TOWARD THE SHADOWY OUTLINE OF HIS aunt Brunetta's face. He could see her lips moving through the glass pane, but the swirl of voices and body odor made it difficult to focus. He was desperate to get back upstairs.

"I let you out of my sight and look what happens . . ." she spat into the window speaker, arm stretched out against the wall.

Brunetta reminded him of a mafia boss, hard-nosed and always focused on an endgame beyond his view. She would defend him to the hilt when the police were involved, then seemed to forget him the rest of the time. He often wondered why he and Mamie had ended up with her—why she was so determined to be the guardian of children she couldn't care for.

"Boy, let me tell you somethin'." Brunetta turned her voice low, and now he could hear her every word. "You in a place where they fuck over boys. *You beat their fuckin' ass.*"

He pushed a knuckle into his eye. He didn't know what she meant by that, and he didn't want to.

None of this was happening the way he'd imagined. He thought the Oregon authorities would question him and then return him to Mount Hood. Instead, they'd left him for over a week in a solitary jail cell before handing him to two officers from the New Orleans Police Department. No one—not the sheriff's office in Oregon, nor the judge who signed the extradition order, nor the New Orleans detectives who came to collect him, seemed to care that he knew nothing of the crime. On the contrary, they treated him as though he was already condemned.

Brunetta said she would return with some boxer briefs and put a few dollars on his account. Then a deputy took him upstairs and sat him on a chair in the hallway.

Central Lockup was part of a sprawling collection of austere buildings near the corner of Tulane Avenue and Broad Street that made up the Orleans Parish Prison. Calvin had been there before. When he worked in the French Quarter, the police had arrested him more than once for "obstructing the sidewalk" while walking home from a late shift, throwing him in their patrol van along with other Black kids they wanted out of the tourist hotspot. He could usually count on Brunetta to get him out by morning, charges dropped. But this time, he wasn't going anywhere. He'd been booked on a charge of first-degree murder.

Minutes turned into an hour. His mind raced with questions. How did he end up here? Who was the person he was accused of killing? The television news reported the victim's name was David Yeager, but Calvin had heard nothing else about the man. Why did the police decide he was a suspect, and what made them want to come all the way to Oregon to arrest him? Probably because the murder happened on Esplanade Avenue, he thought.

Finally, two deputies came to collect him. They pulled him aside and ordered him to take off his jail uniform of army fatigues. Calvin fixed his eyes on a point on the wall, trying to conceal his rage while the deputies moved their gloved hands over him. They snickered at his nakedness the way his cousins used to snicker at his sores during a bout of Indian fire. He swallowed hard, knowing he would have to endure this torment every time he was moved within the jail. He retreated in his mind to Timber Lake, willing the memory to steady him.

The deputies told him to dress and returned him upstairs to the third floor of the House of Detention. Built in 1965, the "House of D" was where individuals were held in custody until their first court appearances or until they made bond. Everyone was lumped together, regardless of their alleged offenses, from DUIs to serious assaults. With minimal oversight and guards delegating authority to favored detainees, it was a chaotic environment where physical strength often prevailed.

The deputies shoved Calvin into a hallway and waited as he walked to the third cell. When he was first moved there late the night before, he was too exhausted to take in his surroundings, still hopeful that he would be bonded out.

Now he counted ten beds and two toilets, with as many as thirty men packed inside, and as he stepped forward—hearing the door slide shut behind him—he knew he was on his own.

The strongest men had already claimed the bunks, and the extra mattresses on the floor were also occupied. Disheveled men in the throes of withdrawal and wide-eyed teens, the most vulnerable of the bunch, had to sit on bare concrete by the toilets, where vomit and feces were backing up in the bowls. Calvin choked at the stench.

Surely, this was the place Brunetta had warned him about.

He noticed an old classmate from high school across the cell and nodded, but the boy quickly looked down at the floor. It wasn't a coincidence that Calvin would see people he knew in jail. For many in his circles, stints in prison were a part of life—a sign of luck, even, because at least you hadn't been killed on the street.

With the deputies out of sight, Calvin watched as the more formidable men sized up their marks, coaxing the younger ones with promises of protection. When necessary, they flashed a shank. They extracted what they wanted with ease: jewelry, a pair of shoes, a blow job. Calvin was stunned to see his former classmate having sex within minutes of the cell door closing. He wasn't sure whether to call it rape. He only knew he would never presume that older men deserved respect again.

Cortisol had been flooding Calvin's brain for two days straight. Despite his weariness, he stayed alert through the night, watching for any movement from the corner of his eye. Whatever happens, he thought, I'm gonna leave this jail a man.

The following day, while some of the men were out on the tier, Calvin retreated to a mattress by the bars, content to be on the floor, where it was cooler. He'd bartered with another guy in the cell for a box cutter blade, which he'd tucked inside his drawers. Feeling more secure, he stretched out his fatigued limbs on the mattress, shoulder blades digging into the floor.

Sleep tugged at him, an outgoing tide trying to pull him away. He gave in and closed his eyes. Gazing into black, Mount Hood appeared, filling his vision with ice and rock. He felt a snap of cold; smelled sweet violets in early bloom. Then a noise stirred him awake—the rattle of the commissary cart—and he realized where he was, his momentary peace shattered.

The commissary brought the men to the bars. Heavy-bodied, Calvin willed himself to follow. He needed stamps. If he wrote Mack Ferrick and Bob Hartsuyker, maybe they would keep a place for him at Timber Lake until he could return.

At the cell door, he spotted Lorenzo, a distant cousin, nodding him over.

Only two years Calvin's senior, Lorenzo was already known as one of the more dangerous men in New Orleans. He had survived multiple shootings, seemingly impervious to bullets.

"Hey, brah." They dapped through the bars. "It's been a while."

It was close to a hundred degrees in the cells, and the only windows were on the walkways, so, like the others, Calvin had stripped down to his underwear. Lorenzo pointed at the briefs Calvin had received from his aunt, which hugged his thighs.

"You can't walk around in those come-get-me drawers," he said, grinning. "Get changed, quick."

Embarrassed, Calvin hurried to put on his army fatigues.

Lorenzo explained he was the "tier rep," a special status that allowed him to spend most of his day outside his cell and control the food portions, giving him leverage over the rest of the tier.

Despite their connection, Calvin was under no illusion that knowing Lorenzo would spare him from harm. In here, it was every man for himself.

GOD HAD BEEN PREPARING CALVIN TO SURVIVE A PLACE LIKE ORLEANS Parish Prison all his life. From a young age, he learned to maneuver through danger and grit his teeth through indignities, determined that one day he would escape them.

Calvin's mother, Mary Ann Duncan, who went by "Tiny," had died of breast cancer in her late twenties—or so the aunts said. No one in the family ever spoke about Tiny after she was gone, and Calvin had his doubts that she was dead. He knew his sister doubted, too, the way she cried for their mother, as though Tiny might still hear her and suddenly appear.

Neither child could recall their mother's face. They had no photos of her, no stories to give her form. Their last memory was being separated from her just weeks after they'd returned to New Orleans from Baton Rouge, where she had been trying to flee an abusive partner (something she'd attempted repeatedly before). They moved in with Brunetta, and soon after, their mother vanished. Calvin had no recollection of her dying, only that one day she was gone, and they never heard from her again.

Tiny also had two older sons, but by then, they had gone to live with their father, Terry Duncan. Though Calvin and Mamie were named after Terry, a revelation unfolded with time: they were not Duncans at all. In truth, their biological father was Herbert Owens, the man from whom Tiny had been trying to escape. At least, that's what the aunts said.

It was during a separation from Terry Duncan that Tiny first noticed Herbert Owens, recently returned from Angola prison, at a neighbor's house and asked to meet him. Though their connection was immediate, the neighbor forever regretted making the introduction. It wasn't long before Tiny was held captive in the relationship and forced to live with another woman. The woman conceived Owens's child only weeks after Tiny conceived Calvin—a half sister Calvin would never know.

After a time, Tiny managed to escape from Owens, but only by staying in hiding. As a result, Calvin and Mamie also lived invisible lives. It wasn't until the second grade, after his mother was gone, that Calvin first attended school regularly. His excitement at finally being in a classroom was tempered by the realization that, though he understood the spoken word perfectly well, the written word—which his classmates already seemed to grasp—was a mystery to him. Even the alphabet was unfamiliar, and the shame made him shy.

In the years that followed Tiny's disappearance, Calvin and Mamie moved eleven times and attended seven different schools. They never stayed somewhere they knew to call home, only a confusing rotation of apartments and houses they were thrust into without warning and pulled out of just the same.

The place they typically found themselves was the one they despised the most—a white double shotgun on Clouet Street in the Desire neighborhood, where their aunt Nema and uncle Trim lived.

Calvin didn't know Aunt Nema's real name or relationship to his mother, only that she was a great-aunt with whom Brunetta had some financial arrangement. Brunetta left Calvin and Mamie, as well as her own daughter, on Nema's doorstep whenever she went away. Since she was a horse groomer who traveled with the races, they were left there often.

In Calvin's memory, the house on Clouet Street was nothing short of a war zone. Of Nema's six children, four—all in their late teens and early twenties—still lived at home, and for reasons beyond Calvin's understanding, they regarded their much younger, orphaned cousins with contempt.

During middle school, Calvin frequently contracted impetigo in the summer months. The neighborhood kids called it Indian fire for the clusters of stinging blisters that wept fluid and spread when he scratched. Though a quick trip to the doctor would have cured Calvin, Aunt Nema wouldn't arrange it. So he endured the painful rash for months on end, hiding his legs beneath long pants at school. His gym teacher punished him with F grades for refusing to wear shorts in class, never investigating the reason for his disobedience.

Calvin didn't know whether it was under the guise of "treatment" or openly a game, but his cousins frequently ran baths of hot water with generous helpings of salt and chased him through the house until they had him in hand. The burning sensation when they plunged him into the salt water was unlike anything he'd experienced. But his screams didn't summon help from Aunt Nema; instead, she stood by while her children laughed.

Other flashes of cruelty would later stick in Calvin's mind: Aunt Nema throwing his and Mamie's food on the floor, yelling, "Here, dogs; here, dogs," while her children ate at the table. Or the sneer in her voice when she told him, "I'll be glad when Brunetta come get y'all." Even as a young boy, he knew it was strange that an adult would hate children the way Aunt Nema hated him and Mamie. Still, he was powerless to change it.

He responded by trying to make up the difference, taking charge of his and his sister's care. At night, he washed their few pieces of hand-me-down clothing in the bathroom basin for school the next day and mended holes in their pants with dental floss. At age ten, he began helping a man named Mr. Brown cut people's lawns in the summers; at twelve, he was working shifts at a corner store. He longed to be old enough to choose where he lived, to buy himself and Mamie their own food and clothing, to overpower his cousins in a fight. He bided his time, reminding himself that before long he'd be a man.

In time, Calvin and Mamie did find a way to escape Aunt Nema's house, though their lack of a stable home entailed new dangers in their teens. While Calvin's forays into burglary and selling stolen goods got him into trouble with the law, he worried more about his sister, having witnessed older men use money and drugs to lure young women into prostitution. As they grew older, Calvin was a strict guardian, monitoring Mamie's interactions and ensuring she had enough money to stay out of trouble. Despite being only a year apart, their relationship resembled that of a parent and child.

Whenever Calvin tried to piece together his early life, he confronted an unsettling truth: he understood remarkably little. A nurse at the Texas Job Corps revealed he was blind in one eye—a fact that had somehow eluded him. The same mystery surrounded the winding scars circling his lower leg. It became clear that his family had withheld information from him, another reason he refused to accept his mother's death. Certain incidents, like the Indian fire, seemed to lie dormant in his memory, only to be awakened by a present torment, like being strip-searched in the House of Detention. He lived with a lingering disquiet, a pervading sense of uncertainty that made life in a place like the parish jail, unpredictable and manipulative as it was, somehow more manageable.

His best chance at survival was to focus on the future. Mount Hood, once beyond his imagination, was now his surest hope.

THOUGH THE LAW SAID IT SHOULD TAKE ONLY THREE DAYS FOR A DE-fendant to be brought before a court after his arrest, nineteen days passed before Calvin made his first appearance in front of a judge. In the New Orleans jail, these sorts of civil rights violations were common, and most people were too poor to afford counsel, let alone seek recourse.

The men in Calvin's section of court were brought up from the jail in fatigues and slippers, their shackles locked together in a long chain. As they shuffled down the grand marble hallway of the courthouse's second floor, white spectators, mostly lawyers, stopped their conversations to watch the line of Black men pass by.

Once seated on a bench at the front of the courtroom, Calvin turned to find his aunt Gail already waiting in the gallery, with Mamie beside her. He met his sister's gaze, and she gave one of her half smiles, anguish tugging at the corners of her lips.

Aunt Gail pressed a hand to her chest and opened her mouth in a silent cry. Calvin nodded to her, signaling he was all right.

Gail was Herbert Owens's cousin and the aunt who had whole-heartedly embraced Calvin and Mamie as her own. She once confided that before their mother died, Tiny had asked her to take them in. But when the time came, Brunetta refused to let Calvin and Mamie live with her. Calvin often wondered how their lives might have turned out if they'd grown up in Gail's care.

Seated on her other side was Earline, cradling an infant in her lap. She gave Calvin a small wave.

It was Calvin's first time seeing his daughter. Earline gently turned Ayana around, revealing her long lashes and bright eyes to him. Although Earline had sent pictures after her birth, nothing compared to seeing his daughter in person. Calvin absorbed every detail, hungry to discover all he had missed. But as he continued to observe her from afar, an uneasiness crept in. He had been absent from her entire beginning, a stranger she would meet for the first time in handcuffs. Would she even know who he was? He turned back to the front of the room, troubled.

The bailiff announced Judge Frank Shea. The gallery stood as a robed man with deep-set eyes and graying hair took his seat at the bench, lighting a cigar. Elected in 1963 as the youngest judge in Louisiana's criminal courts, Shea had long since become a fixture of the system. His early campaigns promised a lightning-fast docket, and he delivered, cutting motion hearings and trial times to the bone.

Shea often inserted himself into proceedings, questioning witnesses and jurors directly while curtailing lawyers' ability to do the same—a reckless devotion to speed that trampled basic protections for the accused. He even barred attorneys he disliked from practicing in his courtroom.

Calvin watched in astonishment as the judge churned through the docket like a butcher at a meat market, shouting case numbers and ordering lawyers about as lackeys. He hurled insults at any person who was slow or unprepared, and the lawyers responded with total acquiescence. Nobody in the room seemed concerned with whether the shackled men understood what was happening. All that mattered was placating the lion on the bench.

At some point in the chaos, Calvin heard his name. Across the room, a white man in a suit announced that Duncan was a capital case. A lawyer rose to tell the judge that he was Calvin's counsel for the arraignment. He motioned for Calvin to stand up and answer the charge.

"Not guilty, Your Honor."

The judge set a hearing date for pretrial motions, including a motion to suppress the confession, then sped on to the next case.

Calvin sat down again, bewildered. No one explained what would happen next. As he was filed out of the courtroom moments later, one question gripped him: What confession?

Aunt Gail brought Mamie to the jail after court. Calvin had been longing to see his sister for months, but now he found himself distracted.

"How's things?" he asked her through the mesh.

"I'm fine."

The aunts always said he and Mamie looked like twins, with

plums for cheeks and hazel eyes. But Calvin never forgot that he was the older one.

"You stayin' by Gail?"

"Yep, at least for a few months."

"Don't let Chanisse get you in trouble."

She rolled her eyes. "I won't. Listen, when you think you'll be getting out of here?"

"Soon, Mamie."

She tried to smile, but the flex of her lips was so slight he could barely make it out through the wire.

Calvin turned to Gail, hoping she would know what to say.

"Brunetta says she's found a lawyer."

Calvin flushed with relief.

"Once I got a lawyer, this is gonna get sorted out," he said, turning back to Mamie.

She smiled again, and this time, he could see it.

"I can't wait for you to come home," she said.

AFTER HIS ARRAIGNMENT, CALVIN WAS MOVED TO THE TENTH FLOOR of the House of Detention to await trial.

"It's Tuesday," Lorenzo reminded him as he was being moved. "Everyone that gets a visit today is most likely gonna get money on their books. You need your tennies on tonight. Gotta be quick on your feet."

Calvin approached the upper floor with dread, knowing he would have to negotiate his place in the new cell.

Eyes turned on him as he entered. Once again, all the beds were occupied, and the cell was crowded. He was grateful to find an empty mattress on the floor.

Dinner was a tray of white bread soaked in gravy, unidentifiable chunks floating in a tepid pool. Calvin pushed the mess around his plate until he worked his way up to eating it.

After dinner, the door to the cell slid open. The men quickly moved onto the tier, where a row of tables was bolted to the floor.

The atmosphere was stiff with tension, games of chess and checkers already humming at the tables. Calvin recalled Lorenzo's warning.

He spotted a card game and sat down to join, hoping to turn a profit with the few dollars Aunt Brunetta had put on his account.

Once the game was underway, he threw his cards aggressively onto the pile. One of the other players responded at a snail's pace, closely studying each play.

Calvin's frustration bubbled up. "Hurry up, man."

"Why you buggin'?"

"You hopin' I get bored of watching so you can hide your cards when I'm not looking? I ain't stupid."

"Who says you ain't?"

Anger and exhaustion fused in a gratifying blast. Calvin launched himself across the table and punched the kid's jaw. There was an audible crunch. Nearby chess players stepped back as the cards scattered and the boys jumped onto the table.

Calvin was the superior fighter; he'd learned young to be good with his hands. His opponent was considerably larger but slow on his feet, and Calvin landed one more lick before security pulled the boys down.

"Dungeon!"

Calvin looked out at the tier in triumph as a sheriff's deputy hauled his hands behind his back. Time in isolation was a small price to pay. He had proven himself, and most important, he had done it where everyone could see.

ORLEANS PARISH PRISON PROVED MORE HELLISH THAN CALVIN HAD imagined. It was the era of the "War on Crime," and nationwide incarceration rates were about to double under President Ronald Reagan. State legislatures were passing laws that expanded criminal codes and required harsher, often mandatory, sentences. Louisiana was no exception. As elsewhere, the Black community in New Orleans, particularly in working-class neighborhoods reeling from middle-class flight and racially targeted policing, suffered the most: 90 percent of the city's jail population was African American. Despite regular construction of additional facilities, terrible overcrowding plagued the jail, continuing a decades-long trend. Mental health crises and physical ailments went unchecked. The number of avoidable deaths and suicides was on the rise. The buildings themselves were in various states of disrepair; one of Calvin's acquaintances was lucky to survive after being electrocuted while trying to move a broken light.

A pervasive sense of scarcity corroded human compassion at every level. Given the limited supervision of the cells, perceived slights could easily end in shankings. Tier reps controlled the food portions, meaning men they had a conflict with starved while those they favored got double portions. Once, when Calvin was in the dungeon for fighting, one man threw a cocktail of human waste into another man's cell, and the tier was besieged by a mushroom cloud of microscopic shit droplets that hung stubbornly in the humid air. Calvin went to sleep with a damp washcloth over his nose and mouth, hoping the stench would be gone by the time he woke.

More than the angry outbursts, it was the relentless jockeying for power that bothered Calvin. Day in and day out, verbal attacks were strategically deployed to test one another's resolve. Responses had to be quick and severe. The vigilance it required was exhausting.

But in the end, it wasn't the men on Calvin's tier that posed the biggest threat to his safety. The guards were the ones he came to fear most.

In his first few weeks, a shank was discovered beneath a mattress during a shakedown of his cell. One by one, the cell's inhabitants were taken upstairs to be interrogated by a group of six deputies. When Calvin's turn came, he refused to let them close the door. Speaking to the deputies alone would signal he was a rat, a fate far worse than being locked up for disobedience. But the deputies had a different view. They made an example of him, throwing him against the wall and repeatedly kicking his chest and lower back after he fell. After a week in isolation to recover from his injuries, they charged him with assaulting a peace officer.

Another day, when Calvin got into a fight on his tier and clocked a deputy in the jaw, security moved him from the dungeon to an open dormitory with people who had already been convicted of serious offenses, hoping he would be preyed upon by older, stronger men. Luckily, Calvin discovered a familial connection with some of the guys in the dorm, which spared him the worst. According to the jail's moral code, fights between people from the same neighborhood had to be "fair ones," meaning one-on-one, with no crowding.

Still, he wasn't spared entirely. Catkiller, sentenced to ninety-nine years for armed robbery and renowned as one of the jail's biggest shit-stirrers, took great pleasure in hazing the new kid.

Late one night, Calvin awoke to Catkiller's voice hissing at him in the dark. "David Yeager's looking for you, brah."

Calvin's heart hammered at the mention of his case's victim.

"He lookin' for you," Catkiller repeated.

"What the fuck you talkin' about?" Calvin demanded.

"When I was sleeping just now, David Yeager came to me in my dream."

The bunks began to titter. Confused, Calvin rubbed sleep from his eyes.

Catkiller continued. "He told me: That motherfucker Calvin Duncan gonna *pay* for what he did."

Raucous cackles echoed across the dormitory, and Calvin, recognizing the bait for what it was, sank back onto his mattress, cursing himself for having fallen for the dig.

On another morning, Calvin awoke with the ominous view of a toilet bowl's underside hovering above his face. Disoriented, he took a moment to grasp that his mattress had been dragged across the floor while he slept, positioning his head beneath the commode. Others in the dorm had carried on using it, looking down over a sleeping Calvin while they evacuated their bowels. Furious, he sprang to his feet, only to find Catkiller on a nearby bunk, tears of laughter wetting his cheeks.

BY MID-SEPTEMBER, CALVIN'S FAMILY HAD RETAINED A LAWYER, Arthur Harris, an affable man with an open face and eyebrows that danced as he talked.

At their first meeting, the lawyer laid out a plan to file a series of motions at the next court hearing, which had been set for October. He would also argue the motion to suppress the confession.

"The law is clear," he said with a confidence that gave Calvin heart. "If a defendant is denied his right to an attorney while being questioned by police, whatever he says can't be used against him in court."

"I didn't confess anyway." Calvin scowled.

Harris sat forward in his chair. "Your cousin Benny, do you remember helping prepare for his birthday party last year?"

"Yeah," Calvin replied vaguely, confused by the lawyer's question. "I painted a couple of the rooms in my aunt Gail's apartment."

"Do you know what day of the week that was?"

Calvin shook his head.

"Your aunt remembers: a Friday. Same night as the crime. Good news, son. You've got an alibi."

Calvin slumped in his chair, relief washing over him.

"How old are you?" Harris asked.

"Nineteen."

"You know they're seeking the death penalty in your case, right?"

Calvin shrugged. "Sir, people been tryin' to kill me all my life."

He returned to the dorm, his hope renewed. Finally, someone was fighting for him. He could begin to think beyond the misery of the jail and start planning for what lay ahead.

While waiting for his court date, Calvin worked on his reading skills. He hoped to return to the Job Corps in time to graduate at the end of the year, but he had catching up to do. He'd entered jail with a ninth-grade education, and the only accessible book on the tier was the Bible, which Aunt Gail insisted he read.

An old-timer, Slim Jenkins, back on a court order from the state penitentiary, noticed Calvin's efforts and offered to tutor him. Calvin had learned a golden rule in jail: owe nothing to anyone. But Slim didn't seem to use kindness as a currency, so Calvin accepted his offer, and his reading gradually improved under the old-timer's steady guidance.

As he navigated through the Old Testament, Calvin began to worry his arrest was a form of divine retribution for the homes he'd burglarized in his youth. One proverb in particular unsettled him: "I will mock you when disaster overtakes you—when calamity overtakes you like a storm. . . . They rejected my advice and paid no attention when I corrected them."

Yet Calvin noticed God also used imperfect people, like Esther and David, to achieve remarkable things. When they chose the right path, God met them halfway. Maybe, Calvin thought, He'd do the same for him.

The night before court, Calvin's lawyer came to see him at the jail. He shook Calvin's hand weakly, his demeanor changed.

"I'm getting off your case, son."

Calvin stared at him blankly. "I don't understand."

"Your aunt hasn't been paying my fees. I think she pooled money from your family for my retainer and then spent it on herself."

Calvin turned his eyes to the ceiling and saw that rust was corroding the metal beams. He felt too stupid to speak.

"I'm sorry, son," Harris said.

Calvin shook his head. Brunetta had been doing this all his life. Why should he have expected anything different this time? The fact that he was fighting for his life didn't change who she was.

"I know this isn't your fault," the lawyer added gently. "I'll argue those motions in court tomorrow like we talked about. But I'm afraid I'll have to ask the judge to remove me as counsel after that."

Calvin nodded. "I appreciate you helping me at all."

He stood and extended a hand, not wanting to take any more of the lawyer's time.

The following day in court, things went even more poorly than Calvin had anticipated. Judge Shea rushed through the proceedings, making it difficult for Calvin to keep up with what was happening. Calvin's attorney argued the motion to suppress the confession, but the judge immediately denied it, leaving Calvin in the dark about what the motion was or why it had been rejected. Then, when Harris removed himself as counsel, a court-appointed lawyer was brought in to take his place.

In the jail, the men adhered to a proverb of their own: "The better the shoes, the better the lawyer." There was a prevailing belief that court-appointed attorneys were pawns of the government, often second-rate and inclined to betray their clients for a paycheck. After all, in a profession where appearances mattered, personal pride was paramount. If your lawyer didn't even care about his shoes, it was a sure sign you were about to be sold down the river.

Since 1963, when the US Supreme Court established a right to legal representation for people accused of serious crimes, Orleans Parish courts had relied on a roster of part-time contract attorneys to represent people who couldn't afford counsel. Since the state legislature refused to fund public defense, these attorneys' contracts were mostly paid from traffic and court fines—an unpredictable and inadequate source of funds cobbled together on the backs of the city's poor. The lawyers' low pay made hiring investigators, enlisting experts, visiting crime scenes, or preparing witnesses to take the stand nearly impossible. Back at their firms, they had wealthy customers to prioritize. What's more, each one was assigned to a single courtroom in the courthouse, meaning they had to answer to the same judge every day—an arrangement that incentivized compliance.

When Calvin's new attorney rose to address the judge, Calvin looked down at the man's worn penny loafers and knew he was in trouble.

"That guy's gonna march you to the death house," Catkiller confirmed when Calvin reached the dorm. "Your ass gonna definitely get the death penalty now. That jury gonna say, 'Oh, that mean-muggin' dude killed that poor little white boy. Fry his ass.'"

Calvin's temper flared. "Cat, not today."

"Don't mind that clown," Big Dugger remarked from a bunk nearby.

Big Dugger, one of the dormitory's elder statesmen, had already spent four years under sentence of death and was waiting to learn if the Louisiana Supreme Court would overturn his case on appeal. His attorney—the very same one who had just been appointed to Calvin's case—had neglected to put on any witnesses during the sentencing phase of his trial.

"Cat's not wrong, you know." Big Dugger slid off the bunk and posted up next to Calvin on the wall. "They've stuck you with the same lawyer I had. Make no mistake, that dude ain't never comin' to see you."

Calvin was defiant. "I ain't worrying about no lawyer, man. I just need my trial. Once the jury hears my case, they'll send me home."

At this, the older man scoffed. "Listen. We all had the same lawyer as you, and we all on death row now. Your victim was white, your witness is white, you got the same judge I had, Frank Shea—a madman.

I know you don't understand what's really goin' on yet. But if you think your case is comin' out any different than ours, you deluding yourself."

Calvin turned on him. "No disrespect, brah, but how does that help me?"

"People go two ways in here. Either you play prison games"—Big Dugger shot a glance at Catkiller—"or you put your mind to getting free. It took me a long time to figure that out. It's too late for me now. But you still got a chance."

"But you're sayin' I'm gonna lose! How am I supposed to help myself?"

"For starters, put down that Bible I always see you reading and pick up a law book."

Big Dugger leaned so close that Calvin could smell the beans from lunch on his breath.

"You wanna help yourself? You better get a real lawyer. And if you can't pay for one, then you *become* one."

1983

The new year only brought more uncertainty. Calvin heard nothing from his new attorney, and no trial date was set. He found himself pondering Big Dugger's advice. It was clear that no cavalry was coming; deliverance lay in his own hands.

Attempting to learn the law in jail was like training for a marathon barefoot. Law books and court opinions were rare gems. He was lucky to get hold of a dictionary. He slept with his pencil and legal pad under his pillow to keep them from being stolen.

Men on the tiers dubbed "lockerbox lawyers" gave legal advice and drafted motions in exchange for cigarettes. But Calvin quickly realized their advice was inexpert, and their motions were regurgitated from other pleadings. He filed one or two of their briefs—a motion for a speedy trial and a change of venue—but Judge Shea predictably ignored them.

Occasionally, guys on the tier would offer up briefs filed by their lawyers, and Calvin would study them line by line, breaking down every word until he grasped its meaning. He could spend hours looking up terms in the dictionary only to find he hadn't yet made it to the end of a single page. In moments of fatigue, he set his reading aside and returned to the card games and the television in the dayroom.

In February, he received word that his case had finally been set for trial in April.

He waited eagerly for his day in court, his interest in the law usurped by thoughts of going home. His mind returned to Timber Lake, and he dug out the letters he'd kept from Hartsuyker and Ferrick promising they would save him a place there.

On the morning of trial, Calvin sat in a holding cell below the courtroom with other men scheduled for the docket. He watched each one be called, hoping he was next.

When the clock showed eleven, he realized he'd been fooled. Judge Shea went to lunch at noon—there was no way he was starting a trial now. Calvin curled over his knees in despair.

When a deputy told him to get up, he braced himself to return to the jail. But instead of walking him to Central Lockup, the deputy led him upstairs.

He was taken to a side room off the courtroom, where Gail and Mamie were waiting.

"What happened in there today?" he asked.

"Your lawyer was out sick," said Gail. "The judge put the trial off until June."

She hugged him tight. He must have smelled awful in his prison clothes, but she clung to him anyway.

After a pause, she stepped aside for Mamie. His sister remained motionless, as if rooted to the floor, her expression hesitant—the same look she had when he used to catch her in the projects between the cuts with a boy.

Gail glanced back and forth between them. "That girl's got something to tell you."

A pit formed in his stomach. "What?"

Mamie wouldn't answer.

"She's pregnant," said Gail.

Calvin turned on his sister in disbelief.

How you gonna take care of a baby? You're eighteen. You can barely take care of your damn self!

As if hearing his thoughts, Mamie's chin quivered, lowering toward her chest, and a tear slipped onto her cheek.

"Don't you look at her like that," Gail warned him.

Calvin clenched his jaw.

His one job in the world was to protect his sister, and he had left her alone. This was his fault.

He let out a long breath, his gaze softening, and in the silence, Mamie finally met his eye.

"Congratulations," he said.

ONE OF THE GREAT PARADOXES OF CALVIN'S LIFE WAS THAT HE GREW up an orphan, yet his father was not only alive but lived just across the street.

He couldn't recall the moment he discovered that the man living across from Aunt Nema and Uncle Trim in the renovated yellow school bus was his dad. Nor could he remember when they began walking past each other on the street, each pretending the other didn't exist, stubbornly fixing their gazes on some distant point. No observer would have imagined they were father and son. In Calvin's eyes, they weren't.

After Tiny escaped her relationship with Owens, Owens converted the school bus into a trailer and parked it in the side yard of his mother's home. He took up residence there with a woman who became his common-law wife, and over the course of the next decade, they had five children together.

The youngest of Owens's children was often left home alone in the trailer while her parents worked, and on those days when Calvin heard her crying from the street, he would instinctively go to her. As soon as Owens returned, he would exit the trailer, passing him as if he'd never been inside.

One day, Owens's wife left the school bus to run an errand and never returned. To Calvin, this confirmed what he had long suspected—that his own mother had left him years earlier. Leaving suddenly was just something some mothers did.

Owens eventually moved to Pearl River, a small town about half an hour northeast of New Orleans, and Calvin didn't see him for some years. Then, the summer after Calvin turned sixteen, Owens invited him and Mamie to visit.

Mamie was eager to go, having grown close to their half siblings while Calvin was away at the Job Corps in Texas. Although Calvin wasn't particularly interested in spending time with Owens, he had questions he wanted answered, and he didn't want Mamie to go alone. So, they went to Pearl River.

Their father's property backed onto a forest thick with kudzu vines and was more isolated than any place Calvin had stayed before. The neighbors, known members of the Ku Klux Klan, did nothing to ease his reluctance. The house was cramped with children, nearly all in their teens. Calvin was introduced to his siblings by name for the first time, including some younger children he'd never seen. He was surprised to find how kind they were, how excited they were to spend time with him, how quickly they called him "brother." He took to them just as fast.

Less so to his father.

Owens, a mechanic who had come to religion later in life, described himself as a Voodoo priest—though Calvin wasn't sure where he got that designation. He wore a long black shawl and a clerical collar, and always kept a candle burning on the altar in his room. Some mornings, the children awoke to the sound of him praying over acquaintances who sought his counsel, mainly from the Black community on the other side of town.

Calvin believed his father was spiritually connected; he knew things nobody else knew. But that didn't mean his stories were reliable.

Owens seemed to sense his eldest son's skepticism and, over the course of his stay, spoke with him privately several times. Their conversations were tentative at first, but became more direct the longer they were together. Eventually, Calvin gathered the courage to voice the questions that weighed heaviest on his mind.

Owens denied that he had ever been abusive toward Calvin's mother, which Calvin dismissed out of hand. When Calvin asked why he couldn't see well out of one eye, Owens explained that Calvin's older half brothers had been smashing bottles in the projects when a piece of glass kicked up and cut him as a child. Owens knew the story of the mysterious scars on Calvin's legs, too. He said Brunetta's teenage daughter had taken an extension cord that was patched with electrical tape and unwrapped the wires. While Calvin was sleeping, she'd wrapped the exposed electrical lines around his leg and plugged the extension cord into an outlet.

"Who do you think was the one getting you out of trouble all those times you was arrested in high school?" Owens asked.

When Calvin replied, "Brunetta," Owens shook his head.

"It was me; I was praying for you."

Owens probably thought he was gaining favor with his son by filling in these gaps, but in truth, Calvin's hurt was only deepening. If Owens knew what was happening to him and Mamie on Clouet Street, why had he never rescued them?

Owens said the aunts kept moving Calvin and Mamie around and he couldn't pin them down. It was an obvious lie—embarrassing, really—but it confirmed one important fact: Calvin couldn't trust his father, either.

At one point, one of his half sisters took Calvin aside to reveal the truth. Owens had never come for him because he was convinced that, given the first opportunity, Calvin would kill him out of hatred. Calvin was willing to accept this explanation at face value, but it baffled him that his father would assume such intensity of feeling from a boy who didn't know him at all.

After four weeks in Pearl River, he was ready to leave. His siblings had won his affection, but his impression of his father had changed little. He and Mamie were still orphans and always would be.

BETWEEN JUNE AND DECEMBER 1983, FIVE MORE TRIAL DATES WERE put off, mostly at the request of Calvin's lawyer, who had yet to visit him in jail. An older Cuban man with broken English called Calvin

"Dog" because of the way his feet wagged back and forth when he was falling asleep. Calvin had embraced the nickname, especially amused when he and Catkiller were dubbed "Cat and Dog." But now, the guys on his tier started calling him "Setback," a nickname he despised.

While he waited for his case to move, he redoubled his efforts to learn the law. He began tearing articles about police investigations and court hearings out of the daily papers and sticking them to scraps of paper with chewed pink bubble gum. At night, he took notes while he watched the news, listening for stories that involved cases in criminal court. Occasionally, Earline would go to the state supreme court library for him and send copies of new legal decisions she found. It was a favor reminiscent of their early days together, when Earline used to help with his homework on the bus home from school. Even now, though she had moved on to another relationship, she was loyal to a fault, attending his court dates and bringing cases to the jail. Over a period of months, he compiled an impressive collection of articles and papers—a makeshift law book of his own.

Occasionally a dictionary would appear on the tier and he would vie for it, eager to decipher more of the legal jargon he didn't know. He concluded that the language of the law was needlessly confusing: "mandamus" meant a command, "indigent" referred to the inability to pay, and a "motion" was just a request. The purpose of legalese, it seemed to him, was to ensure attorneys got paid while poor people were kept in the dark. He was determined to understand it as well as any lawyer.

A full year and a half had now passed since his arrest. He'd still never met with his court-appointed attorney, and the cycle of setting and resetting trial dates was driving him to despair. In dark moments, Calvin wondered if he was lost to Orleans Parish Prison for good.

In early 1984, after yet another court hearing failed to materialize, sheriff's deputies escorted him from the holding cells to the courtroom to meet with his family.

He presumed it would be Aunt Gail waiting, but when he reached the door leading to court, he heard a child on the other side of the wall.

"I want to see my daddy!"

His chest knotted at the sound of Ayana's voice.

She spotted her father as soon as he came through the doorway, running down the aisle to tackle his shackled legs. He squatted to meet her. When she found his shoulders, she pushed her face into his neck, her cheek hot with exertion. Calvin forgot the courtroom and the deputy at the door, taking in only her warmth and the feeling of her tiny body curled into his. Whatever rejection he'd feared at a distance was gone in her embrace. He tried to wrap his arms around her, but his restraints jarred his wrists in mid-flight. Being unable to hold his daughter was worse than any beating he'd taken in the jail.

"When are you coming home, Daddy?" She pulled back to search his face.

She was a toddler now, and he watched her eyes taking him in, terrified at how quickly she was growing. Soon, she would comprehend that he was locked up. A wash of grief pulled his eyes to the floor.

"Soon." He swallowed. "Are you being good to your mama?"

Earline stood a few paces behind, a bump visible beneath her blouse. She was pregnant with another man's child, and though Calvin had been hurt when he first learned the news, he quickly moved past it. He was just grateful that she continued to visit.

"Time's up," said the deputy.

Calvin pressed his face into his daughter's hair. She hugged him again, more tentatively this time, and he discerned her confusion. He promised to see her soon, then turned away, unable to bear the sight of her leaving.

AFTER ANOTHER SCUFFLE ON THE TIER, CALVIN WAS BACK IN THE dungeon, huddled over a yellow legal pad. He was glad to be alone in a cell tonight. He had work to do.

> May it please the court,
>
> Petitioner is incarcerated in Orleans Parish Prison and there are no Law Library Facility located in this prison system. Petitioner is indigent, so petitioner is unable to buy a Code of Criminal Procedure (1984, Paperback). . . . Petitioner is in custody in the Orleans Parish Prison accuse of a capital offense—First Degree Murder, a crime Petitioner did not commit. Wherefore, Petitioner Calvin F. Duncan prays that this honorable court consider petitioner motion and provide petitioner with a Code of Criminal Procedure Law Book.

He sat back and ran his eyes over the red ink, wincing at the garish color. It looked amateurish, but he had no choice. He was stuck in the cells without a black pen.

The Code of Criminal Procedure was the state's legal rule book governing how criminal trials worked in Louisiana. Every prosecutor, judge, and criminal defense lawyer had one. He needed one, too.

He printed a title across the top of the page: "Motion for a Law

Book." After reading through it one last time, he tugged the yellow pages away from the notepad, guarding the perforations so they wouldn't tear. Then he tucked them into an envelope addressed to the state's highest court. If the justices at the Louisiana Supreme Court knew anything of the conditions at Orleans Parish Prison, they would surely answer his call for help.

When a response from the court arrived weeks later, however, Calvin realized his mistake. The order, only two sentences long, said the court lacked jurisdiction because his motion wasn't first adjudicated by the lower courts.

The motion was sent back down to the court of appeals, which in turn sent it back down to the trial court, to Judge Shea.

Calvin figured the motion was doomed—Judge Shea would only ignore it.

At his next status conference, just as another uneventful hearing unfolded, Calvin was preparing to be taken back to the cells when an unexpected movement caught his eye.

Judge Shea instructed the bailiff to hand defense counsel a copy of the Code of Criminal Procedure. Calvin's lawyer raised his brows as the bailiff set the hulking book in his hands. Astonished, Calvin turned toward the judge, but Shea continued the proceedings, never meeting his gaze.

When court adjourned, Calvin's lawyer met him in the holding cell with the book. "Apparently you asked for this. Don't let them take it away," he warned.

Calvin knew the rules: nothing was allowed back on the tier. Even a law book was deemed contraband.

He approached the sheriff's deputy at the door to the stairwell with caution, but the deputy let him pass. So did the next. When he made it all the way to his cot with the book tucked safely under his arm, he felt like Moses parting the Red Sea.

He laid the treatise on his mattress, watching it sink into the thin bedding, heavy with a thousand procedural rules he would need to learn. He stared in disbelief.

He hadn't just filed his very first motion in court—he'd won it.

IN SEPTEMBER, NOW MORE THAN TWO YEARS AFTER CALVIN'S AR-rest, his lawyer was suddenly removed from the case. Calvin wasn't sure whether to feel discouraged or relieved.

Judge Shea appointed two attorneys from the Indigent Defender Board in his place: Phil Johnson and Numa Bertel. Then he set a trial date for October.

Johnson raised a finger. "This is a capital case, Judge—mightn't we need more than four weeks to prepare?"

Judge Shea chewed his cigar with exaggerated annoyance. "January twenty-eighth, then. But nothing short of the Second Coming will stop it this time."

Despite the severity of his charge, Calvin still knew little of the crime he stood accused of. Police reports weren't a matter of public record, and his attorneys were none the wiser. He'd seen in an old copy of a news report that a man in his early twenties named David Yeager had been shot at a bus stop after two Black youths tried to rob him and his girlfriend. That was it. Unless his defense team put resources into an investigation, Calvin wouldn't learn what evidence the state planned to use against him until his trial.

Most of what was known about David Yeager's murder had come from statements provided by his girlfriend, Kristie Emberling.

Kristie, fifteen, told police that David, twenty-three, had been staying with her and her mother at their home on North Roman Street. The pair had met two years earlier through a mutual friend at Kristie's school, before she dropped out in the seventh grade. On the night of David's death, they had been together for seven months.

The couple left Kristie's house late in the evening to eat at a nearby diner called Tastee Donuts, just a short ride up the road.

While Kristie and David waited at the corner for the bus, two young men approached. The shorter and fatter of the two eyed a promise ring David had given Kristie, then asked if she wanted to buy or sell some weed. When she answered no, he commented on her ring and pulled something from his jacket. At the sight of a gun barrel, Kristie took off running.

Rather than follow, David stayed behind to confront his assailant. Kristie later said David had been in the military and "wasn't scared of anything." The first gunshot struck his leg. When Kristie heard it, she stopped running and turned around to see David being shot a second time, this time in the head. He dropped to the ground, and she ran to his side as the assailants fled.

Calvin was the only person the police ever arrested.

ON THE MORNING OF JANUARY 28, 1985, CALVIN WOKE TO THE SOUND of his name. Though it was only 3 a.m., a sheriff's deputy was already calling the men scheduled for court.

He rubbed thick grains of sleep from his eyes. His lawyers had briefly seen him the night before to make sure he had a suit to wear—

the only jail visit they'd ever paid him. They said his trial was going ahead this time.

At seven thirty, he was taken to a holding cell beneath the court-room, where his pants and shirt were already hanging. A deputy instructed him to put them on.

When his case was called a little after nine, Aunt Gail, Brunetta, Mamie, and a handful of his younger cousins were waiting in the hall. The deputies allowed Calvin to greet them briefly before ushering him into the courtroom.

As he approached the defense table, two anxious-looking men caught his eye. It took a moment to register Bob Hartsuyker and Mack Ferrick. Ferrick gave a small wave and Hartsuyker attempted a smile as Calvin, wrists shackled, dipped his head in appreciation. He was stunned to see that these men had flown across the country to be there. After all this time, they still believed in him.

The deputy instructed Calvin to sit down at the counsel table and unchained his wrists. By law, he was to appear a free man in front of the jury. Judge Shea ordered the first batch of potential jurors in.

Since it was a death penalty case, the prosecution and defense would question each juror about their views on capital punishment. Capital trials were largely won or lost at jury selection. The defense needed to ensure that at least a few jurors with meaningful reservations about the death penalty remained in the box; otherwise, their clients would be in jeopardy. Not only were jurors who believed in capital punishment more likely to vote for death, but research showed they were also more likely to convict.

Shea barked at the lawyers not to waste time.

Bruce Whittaker, one of the prosecutors, a white man in his early thirties, positioned himself in front of the jury box and began his presentation. Glynn Alexander, his assistant, a Black man in his late thirties, remained seated at the state's counsel table.

Calvin observed that every potential juror who admitted to having moral or religious reservations about imposing a death sentence was dismissed from the jury box. The only jurors who remained were the ones who said they would be able to give the death penalty. His unease deepened.

With twelve jurors seated, the prosecutor stood to deliver his opening statement. Calvin glanced in the direction of the family sitting behind Whittaker and guessed from the creases of worry at their brows that they were kin to David Yeager.

The prosecution began with a description of the crime. Whittaker recounted the altercation at the bus stop, the shooting, and Kristie's efforts to comfort David's motionless body. He noted that after the shooter ran off, his partner returned to check David's pockets while Kristie was bent over his chest, listening for a heartbeat. Wallet in hand, the assailant took off in the same direction, disappearing around the corner and into the night.

Whittaker paused to let the scene sink in.

The jurors would hear testimony that when the police showed Kristie a photographic lineup, she singled out the mugshot of Calvin Duncan, he continued. They would also hear that when Calvin was arrested for the crime, he shared details only the killer could have known. The totality of the evidence would leave no doubt in the jury's mind that Calvin Duncan had killed David Yeager in cold blood.

Calvin sat frozen as Whittaker returned to his seat.

Despite his lawyers' advice to maintain a stoic expression for the jury, he trembled with rage. He wanted to push back his chair and yell that the prosecutor was a liar.

Numa Bertel rose to give his reply.

There was no way that Calvin could have been at the site of David Yeager's murder, he said. Multiple witnesses saw him painting his aunt's apartment on the night of August 7, 1981, more than a mile from where the crime occurred. It was the state's burden to prove that Calvin was guilty beyond a reasonable doubt, Bertel reminded the jury, and they would surely fail that standard here.

Battle lines drawn, the two sides looked to the judge, who ordered the prosecution to begin calling witnesses.

After testimony from a forensic pathologist, Whittaker announced, "State calls Kristie Emberling."

The courtroom fell silent as the prosecution's star witness came through the door and made her way up the aisle.

As Calvin watched her take a seat, a realization dawned on him: Kristie had been waiting for this day just as long as he had, and one of them was going to leave the trial in ruins.

"Who was David Yeager?" the prosecutor asked.

"My fiancé," she replied.

"Where were you going that night?"

"Tastee Donuts, on Broad and Esplanade."

"Was anybody waiting at the bus stop with you all?"

"Not at first. That man over there"—she pointed at Calvin—"and another man walked up to the bus stop from off Roman Street."

The jury followed Kristie's gaze. Calvin gripped the pen he was using to take notes.

"When you say, 'That man,' would you describe him right now for the jury, what he looks like today?" Whittaker asked.

"Well, he has lost a lot of weight. He has on a pair of gray pants, and a shirt."

Calvin leaned over to his attorneys. "I haven't lost weight—I *gained* it since being in jail."

Phil Johnson nodded.

"I turned around and I looked and I saw this man with a gun," Kristie continued. "And he just shot him right in the head, and David fell."

Though the trauma of the memory was plain on Kristie's face, her speech didn't falter.

Johnson rose to conduct the cross-examination. Questioning a victim in front of a jury was an unenviable task, and he approached the witness box carefully.

"Did the detective say anything to you about the photographs before asking you to pick one out?" he asked.

Judge Shea cut him off. "That's irrelevant."

Johnson tried a different tack, and again the judge intervened.

"But Your Honor . . ."

"I don't argue with lawyers. When I rule, I rule."

Despite more interruptions, Johnson managed to extract a few crucial details.

First, though Calvin had gold caps on his front teeth, Kristie didn't observe any on the shooter. Second, before Kristie identified Calvin in a photo spread, Crimestoppers had broadcast his mug-shot on television, and Kristie had watched a Crimestoppers re-enactment of the crime being filmed near her house. She also saw a broadcast of Calvin being led to a patrol car in handcuffs after his extradition from Oregon before identifying him in a physical lineup.

As Kristie stepped down from the box, Calvin noticed her shoulders hunched in exhaustion. He wondered why she had singled him out. What possible reason could this girl have for falsely accusing him?

Whittaker called his next witness, a detective from Oregon.

Calvin was anxious to hear what Lieutenant Reed had to say.

Instead, the lanky officer, Peterson, appeared in the doorway.

"Detective Peterson, I want you to think back to August 6 of 1982," Whittaker said once the officer took the stand. "On that date, did you have the opportunity to come in contact with a subject identified as Calvin Duncan?"

"Yes, I did."

"Briefly, what did he tell you at that time?"

"After being advised that there was a warrant for murder, he said he did not kill any white man in New Orleans, nor did he know any white lady witness in New Orleans."

Calvin realized with horror what the detective was doing.

"This dude is gonna lie on me," he whispered to Johnson. "He wasn't even the one that questioned me!"

"All right," Johnson murmured. "I'll bring it up on cross."

Johnson asked to see Peterson's written report. Predictably, the judge denied the request.

Calvin had never even seen a copy of the statements he supposedly made.

"Is it not necessary for Mr. Duncan to review his own statement to see if it's correct?" Johnson probed Peterson. "He doesn't even get to *read* it?"

The detective was indifferent. "No, he did not read it."

Marco Demma, the detective from New Orleans, was called next.

Whittaker asked Demma how Calvin came to be a suspect in the first place, something Calvin had long wondered himself.

An unidentified male caller called Crimestoppers with an anonymous tip, Demma explained. The caller said, "Calvin Duncan shot David Yeager."

When Demma searched for Calvin's name in the police database, he discovered an arrest record for shoplifting dating back to when Calvin was fourteen. He presented Calvin's mugshot from that arrest to Kristie in a photo spread, and she identified him.

On cross-examination, Bertel pointed out that it had taken the police six months to identify Calvin as a suspect and just as long to arrest him. There were numerous discrepancies in the police's descriptions of the perpetrator. Early newspaper reports described the shooter as "short and fat," five foot six, and wearing a short-sleeve shirt. However, at trial, Kristie had said the perpetrator was five foot eight or nine, 180 pounds, and wearing a leather jacket and a knit cap.

Demma denied that the descriptions in the newspaper came from his office, and after submitting its evidence to the jury, the state rested its case.

Calvin wondered how things looked from the jurors' perspective. While the police investigation had clearly been half-baked, the image of a stricken Kristie would be difficult for jurors to forget. His attorneys needed to fight back, and hard.

The defense called Calvin's alibi witnesses, summoning Aunt Gail and her children to the stand. Each of the children testified that Calvin had been at their home on Pleasure Street on the night of the crime, painting the living room and the kitchen in preparation for their cousin's party the next day. He'd finished working around midnight, then took a bath and went to bed.

On cross-examination, the two youngest admitted that they had gone to sleep around eight o'clock and couldn't have known if Calvin was in the apartment for the rest of the evening. The eldest filled in those hours, saying she didn't fall asleep until after *The Midnight Special* had begun on television, when Calvin was washing up for bed. Though Aunt Gail echoed her testimony, the prosecution attacked their credibility, suggesting they were lying to protect him.

Calvin winced. The case was slipping through his fingers. He would have to save himself.

Johnson called him to the stand.

As he stepped into the witness box, he sensed the spectators' eyes tracking his every move. He raised his hand and swore to tell the truth.

"Tell us your side of what happened on the night of August 7, 1981," said Johnson.

Calvin described painting his aunt's apartment: first the living room, then the kitchen. The only time he stopped working was to join his family for a meal of hamburgers and fries at the kitchen table.

Johnson asked whether Calvin owned a knit cap or a gun.

Calvin shook his head.

Johnson asked about the circumstances surrounding Calvin's departure from New Orleans.

He didn't know anything about a murder when he left the city in January of 1982, he told the jury. He was having trouble finding work, so he hitched a ride with a cousin to Los Angeles, thinking he'd reapply for the Job Corps.

On cross-examination, Whittaker stepped close to the witness box.

"You heard what the police officer said you told them?"

"Yeah, I heard them testify to that," Calvin said.

"You deny you made those statements?"

"Yeah."

"They just made it up?"

"They had to."

"They could have put words, any words in your mouth they wanted?"

Calvin shrugged. "My name ain't on the paper."

"If they wanted, they could have said you confessed to the whole thing, right?"

The blow landed with targeted precision.

"Yeah, they could have."

Whittaker gave the jury a knowing glance.

The sound of Calvin's heartbeat filled his ears. How had the prosecutor managed to twist things like that?

The judge dismissed him from the witness box, then told the lawyers to prepare for their closing arguments. Shea was determined to push the proceedings to a conclusion, though it was already dark outside.

Whittaker delivered his remarks first.

"Kristie Emberling saw that man take a gun and put a bullet into David Yeager's head. She got a good look at that face. We got a picture of Calvin Duncan. We showed those pictures to Kristie Emberling, six pictures. Out of all the people in the world, she looked at those pictures and said, 'Calvin Duncan, he's the one that shot David Yeager, I'm positive.'"

He pointed a finger at Calvin like he was brandishing a knife.

"This is just some innocent guy who decided to go to Clackamas County, Oregon? Don't bet on it."

Johnson used his final argument to point out inconsistencies in the state's evidence and the inadequacies of the police investigation.

Then Whittaker spoke in rebuttal before Judge Shea dispatched the jurors to deliberate.

The lawyers exited the courtroom to make phone calls while witnesses lingered in the hall. Judge Shea retired to his chambers, leaving the courtroom all but empty.

Calvin sat alone at the defense table, staring at the pale glow of the wall sconces.

They could still win, but the certainty he'd clung to before trial was wavering. His mind returned to the moment when Kristie declared he was David's murderer; the way the jurors tensed at the sight of her tears.

He pressed his index fingers against the bridge of his nose, elbows on the table.

If his lawyers had been able to investigate and properly prepare for trial, the state's case would have fallen apart. The identification, his supposed statements to police—it was all bullshit. But he had no way of knowing what the jury was thinking.

Early the following morning, Calvin received word that the jury had finished deliberating. He stood as the judge resumed the bench.

He'd fantasized about this moment for two and a half years, yet suddenly he wasn't sure he wanted it to pass. He readied himself in a wordless prayer as the foreperson read the verdict.

"We, the jury, find the defendant, Calvin Duncan, guilty of first-degree murder."

Murmurs rippled through the room.

Calvin pulled his body tight like a string, worried his knees might give way. Out of the corner of his eye, he saw the prosecutor smooth his tie.

As news of the verdict carried out into the hallway, an almighty wail exploded through the wall.

Calvin recognized his aunt Brunetta's screams as she began kicking the double doors. *Bam, bam, bam.*

The jurors and court staff turned their heads as the sheriff's deputies rushed to lead Brunetta away. A small group gathered around Whittaker to congratulate him, ignoring the commotion outside.

Calvin watched on, aghast.

This wasn't supposed to happen. The truth was supposed to come out.

The higher courts would fix this. They had to.

Brunetta's cries, now distant down the hall, disturbed him even more than the verdict.

His mind veered back to the beginning, to the phone call where this had all started.

His aunt had been so worried when she saw his face on the news, but he'd reassured her it was nothing, confident the police would move on.

She had warned him on his first morning in the jail, before he knew what was waiting for him in the House of D: *"You in a place where they fuck over boys."*

Somehow, Brunetta always saw the worst coming.

He wondered what she saw now.

1985

Calvin was desperate to get to Angola. Big Dugger, who'd contin-ued to act as a mentor, said the Main Prison contained the larg-est law library of any in the state. In the 1970s, a series of US Supreme Court decisions, along with the efforts of determined jailhouse law-yers, had compelled the Department of Corrections to expand its collection of law books and improve access to other legal materials. Calvin needed all the help he could get to prepare for a new trial.

Calvin's jury hadn't been able to agree on whether or not to give him the death penalty, so, by law, he was automatically sentenced to life at hard labor without the benefit of probation, suspension of sen-tence, or parole.

Brunetta said they would let him come home after ten years and six months if he behaved himself, but the older guys in the jail said that wasn't how the law worked anymore. That life in Louisiana meant life. He didn't know what to believe, but it didn't much matter; he was going to get out soon when his appeal was granted.

Nearly all Louisiana's long-termers were sent to Angola to serve their sentences, yet the jail was in no hurry to send Calvin. A shift toward more punitive sentencing combined with a newfound reluctance on the part of governors to use their commutation powers was rapidly increasing the length of prison sentences in Louisiana. Even though Angola was an eighteen-thousand-acre compound of camps and farmland, and the state had opened two additional prisons in recent years, the Department of Corrections was grappling with chronic overcrowding. It sought a temporary fix by paying local sheriffs a daily per diem to keep state prisoners in their facilities, but the sheriffs were getting used to the additional revenue and sought to solidify the arrangement. The Orleans Parish sheriff, Charles Foti, intended to keep Calvin and others like him right where they were.

Calvin could feel his mental strength deteriorating with each passing day. The trauma of being convicted for something he didn't do and his now stateless existence in the jail were beginning to drive him mad.

Many men dealt with their anger by provoking fights or lashing out at guards. Violence was one of the few ways they could regain some fleeting sense of control in an environment designed to infantilize them. Calvin's urge toward combat was equally fierce, but he felt guilty over a recent altercation with a disruptive dorm partner, recognizing that fighting was just an outlet for the rage he couldn't direct at his captors. The more he considered his situation, and watched others devolve into cruelty, the more determined he became to make the law the site for his battles, where winning would build character rather than destroy it.

So, he set his mind to learning how to file lawsuits.

To take legal action against the jail, people in custody first had to file a grievance with the administration. If the jail denied or declined to address the issue, then they could try to file a lawsuit against the sheriff in federal court. In theory, this process allowed the jail to fix problems on its own, sparing the courts. In reality, it permitted jail administrators to stall or carry out the bare minimum to avoid sanctions.

Calvin learned to draft suits by copying ones that circulated on the tier and speaking to guys who had some experience filing them. Broom, a friend from childhood, was also eager to learn, so he and Calvin exchanged drafts and critiqued each other's work.

The first suit Calvin prepared on his own was over the jail's failure to provide him with a high-fiber diet. A doctor had ordered that he eat raisins and bran cereal as a remedy for a bout of severe intestinal pain, yet the jail continued to serve him the same food as everyone else. When the trial date for his lawsuit arrived, Calvin was taken to court to represent himself.

The judge nicknamed the lawsuit the "Case of the Missing Raisins" and ruled in Calvin's favor, and the jail began providing him with the proper diet. Months later, he received a check for $250 in damages, which he used to purchase a legal dictionary and a legal writing textbook.

His first suit a success, Calvin began filing suits about other sorts of dehumanizing treatment: when the shakedown crew confiscated his legal work while turning over the cells, or when he was beaten by deputies. Each filing gave him a better feel for how the law worked in practice. He started to file suits on behalf of other men, many of whom were enduring worse conditions than he was. He helped them file over the lack of medical care, arbitrary disciplinary procedures, inadequate food portions that were leading some people to starve, and failure to provide mental health treatment. Having been demoralized for so long, Calvin found that defending others helped him regain a sense of purpose. One lawsuit in particular showed him how powerful the law could be.

Old-timers sent back from Angola to the parish prison for court appearances weren't being provided dentures when they were placed in the jail. (Indeed, there was no dental care provided in the jail at all, save for tooth extractions.) As a result, they couldn't properly chew their food. Calvin watched them suffering over their meals and losing weight by the week. He filed an emergency suit on their behalf, arguing that the Eighth Amendment to the Constitution guaranteed their right to be free from cruel and unusual punishment. The sheriff fought the suit initially, but once it became clear that the judge wasn't going to dismiss it, he gave the men their dentures to moot the case.

When Calvin saw the elderly men able to eat—that simple, precious act—he fell in love with the law. He could wield the very thing holding him in prison to challenge those who had taken his freedom. The law gave him a way to fight back.

After a string of wins, the guys in the jail dubbed Calvin "the Snickers Lawyer," referring to his policy of accepting only a candy bar for helping with a suit. He wouldn't accept any other payment for his work.

Alongside his civil cases, Calvin was working hard on his brief on appeal. Months passed without any word from the lawyer assigned to his case, and as Calvin's due date approached, he worried that his attorney might not file anything at all. So he began preparing his own supplement to file pro se—that is, on his own.

On direct appeal, the court of appeals was limited to reviewing the trial record for legal errors and ensuring procedural fairness. Defendants were not allowed to introduce new evidence or argue that their trial lawyer had made mistakes, that a juror had acted improperly, or that the state had withheld evidence. Their only recourse was to demonstrate that errors in the trial judge's rulings or the state's presentation of the case somehow violated their constitutional rights. Being innocent wasn't itself a legal claim.

Calvin decided he better get acquainted with the Constitution if he was going to articulate how his rights had been violated. The right to remain silent, the right to be free from cruel and unusual punishment, the right to equal protection under the law: they were terms that got thrown about in the dayroom, but Calvin sensed few men understood what they really meant.

One evening, he remarked on this to Joe Washington, a brilliant but elusive figure who had been in the jail about a year longer than him. Joe had grown up in the Lower Ninth Ward, but no one from that neighborhood seemed to know him. He was one of the few in the jail who had attended college before his arrest and had a sharp understanding of the legal system, which made Calvin think he might have taken law classes. Calvin never asked, though—it was clear Joe didn't want to talk about his personal life.

"Ain't it crazy that the only time we come to learn about our constitutional rights is when we're trying to stop them being taken from us?" he said.

Joe smirked. "These dudes all think they have 'inalienable' rights."

He waved a finger at the men glued to the six o'clock news. "*Constitutional rights.* What they don't understand is that all we have is what a five-person majority of the US Supreme Court says we have."

Calvin cocked his head. "What do you mean?"

"We're only protected by the Constitution as much as those five justices want us to be protected. When the judges on the court change, so do our 'rights.'"

"I hadn't thought about it like that."

Joe pulled a paperback as thick as a telephone book from his waistband. "Here, you need to read this."

"*The Brethren?*"

"It's about the Supreme Court. How it changed in the sixties and seventies." Joe planted the book in Calvin's palm. "There's no such thing as constitutional rights. There's just a pendulum that swings backwards and forwards. In the fifties and sixties, Earl Warren's court gave Blacks and convicts and women rights they'd never had. But when Nixon came in, he shook a bunch of the justices loose to put an end to all that. He found judges who would decide cases based on *his* agenda. Sent that pendulum backward."

Calvin thanked Joe for the book. Though his reading was much improved, it took weeks to get through Bob Woodward and Scott Armstrong's six-hundred-page opus. He kept at it, riveted by the story of Supreme Court justices maneuvering around one another and leveraging external pressures to influence the court's direction.

Before he started speaking with Joe, he'd had no idea that a prisoners' rights movement existed or that its success was the reason he could now file complaints through a grievance procedure against the jail. Nor had he known that prisoners' rights were tied to other justice movements of the civil rights era, like Black Power. Through his reading, he learned that politicians like Nixon orchestrated a deliberate strategy to paint these movements as violent, destabilizing forces. In essence, law-and-order rhetoric was developed as a counterpoint to the civil rights movement.

Calvin finished *The Brethren* with a keener understanding of what he was up against. He realized his struggle to even get legal materials in the jail reflected a deep skepticism about whether people who had committed crimes deserved access to the courts. The Supreme Court was turning its back on prisoners, Joe warned, and the worst was yet to come.

WITH HIS APPEAL LOOMING, CALVIN NEEDED SOME BASIC RECORDS TO substantiate his legal claims. Long before trial, he'd tried to get his police reports, but the NOPD and the clerk of court failed to respond to his requests.

During his trial, he met an investigator from the indigent defender's office and kept his business card. He decided to write to the investigator, offering $350—an unexpected inheritance from his estranged grandfather's estate—to copy his police file.

The investigator accepted the job, and Calvin sent him a check to retain him. A few weeks later, however, the investigator came to the jail and said he had changed his mind. He didn't feel comfortable retrieving the copies since they weren't a matter of public record.

The investigator didn't return Calvin's check, and soon he stopped responding to his letters.

After months of silence, Calvin realized he would have to sue to recoup his money.

He filed a lawsuit, but still the investigator didn't respond. With no opposition, the judge ruled in Calvin's favor, ordering the investigator to pay him $350 plus interest.

When the investigator ignored the judgment, Calvin requested the judge garnish his wages.

Eventually, monthly checks began arriving in the mail. The whole ordeal had taken two years, and he still didn't have his police reports.

He did have one piece of luck regarding his trial transcripts, though. Mamie, who had recently been convicted of shoplifting and ordered to do community service at the courthouse, visited Calvin after one of her shifts and revealed that a clerk had taken a liking to her.

"Does he work for a judge or in the clerk's office?" Calvin asked.

"The clerk's office." Mamie's eyes brightened. "Why?"

"I need the transcripts from my trial. Tell him you're trying to help your brother and ask if he'll copy them for you."

"Your trial transcripts?" she asked.

"Yeah. They charge a dollar a page. There's no way I can get them on my own."

"I'll ask him," she promised.

Days later, the transcripts arrived in the mail. Calvin's heart swelled with gratitude when he saw the envelope. He stored the papers under his pillow, unwilling to let them out of his sight.

As he carried on researching legal claims for his appeal, a deeper truth hidden in the pages of *The Brethren* began to reveal itself. The story was not merely about Nixon's political maneuvers and the Supreme Court's conservative shift, he realized. It was a saga tracing back to the nation's very founding. Calvin had secured a copy of Alex Haley's *Roots*, which was circulating on the tiers, and as he read about Kunta Kinte and the early experiences of enslaved people on US soil, connections began forming in his mind about the nature of the law, how it was designed, and who it was for.

In a land where the founding fathers harbored a deep mistrust of central authority, he learned that the Constitution was crafted more as a check on federal power than an endorsement of it. The Bill of Rights granted specific powers to the federal government, leaving all others to the states or the people. As Joe Washington often noted, before the Civil War, "the people" primarily referred to white male property owners. For much of the nation's history, states had the authority to enforce oppressive local practices without federal oversight or intervention.

Through this historical lens, Calvin recognized the fleeting nature of the Warren court's fifteen years of progress—a brief moment of advancement that was over in the relative blink of an eye. Just a decade later, he and Joe were witnessing a rollback of the constitutional protections that the Warren court had once deemed absolute. According to *The Brethren*, the current chief justice Warren Burger's judicial philosophy of deference to law enforcement, along with his skepticism of protections for the accused, was precisely what motivated Nixon to nominate him to the court.

Calvin noted with some irony that while he'd waited for trial in the Orleans Parish jail without a single visit from his court-appointed attorney, the Burger court had issued two decisions in 1984 that undercut the Sixth Amendment right to counsel, making it even more difficult for defendants to challenge inadequate legal representation as a constitutional violation. Other rulings that year weakened protections against unreasonable searches and seizures, and the right against self-incrimination. Rather than a tale of linear progress, then, the court's precedents were better understood as a site of fraught negotiation, an elastic band for which every stretch was seemingly followed by a stinging contraction.

Calvin concluded that the Bill of Rights was never *for* people like him—not for Black people or for poor people, however much the Warren court tried to make it so. The battle he was facing wasn't for "rights"—it was for survival. Far from deterring him, this revelation served as fuel; his struggle was bound up in the fates of those who had come before and was symbolic of what many in America were still facing. He was grateful that *Roots* and *The Brethren* had lifted the scales from his eyes. He would fight smarter knowing his opponent.

IN EARLY 1986, CALVIN LEARNED ABOUT A NEW US SUPREME COURT case, *Michigan v. Jackson*, which established that once a suspect requests an attorney, they cannot be interrogated further without the attorney present. He requested a copy of the decision from the court—no easy task from inside the jail—and used it to support his appeal, arguing that his statements to authorities after his extradition hearing should have been excluded from trial.

He sent the handwritten appeal to the Fourth Circuit Court of Appeal, the state appellate court that handled appeals of criminal cases from New Orleans, just in time to meet his deadline. Despite his constraints, he was pleased with the brief.

When his lawyer finally sent him a copy of what he'd filed, Calvin was incensed. It was only two pages long and contained a single claim. Worse, the trial lawyers hadn't objected to the issue, meaning it wasn't preserved for appeal. His appellate lawyer hadn't even read the record closely enough to realize he was filing a meaningless claim.

Calvin prepared a bar complaint against the attorney, but he knew that wouldn't save him in court. He tried to reassure himself that his own brief would be enough to win a new trial, even without his attorney's help. While he waited for the court to rule, he focused on getting to Angola so he could access the law library and prepare his defense.

The opportunity finally came when Calvin saw the sheriff's attorney at the jail one day. They recognized each other from prior court hearings on Calvin's many suits. Calvin called him over to the bars.

"If you get me transferred to Angola, I'll drop all my lawsuits," he offered.

The lawyer's brows twitched with interest. "I'll see what I can do."

A few weeks later, Calvin was on his way.

1986

As the prison bus turned onto Highway 61, Calvin recalled a nursery rhyme from his youth.

> Angola . . . When I was one, one, one, one
> They booked me . . . for shooting that gun, gun, gun, gun
> Way down yonder on that farm
> Pickin' that cotton all day long
> Angola . . . When I was two, two, two, two
> They booked me . . . for sniffing that glue, glue, glue, glue
> Way down yonder on that farm
> Pickin' that cotton all day long
> Angola . . . When I was three . . .

He and his friends had jumped rope to the tune as preschoolers, onlookers tapping the syncopated rhythm at their sides. The state penitentiary had been in Calvin's consciousness for so long that he couldn't remember a time without it. Like Hurricane Betsy, which had ravaged the Gulf Coast in 1965, Angola prison loomed large in old-timers' stories and children's imaginations. Calvin had heard tales of knife fights and guards on horseback as if torn from the pages of a perverse Western, never sure what was real. After four years in Orleans Parish Prison, he was about to find out for himself.

It was a terrifying journey down the winding road. Though the highway was little more than a muddy track, the bus charged on at breakneck speed. It lurched at every corner, threatening to fly off into one of the deep ditches along the edge. Wrists shackled, Calvin struggled to hold on, his body sliding right and left while he prayed that the next turn wouldn't be his last.

As the bus charged deeper into the woods, he couldn't deny his fear. The guys in the parish had told far more worrying tales than those he'd heard on the street: of young men being used as sex slaves, of others mutilating themselves to get out of dangerous cells, of a sprawling farm in the middle of nowhere that was impossible to escape.

Still, he was convinced he'd made the right decision in getting moved. The law library was his only hope.

He stared out at the roadside trees, their lean shapes disappearing in a strangle of kudzu vines.

THE NEXT MORNING, CALVIN AND THE OTHER NEW ARRIVALS WERE taken to the hospital and shuttled into a windowless, airless room called the bullpen. They'd spent their first night in the cells, and now they were waiting for a doctor's assessment so they could be sent to the fields.

In the narrow room where they entered, a group of older men were already waiting on a bench to one side. The new arrivals were led to a bench on the opposite wall. Every face in the room was Black except one. Since slavery ended in Louisiana, long and life sentences had been primarily reserved for Black prisoners, who still made up three quarters of Angola's population.

A guard cracked open the door and called out a name. A man with swollen, red eyes got up and shuffled out, his shackles pinging against the concrete floor.

Calvin's shoulders and hips ached from the bus ride the night before. He leaned his back against the cinder block, preparing for another long wait. Doing time was no misnomer: so much of incarceration was about being rendered useless. Enforced nothingness. Waiting.

An unexpected movement caught his eye, and he noticed one of the older guys on the other side of the room tugging at his wrist. It looked like he was shoving the plastic stem from a cigarette lighter into the keyhole of his handcuffs. Within seconds, he had jimmied a hand free.

Calvin watched the man rise from his seat. He was wild-looking, with hair sticking out at odd angles and a mean stare. He glanced toward the closed door, then sauntered over to Calvin's side of the room, the others on the bench watching now, too. In seconds, he had snatched something from one of the new kids' throats. The room fell silent. All eyes fixed on the gold chain dangling from the man's fist.

Surprise, then anger, twisted the face of the kid who had been robbed. He was no more than twenty and skinny; Calvin recognized him from the bus. He lurched up from the bench in his shackles and blundered over to the man holding his chain. Whoops and whistles rose up from the onlookers.

"Come on," the older man taunted.

He grabbed the kid by the shoulder and plunged a fist into his stomach, the chain still threaded through his fingers.

Calvin heard the air leave the kid's lungs as he doubled over in pain. His opponent didn't wait for him to recover. He thrust a fist downward in the same moment the kid threw his head upward, and the contact made a hard, slapping sound. Blood splattered across the floor.

Calvin egged the young man on under his breath, urging him to fight back. If he cowered, he would be tagged as weak and made a target for future violence.

Why would they leave us alone in this room without anyone watching us? he wondered. But the door never opened.

The kid was bucking his head like a wild horse now, flailing aimlessly to keep his attacker away. The older man stood back, enjoying the spectacle he'd created.

A scene arose in Calvin's mind, from when he was eight or nine. He was playing in an overgrown yard with his cousins Brian and Anthony. Brian was chasing Anthony and Calvin through tall grass, one hand cocked like a gun. When he finally caught the pair by their shirts, he yelled, "Police! Stop!" Then he leaned over and thrust his knee into their backs.

Three of the boys' older cousins, Tyrone, Melvin, and Pee See, turned the corner. Even from a distance, they smelled of liquor and weed. Calvin tried to shrink into the grass.

"Look at our little fighters here," said Tyrone. "Come on then, what are you waiting for? Fight."

The youngsters clambered to their feet as the older cousins formed a loose circle. Calvin's chest tightened. Anthony and Brian were first cousins, he was a distant second. He shot them a pleading look, but it would be worse for all three if they didn't do what Tyrone and Melvin said.

Anthony and Brian came at him at once. Brian swung a punch at Calvin's midsection while Anthony bit the flesh of his arm. The fighting was vicious and ragged, nothing like the game of cops and robbers moments before. The men hollered and clapped, their drunken mouths gaping at their young gladiators.

"Manny Boteler!" Calvin was pulled from the memory by the yell of a guard.

The fight between the kid and his attacker broke up at the sound of the door. Another man rose to the call of his name and shuffled out.

It was as though nothing had happened. The kid leaned against the wall, blood running down his chin. The older man tucked the gold chain into his pocket and replaced his handcuffs. People resumed their muffled conversations and waited for their turn to pass through the door.

As he waited to be weighed and inspected for his fitness to work, Calvin braced himself. He knew this place posed threats he was only beginning to understand.

The moment the bus had arrived the night before, he'd been gripped by an instinctual terror. Though it was pitch black, the prison's isolation felt otherworldly, the ghosts of its plantation past seemingly lining the path to the front gate in warning. In New Orleans,

Calvin had always stayed on his side of Canal Street, a dividing line he knew not to cross. Angola offered no such boundary—it was absolute.

He knew little of the penitentiary's origins, which dated back to the early nineteenth century, when local Indigenous peoples were driven from the land so it could be conferred to white settlers through Spanish land grants. A Tennessean slave trader formed a plantation by consolidating several neighboring estates that came to be known as "Angola." After the Civil War, Major Samuel L. James bought the Angola Plantation from the slave trader's wife, who could no longer make it profitable without free labor. Amid allegations of bribery, James won a contract to manage the state's convicts. He moved prisoners into the old slave quarters at Angola and leased the male workers, including children as young as ten, to former planters in surrounding areas who wanted cheap labor to build levees and grow cotton. Women were made to work as domestic servants or in the fields. Criminal laws were purposefully created and enforced against Black people such that James had no shortage of hands. He operated without accountability, routinely working those in his charge to death.

Brutal conditions and the profit motive remained unchanged once Angola was bought by the state in 1901. The only difference was that the government now bore the cost of running it. The farm was expected to at least cover the cost of its operation, and every capable man or woman (women were confined at the penitentiary until 1961) was forced to work as a condition of their punishment.

Nearly every job on the prison farm—from cooks to electricians to clerks—was done by an individual in custody. "Field hands" earned four cents an hour (later, only two cents) to harvest cotton and hay and grow vegetables, the best of which were taken outside the prison to be sold in stores.

The old-timers in the parish jail had warned Calvin that he would have to start in the fields like everyone else, but with any luck, after a few months, he could make his way into a less physically punishing job. This was far from assured; some people got stuck in the fields for years. Yet these same old-timers insisted that conditions at the prison had improved over the past decade—that newcomers like Calvin had no idea how lucky they were.

Since the 1940s, the prison had faced, and resisted, sporadic calls for reform, particularly over the use of flogging and the "convict guard" system, where selected prisoners were armed and given control over the rest of the population, keeping security costs low. In 1951, thirty-seven white men dramatically slashed their heel tendons in protest of overwork, inedible food, and torturous floggings, prompting outrage and, eventually, plans for reform. Outside penologists were brought in to modernize the system, but their efforts were blunted in the '60s by an apathetic governor and the long-standing influence of politics and patronage that had plagued the prison from the start.

In 1971, a pivotal lawsuit filed by four Black men—Lazarus Joseph, Hayes Williams, Lee Stevenson, and Arthur Mitchell—forced federal courts and the Department of Corrections to confront Angola's pervasive violence, racial segregation, and arbitrary disciplinary procedures. Throughout this period, political organizing by men like Herman Wallace, Albert Woodfox, and Robert King (later known as the Angola 3), along with fearless reporting by incarcerated journalists such as Wilbert Rideau, advanced efforts for safer labor conditions, desegregation, and ending widespread sexual abuse. Despite these efforts, without funding from the legislature, conditions remained dire. In 1975, a federal judge declared the prison would "shock the conscience of any right-thinking person."

Angola was eventually brought under a federal consent decree, which was still in place at the time Calvin arrived. The federal court's intervention led to significant, permanent reforms. Even so, many practices at Angola, including field work, remained a psychologically and physically grueling echo of the old plantation, seemingly crafted to invoke the agonies of the modern-day workers' enslaved ancestors as a means of control.

AFTER HOURS OF SITTING IN THE BULLPEN, CALVIN'S NAME WAS finally called.

When he entered the hallway, Catkiller and Burl Carter, another friend from the parish jail, were waiting outside.

"Calviiiiin!" Catkiller called out in surprise. "Man, where you at?"

"Cell Block C," Calvin said.

It was a relief to see familiar faces. Catkiller had left the parish jail only a few months earlier. Calvin noticed that neither of his friends was shackled like him. People in general population—those living in dormitories—seemed to walk around freely, without any physical restraints.

"Oh no, that's where them hoes are at. You one of them hoes?" Catkiller cackled.

"What you talkin' 'bout hoes?" Calvin was confused. He thought about the young lady in denim who had brought him his tray of food the night before. "We got women feeding us over there, man, it's not bad."

"They ain't women, Calvin, they hoes," Burl confirmed.

Calvin flushed with embarrassment.

"I knew it, I always knew you was one of them," Catkiller clucked loudly. "I knew it was in your record. You a ho, man."

The guys waiting on benches in the hallway chuckled. Catkiller hadn't changed one bit.

"For real, though, Calvin." Burl turned serious. "That's a weak line, man, for punks and hoes that need protection. You gotta get from over there before you get that reputation."

"What do I do?"

"You beat up your cellie or one of the hoes," Catkiller said.

"Go back there and scuff up your cell partner," echoed Burl, "then they'll put you out."

The nurse motioned for Calvin to come over to be weighed. He turned back to Burl and Catkiller and gave a nod.

CALVIN WAS ON EDGE WHEN HE GOT BACK TO THE CELLBLOCKS.

"What kind of unit this is?" he asked his cellmate. "I heard it's weak."

"Don't believe those people, man, it's just talk," his cellmate said with a scowl. But his voice lacked conviction.

The next time the unit lieutenant came down the tier, Calvin called him over.

"How do I get transferred? I got to get from over here."

The lieutenant scoffed. "We just got you and you already cryin' about being moved?"

"Our bus broke down on the way from Hunt and we didn't get in till late. They stuck me here, but I wasn't supposed to be put on no weak unit."

The lieutenant scanned Calvin from head to toe. "Well, I'd say by the look of you that they would love you down on the walk. Fresh meat. You won't last a second."

Calvin turned away in disgust.

Back on his bed, he watched his cellmate out of the corner of his eye. He was troubled by the thought of having to attack the guy for no reason. Calvin recalled Big Dugger's advice not to play prison games. He wasn't supposed to be here, and he wasn't going to act like he was supposed to be here, either. He'd find another way.

The next morning, a guard yelled that it was time to go outside. "Yard call!"

Calvin quickly gathered up his belongings and stuffed them into a plastic bag. His cell partner watched him warily as he leaned the bag by the cell door.

The doors to all the cells slid open in unison, and the men inside, including Calvin, moved out onto the tier. They walked in a line until they reached an open gate on the covered walkway beyond the tier, then downstairs to the grass below.

The yard was a large square of neatly trimmed grass bordered by fencing topped with concertina wire. A much larger yard abutted it, where Calvin could see hundreds of men from the dormitories, some lifting weights or playing basketball on a patch of concrete. A few recognized him from the parish jail and came over to talk through the wire.

Calvin hadn't been allowed outdoors without shackles in more than four years of confinement. Walking on the soft earth was sublime, like wading into the waters of the Columbia River. He wandered the fence line with the sun at his back, stopping periodically to chat with people he knew from New Orleans. The sheer size of the grassy area was disorienting after years in a concrete pen.

When the call came to return to the cellblock an hour later, the men formed a line at the steps to be shaken down by security. They walked to the front of their cells and paused, waiting for the whistle. The cell doors opened and they moved inside. All except Calvin.

In the parish jail, refusing to leave or enter a cell was a rule violation. If it was the same here, he could get a write-up. And a write-up might get him moved.

"Catch your cell," an officer called from the front of the tier.

"I'm not going in my cell," he called back.

The officer called for the lieutenant.

"Catch your fucking cell," the lieutenant said loudly. "You're holding up the count."

Calvin steeled himself.

"I ain't living on no whore unit," he fired back.

The lieutenant cocked his head as if recalling their earlier exchange.

"Go in that cell, and when I'm finished counting, I'll move you."

Calvin wasn't fooled.

"No, no, no," he called, running forward to snatch his bag of belongings before the cell door could close behind him.

The lieutenant's pale face reddened. "You get your motherfucking ass right here, right now, or I'll beat them legs off your goddamn body."

Calvin hurried to the front of the tier and set his bag on the floor. Heart racing, he held out his wrists for the lieutenant, who slammed down a pair of cuffs.

———

THE DUNGEON WAS A SINGLE-MAN CELL, AND CALVIN WAS ONLY AL-lowed out of it when he showered, which involved standing in another cell at the end of the tier where a showerhead was hooked to the wall.

The days were long, but he was relieved to have a cell to himself. Two-man cells were the hardest place to protect yourself, depending on who your cellmate was. He stayed busy by reviewing his civil cases. Though he had promised the sheriff's attorney to drop all his suits, he kept one or two that were too important to set aside. He used his new law book from the Missing Raisins suit to help him draft new pleadings, following the writing exercises in the back.

One day, two middle-aged men in brand-name clothes came wandering down the tier, law books in their hands. Long before they reached his cell, Calvin spotted them with his peeper, a piece of mirror glass stuck to the end of a toothbrush that he poked through the cell door bars.

He asked his neighbor who they were.

"Inmate counsel," he replied.

The official title was inmate counsel substitute, given to individuals who worked under the supervision of Angola's Legal Programs department, serving as substitute lawyers for others in custody.

"They're convicts?"

"Yep."

One of the men stopped at Calvin's cell. "What's your name, young'un?"

"Calvin."

"Joe Pecker," the man said in reply. (It was always Joe Pecker, never Joe.)

He looked slick, with shiny black shoes, a fitted shirt, and a pen tucked behind his ear. The guys in general population could wear clothes from the street if they had the money to buy them, but Calvin didn't know that yet. He looked at the inmate counsel, confused.

"So, you're a convict?"

Joe Pecker smirked. "As the day is long."

"And what, you help with people's legal work?"

He nodded.

Calvin felt a spark of excitement. "I got a civil suit going in federal court and I need copies of two cases handed down by the Supreme Court last year."

When he named the cases, Joe Pecker's face went blank. Calvin wondered what an inmate counsel had to know if he didn't know the latest cases on conditions of confinement.

"I'll take a look for you," said Joe Pecker.

Calvin nodded. "Say, what does being an inmate counsel involve, anyway?"

Joe Pecker leaned a shoulder against the bars.

"Everyone has different assignments. My thing is, I represent people at disciplinary court, and then I do my rounds here in the cellblocks. Most days I'm in the law library, researching cases, things like that."

Calvin's eyes widened at the mention of the law library. "When do you get to go there?"

Joe Pecker shrugged. "Every day."

Calvin imagined wandering the bookshelves with a pencil tucked behind his own ear.

"If you're interested in a job, see what happens when you get out from behind here." Joe Pecker propped himself back up to move to the next cell. "I could put in a word for you."

Calvin lit up. "I appreciate that, man."

A FEW DAYS LATER, CALVIN WAS CALLED UP FOR DISCIPLINARY COURT. When he entered the office to face the board, he found Joe Pecker waiting for him.

For refusing to go into his cell, Calvin was facing a charge of aggravated disobedience. He'd heard from the others on his tier that Joe Pecker was good at cutting deals with the board.

Calvin had represented himself in all the grievances and civil suits he filed against the parish jail. It was strange to sit back and let another man act on his behalf, but the inmate counsel took charge.

"This dude—he's new here. He was still figuring out how things worked when he refused to go in his cell. I been speaking to him on my rounds and I know he's a good kid, he just needed to gain some understanding."

Joe Pecker spoke to the major and the classifications officer who made up the board with a familiarity and confidence that floored Calvin, as though he was one of them. It seemed to work.

"Camp D working cellblocks," said the major plainly.

He was getting out of the dungeon.

Calvin reached awkwardly to dap Joe Pecker's fist with a shackled hand. "Thanks, man."

"Every ninety days, the boards will come around to check on you," the inmate counsel explained. "If you do well in the working cellblocks, they'll consider moving you to general population."

As if reading Calvin's thoughts, he added, "And that's when you can get to the law library."

IT WASN'T UNTIL 1969, NEARLY TWO DECADES BEFORE CALVIN DIS-covered inmate counsel substitutes at Angola, that the US Supreme Court first recognized the crucial role of "jailhouse lawyers" in safe-guarding the constitutional rights of the poor. Before 1969, those men and women in American prisons who took it upon themselves to assist their peers with legal filings were often labeled rule-breakers and punished. Without the persistence of jailhouse lawyers like William "Joe Writs" Johnson, things might never have changed.

In 1965, while serving time at the Tennessee State Penitentiary in Nashville, Johnson started filing writs of habeas corpus for his fel-low prisoners, challenging the validity of their convictions in federal court. At the time, a Tennessee prison regulation stated that no "in-mate will advise, assist or otherwise contract to aid another, either with or without a fee, to prepare Writs or other legal matters." Johnson paid the regulation little heed, convinced as he was that all people, wealthy or not, had a constitutional right to appeal their convictions—a right he felt superseded any prison rule.

Despite repeated warnings and sanctions from the penitentiary, including retaliatory stints in solitary confinement, Johnson contin-ued filing writs. He charged his clients nothing in return. During a period in isolation, Johnson filed a lawsuit arguing that he was being deprived of the basic materials he needed to do his legal work, includ-ing law books and a typewriter. After litigating his claims in the lower court and losing, Johnson appealed to the US Supreme Court.

In a rare move, the court, led by Chief Justice Earl Warren, agreed to hear the pro se petitioner's case, and Johnson, who was appointed counsel, prevailed in his lawsuit seven votes to two.

Throughout the 1970s, the Supreme Court further fortified the right to access the courts through several pivotal decisions. It struck down regulations limiting the number of law books prisons could maintain and broadened the right beyond criminal appeals to include prisoners' civil rights complaints.

Then, in 1977, the court issued a landmark ruling in *Bounds v. Smith* holding that states have an affirmative obligation to ensure that incarcerated individuals receive meaningful access to the courts. This included providing them with pens, paper, notary services, stamps, and law libraries or other forms of legal assistance. The decision was a crucial victory for prisoners' rights, affirming that access to justice is a fundamental safeguard, even for those unable to afford counsel. In many states, law libraries became the primary means by which corrections departments fulfilled this obligation. Louisiana distinguished itself as one of only six states to implement a dedicated legal assistance program operated by incarcerated law clerks, known as inmate counsel substitutes.

FOUR DAYS PAST HIS TWENTY-FIFTH BIRTHDAY, CALVIN WAS MOVED from Camp D back to the Main Prison.

Angola's vast farmland, edged by forest and swamp, was dotted with outer camps—self-contained units with their own cellblocks, dormitories, and recreation areas. The Main Prison offered more programming and educational opportunities than the outer camps, and after three months away, Calvin was eager to return.

Gazing out from the back seat of the passenger van, he realized how little he had seen of the farm since his arrival. The fields, green from spring rains, were lined with newly sprouting crops.

Calvin wasn't fooled by the picturesque view; he knew he'd be harvesting those crops beneath a scorching sun in the months to come. At Camp D, he had worked as a field hand, cutting grass with a handheld blade under the watch of rifle-armed guards, returning each evening to his two-man cell, exhausted and relieved to have survived the day. When he reached the Main Prison, he would try to enroll in a GED program and find a way out of the fields—hopefully before the summer heat set in.

When the van slowed at an intersection, he noticed a tin shed off to one side. A few men in their forties were gathered out front, one sitting atop a tractor. If he hadn't known better, Calvin would've thought they were free. It was ironic that these men, cast off by society, were so thoroughly trusted by the prison.

As he made his way down the walk at the Main Prison for the first time, tens of pairs of eyes following him, he remembered his first days in the House of D at Orleans Parish Prison and the lesson he'd learned: the cost of freedom was doing without. He'd never give anyone a reason to think he owed them anything.

The old-timers in the parish jail warned Calvin that he needed to keep his guard up at Angola, especially when he used the toilet and the shower, and to avoid being alone in any quarters. While the prison he found in 1986 was not so thoroughly dangerous as the one they had first encountered in the 1970s, strength and "respect" remained vital currencies for survival. Violence and sexual manipulation were daily concerns, especially for the young and newcomers like Calvin. The adage was "You either be a man, or you get a man," meaning you either fought for your own protection or relied on it from a stronger man in exchange for sex and subservience. Once you crossed that line, there was no coming back. Calvin would sooner die fighting.

He was assigned to Pine 2, a dormitory in the East Yard. Standing on the threshold of the dorm, he balked at its size. The Main Prison was the biggest camp in the penitentiary, with the capacity to house more than a thousand people, and now he could understand how they all fit. Four rows of fifteen beds ran the length of the room. Two gigantic industrial fans whirred loudly at each end. In his five years of incarceration, he'd never navigated a sleeping space so large. How would he keep track of everybody? He'd heard of men with a score to settle thrusting padlocks in socks into the eyes of unsuspecting sleepers. He wasn't sure how he would fall asleep in a room this big.

The dormitory smelled of bleach and lye soap. Beneath his shoes, the gray concrete floor shined from years of being waxed by hand. The bathroom next to the dormitory contained four showerheads above an open, tiled floor. Four urinals and six toilets lined one wall, forcing men to wash and shit in front of one another, completely exposed.

The dayroom, a smaller room also attached to the dorm, contained a handful of desks and one television to serve its sixty residents.

Calvin found his cot and took a seat, his weight flattening the mattress pancake thin. The mattresses were made right there on the farm by incarcerated people, like nearly all necessities that sustained life at Angola.

Heart racing, he pulled open two metal lockerboxes at the foot of the bed, pretending not to notice the stares of the men on adjacent bunks. One by one, he placed his belongings inside: deodorant, a razor, soap, a toothbrush, and toothpaste. Two pairs of blue jeans, two white shirts, a denim jacket, four pairs of underwear. A handful of letters from Earline, Aunt Gail, and Mamie. And a few photographs of his little girl, Ayana, who was now five years old. The hardest thing about leaving the parish jail was the distance it put between him and his daughter.

He tucked his trial transcripts, his case files, and several of his lawsuits beside the letters and photos. On top, he piled his legal writing books, his most prized possessions. Then he locked the box.

He was told to sit on his bunk for the count, an interminable process that involved tallying every prisoner on the farm, from the men locked down in solitary cells to those wrangling cattle in far-flung fields. Mistakes or delays could cause it to be repeated two or three times before it was finally completed.

Once the count was over, it was time for chow. On his way out of the dorm, Calvin forged a callout pass, unable to wait even a day to see the law library. Following his friend Broom's instructions, he made his way down the walk to the Education Building after the evening meal and handed it to the sergeant waiting out front. Seeing nothing amiss, the sergeant took the forged pass and motioned for Calvin to go inside.

Calvin followed the hand-painted signs to a door with a wired glass window. He pulled it open and saw a concrete floor extending sixty feet back lined with rows of wooden bookshelves. His breath caught in his throat. He'd never seen so many books.

At the sound of his entry, a familiar face jutted out from among the shelves.

"If that isn't Calvin Duncan," said Joe Pecker, walking over. He was still Cool Joe, a swagger in his step and a pencil behind his ear. "So, you finally made it up here, uh?"

Calvin grinned. "I appreciate your help with the disciplinary board."

"Sure. This your first time to the law library?"

"Uh-huh."

Joe Pecker led the way, and Calvin followed.

"You got the reporters over this side. The legal writing stuff is over this side. Legal theory is up there. The rare books are behind the counter—you gotta ask Norris for permission for those. And you can study at the desks up front."

Calvin thanked him and wandered off to browse the shelves.

The spine of a legal reporter, a book of published court decisions, caught his eye, and he pulled it down to examine it. He felt the grain of the cover between his thumb and fingers and breathed in the musty scent.

At the end of the row, he noticed a small grouping of desks fronted by another hand-painted sign: RESERVED FOR INMATE COUNSEL SUBSTITUTE ONLY.

He pictured himself getting comfortable in one of the chairs, a legal dictionary and notepad in hand.

I'm gonna be the meanest lawyer on the walk, he thought, sliding the reporter back onto the shelf.

CALVIN RETURNED TO THE LAW LIBRARY THE NEXT NIGHT, AND THE night after that.

He already knew a couple of the inmate counsels, like Norris Henderson, an acquaintance from the parish jail. Norris introduced him to Floyd Webb, Checo Yancy, John Siri, Stan Smith, and the head of the program, Henry Hill. Mostly a generation older than Calvin, many of the inmate counsels held leadership positions in the prison clubs as well. The thirty or more clubs and religious groups, which centered around community service and self-betterment, met in the evenings and formed the backbone of Angola's social life.

Norris, known for his generosity, helped Calvin find his footing in the Main Prison. He taught him how to identify and avoid sources of trouble, encouraging him to become a role model for others. If the laws ever changed, or if he wanted to apply for clemency one day, Norris said, he needed to think about his conduct and reputation as well as his legal case. Big Dugger's advice for getting out of prison was to become a lawyer; Norris's was to become a leader.

Calvin appreciated Norris's guidance and recognized the wisdom of his counsel, but what he was thinking—and never said—was that such long-term considerations were irrelevant to him. Other guys might need to rely on clemency or changes in the law to find a way out, but he was going home through the courts, and soon. Any day now, the state appellate court would grant his direct appeal, and Angola would become little more than a brief stop on his journey home.

1987

While he waited for the appellate court to rule on his direct appeal, Calvin went to work on accessing his police reports. His legal research turned up some promising news.

In 1984, the Louisiana legislature had made initial police reports a matter of public record, giving anyone the right to view them. These reports were the first that officers made when they arrived at a crime scene, different from the supplemental reports detectives compiled during an investigation. Calvin hoped to obtain his entire police file, but the initial police report was a good start.

He mailed a public records request to the New Orleans Police Department. In response, the custodian of records demanded twenty-five dollars to copy and mail the report. That would take Calvin months to save, working in the fields.

"Is there an exception for people who can't afford the fee?" he asked the custodian in another letter.

But he wouldn't budge. "It costs twenty-five dollars for everyone."

Calvin sought advice from Tookie Davalie, an inmate counsel who was well-versed in criminal and civil law.

"You could file a writ of mandamus," Tookie suggested, referring to a request made of judges to compel individuals or agencies to fulfill their legal obligations. "Attach an affidavit that you're indigent and ask the court to force the NOPD to comply."

"You think a state court judge would do that? I don't have a constitutional claim," said Calvin.

"It's impeding your right to access the courts, ain't it?"

"Uh-huh."

"Look, get me some cigarettes and I'll do it for you."

Calvin paid Tookie two cartons of Camels to prepare the writ of mandamus, and he filed it.

To Calvin's surprise, the judge signed the writ and ordered the NOPD to produce the records or show cause why they couldn't.

Weeks later, a copy of Calvin's initial police report turned up in the mail.

Calvin took the report to the law library so he could read it without interruption. He sat down at a corner desk and carefully removed it from the envelope.

He saw the document was only six pages long. He read the first page, a chart listing descriptors of the scene.

Incident: homicide. Day/time occurred: 8.7.81 at 11:35pm. Temperature: 79. Lighting: Good.

The report named David Yeager as the victim and Kristie Emberling as the eyewitness.

But it also noted a second witness Calvin had never heard

mentioned: Lionel Glasper, who saw two men fleeing the scene, both five foot ten, one wearing shorts. He marked the name down on his legal pad.

Calvin turned the page and saw more descriptions, this time of the perpetrators. Two unknown "Negro" males, fifteen to twenty-five years old. One was five foot ten, stocky, with a light complexion, and wore a leather sun visor, a light shirt, dark pants, and tennis shoes. The other was five foot six, thin, with a dark complexion, a beard, and a mustache, and wore a dark shirt, tan shorts, and tennis shoes.

The third page described two more witnesses Calvin had never heard of: Gregory Sumas, who lived on North Roman Street, and Martin Laborde, who lived on Esplanade Avenue. Like Glasper, both witnesses only saw the perpetrators fleeing the scene. Sumas saw one man dressed in a light shirt and dark pants, while Laborde saw two subjects running toward downtown. Why hadn't prosecutors brought them to testify at trial?

Calvin opened his files to find the transcript of Kristie Emberling's trial testimony.

Emberling told the jury that the man who shot her boyfriend was wearing a knit cap, a brown vinyl or leather jacket, blue jeans, and tennis shoes.

Calvin had always thought it odd that she described the shooter wearing winter clothes in August. Now, comparing her testimony to the initial police report, he saw that he'd been right to be skeptical.

According to the police notes, the shooter was wearing a sun visor, a light shirt, and dark pants. Calvin noticed more discrepancies: at trial, Emberling said the shooter was the shorter of the men; the police report suggested the opposite. Emberling told the jury that the shooter had a mustache of two to three weeks' growth, but in the report, the facial hair descriptor for the shooter was left blank. Who was to say if the inconsistencies were Emberling's or a product of poor note-taking by the police? Either way, the discrepancies cast doubt on the witness identification.

That evening, Calvin lay on his cot, his mind whirring with all he had learned. While he felt relieved to finally have some answers, the more he dwelled on what the state had concealed, the angrier he became. He put on a cassette of Dr. Martin Luther King Jr.'s sermons that he had borrowed from the library.

> I call upon you tonight not to be spectators on the sideline, not to be individuals who are looking on, but to be involved participants in this great struggle to make our nation a greater nation, and to end all of the evils of racial injustice, poverty, and the evil of war.

An idea cut through Calvin's fury: Why not try to help a bunch of guys at the law library access their police reports? Success was its own revenge. If the state had buried this sort of information in his case, surely they had buried it in others.

The next day, Calvin found a typewriter and began copying Tookie's writ of mandamus, leaving blank fields for names and case numbers. He then mailed the template to Legal Programs, the department responsible for providing legal materials, and requested photocopies.

When the copies arrived, he handed them out in the law library. "Fill this in," he instructed the other callouts.

Weeks later, people's police reports began arriving in the mail. Word quickly spread that Calvin had found a way to secure them, and soon he was fielding requests from all over the Main Prison.

DEFENDING THE VULNERABLE FROM AN OPPRESSOR WAS AN INSTINCT Calvin had developed early in life. It wasn't just because of what his cousins did to him and Mamie on Clouet Street. It was seeing what happened to his uncle Trim, too.

Although technically the head of the household, Uncle Trim likely fell somewhere between his own children and Calvin and Mamie in the hierarchy of Aunt Nema's home. When Calvin was growing up, husbands and wives didn't divorce, and Uncle Trim seemed resigned to endure Nema's slings and arrows with stoicism. A Korean War veteran with a debilitating drinking problem, he mostly kept to himself, spending his days on a leather recliner taking long pulls from a quart of brown liquor.

Trim took a shine to his great-nephew as soon as Calvin and Mamie arrived on his doorstep. Despite his frailties, he strived to support Calvin in every way, helping with his homework and encouraging his creative interests, teaching him to cook, and taking him to the grocery store to buy paint-by-number kits when he found spare change beneath the couch. When Calvin was suspended for fighting other kids who made fun of him, it was Uncle Trim who advocated on his behalf with the administration. His support made school a place where Calvin could feel comfortable, and by the end of the eighth grade, he was earning certificates for best attendance.

Having benefited from Uncle Trim's care, it was difficult for

Calvin to witness his cousins treat their father with so little respect. He was an easy target, a punching bag whenever they needed money to get high.

"We in the same boat, son," Uncle Trim would say to Calvin after a beating. "We both getting dogged out."

Some mornings, Calvin would wake to find salt scattered across the floor. He assumed that Uncle Trim was placing a hex on the household in retaliation for his misery. During one alcohol-fueled outburst, however, when Uncle Trim cried that a terrible curse was already on their family—"Ain't none of us escaping it!"—Calvin realized the salt was his uncle's attempt to chase the demons out.

Uncle Trim died of cirrhosis of the liver when Calvin was fourteen. The loss was profound, leaving Calvin rudderless. A few months later, when he entered high school, he noticed the sidelong glances at his appearance when he wore the same three outfits each week. The shame that had marked his entrance to the second grade struck him again, but this time, Uncle Trim wasn't there to deflect it. Calvin felt all hell break loose inside him then. He lost sight of himself for a time, stealing from people's homes and selling their goods on the street, doing what he knew to survive. Still, he never forgot the compassion he'd learned from Uncle Trim—the sole gift Clouet Street had imparted.

"SO, YOU'RE A CIVIL LAWYER, HUH?" NORRIS WATCHED CALVIN DRAFTing a writ in the law library.

He nodded, still writing. "Who knows when this window's gonna close. These guys need to get their police reports before they change the law on us."

Norris leaned forward to read the draft.

> Though his rights may be diminished by the needs and exigencies of the institutional environment, a prisoner is not wholly stripped of constitutional protections when he is imprisoned for crime. There is no iron curtain drawn between the Constitution and the prisons of this country.

"Is that *Wolff v. McDonnell?*"

"Yep."

Norris studied him. "You interested in working as an inmate counsel?"

At this, Calvin set his pen down. "Yeah. Why?"

"You're young, but I'll tell Mrs. Rabalais you're serious," said Norris, referring to the head of Legal Programs.

Calvin was caught off guard. "Thanks. I appreciate you, man."

Norris was walking away when Calvin stopped him.

"What's she like, anyway?"

"Who? Mrs. Rabalais?"

"Yeah. 'Cause she's security, right?"

Norris looked amused. "I've worked with Mrs. Rabalais about as long as anyone in here, and I can tell you she's got one rule: long as you don't mess up, she don't let anybody mess with her boys."

CALVIN WOKE EACH DAY HOPING TO FIND A RULING ON HIS DIRECT appeal in the mail, and went to bed each evening disappointed.

He'd already decided that he would represent himself at his next trial when the time came. He would hire an investigator and gather the evidence he needed to show a jury how flawed the state's case against him really was. Never again would he leave his fate in the hands of a court-appointed lawyer.

Even as Calvin saved his earnings for an investigator from work assignments and plasma donations, accumulating savings inside the prison was difficult and slow. It was surprising how many ways there were to spend (and lose) money in the penitentiary. For one, the prison charged for necessities such as deodorant, shampoo, and stamps. Beyond those, many people sought momentary relief in dice games and drugs (the most widely used were marijuana and prescription pills known as T's and Blues). And then there were the discretionary purchases that made everyday life slightly more bearable if you could afford them: cigarettes, snack foods from the commissary, and clothes.

Though the prison enforced a dress code of denim jeans, tennis shoes, and white T-shirts, people could also purchase clothing from stores in the free world via mail-order catalogs, provided the pieces weren't too ostentatious. The result was a subtle visual stratification of the population into those who could afford Levi's and Nikes, and those who couldn't.

Calvin couldn't. Yet since his days on Clouet Street, he had cared for what clothing he had with meticulous attention. Even here in the penitentiary, he hand-washed his state-issue shirts and boxer shorts, not content to wait for the weekly laundry day. He also ironed his jeans, which earned him teasing comments from his dorm partners, but he brushed them off. He wasn't foolish enough to waste his hard-earned money on material things. He would have the presentation of a real lawyer, with or without designer jeans.

Nevertheless, he allowed himself one indulgence.

One evening after chow, he received a notice that a package had arrived for him at Classifications. Guessing the contents, he returned to the dorm to open it.

He sat on his cot and loosened one end of the package with his finger, sliding out a cardboard box. As he lifted the lid, a rich, oily scent hit him.

Beneath the sheets of tissue paper, he uncovered a pair of black leather shoes.

He picked one up and examined the thin laces and slim heel, tracing his finger along the stitching at the top of the sole. He knew how valuable a pair of shoes could be. As a child on Clouet Street, he had safeguarded his only pair by walking home barefoot after school, the cuts and bruises a small price to pay to keep his shoes intact. It seemed only fitting that he should have a pair of lawyer's shoes to wear when he won his trial and descended the steps of the Orleans Parish Criminal District Court a free man.

He set the new shoes on the floor and walked a few feet to test them. Pleased with the fit, he halted, unwilling to go farther.

These shoes weren't meant for the penitentiary; they were reserved for the day he would leave this place.

Carefully, he tucked them into his lockerbox and secured the lock.

THE FIRST TIME CALVIN SAW ALVIN ABBOTT AT ANGOLA, HE WAS ON his route from Pine 2 to the law library. Seeing Alvin lifting weights on the Big Yard, he paused at the fence beside the walk.

"Alvin Alvin," he called.

"Calvin Duncan!" Alvin plonked the barbell he was curling on the ground.

Calvin found the nearest gate and bounced down the steps.

They gripped hands.

"I heard you was up here. You know we were in the parish at the same time, but I never saw you," said Alvin.

"I know, I got in a fight my first few months and they stuck me on B-1 with Burl an' 'em."

The pair had been friendly since middle school, when Alvin lived in the Florida Projects and Calvin lived nearby on Clouet Street. The kids in the Florida Area gave each other nicknames by repeating their first names, but Calvin had never stayed put long enough to earn one.

He looked past Alvin to the other guys on the weight pile. "So, you one of these bodybuilder dudes?"

Alvin chuckled. "Gotta keep up my condition for when I get outta here."

"Sam's waitin' on you, uh?"

Alvin and his girlfriend, Samantha, had begun dating in the sixth grade, and they had been together ever since.

"You ever made it to the military?" Alvin asked. "Last time we talked was at your place on Pleasure. New Year's, remember? You said you were getting out of New Orleans."

"I tried. I made it to the Job Corps in Oregon for a while, but they arrested me and brought me back here."

Alvin's face fell. "I always remember that."

"What?"

"That night. We walked out to the front, to get away from everyone hanging in the back. We were talking on the front stoop, remember? Man, I thought you was so grown back then. You seemed like one of them *big* boys."

Calvin gave a chuckle as Alvin continued.

"You'd moved all over to different projects, seen more than I knew there was to see. Even though you were only two years older, there was always somethin' different about you, man. It stuck with me after that night."

Calvin was surprised by Alvin's keen recollection.

"You just seemed real determined to get out of New Orleans. To go do somethin' with yourself. I didn't get it. I didn't know what I was gonna do when I turned nineteen and they wouldn't send me to the juvenile institution anymore. Angola or die, I guess. But you . . ." Alvin paused. "I guess I'm just surprised to see you here."

Calvin was moved by his friend's dismay. Alvin was right—he shouldn't be here.

"Well, I'll let you get back to it," said Alvin. "You headed to the law library?"

"Yeah. By the way, what's up with your case?" Calvin asked.

Alvin waved the question away. "I don't really mess with my case."

They dapped again and Alvin returned to his weights, talk-back radio blaring in the background.

AFTER NORRIS PUT IN A WORD, MRS. RABALAIS SENT FOR CALVIN. HE was instructed to meet her in the A-Building, where Norris said she would interview him.

He put on a fresh gray sweatshirt and made his way down the walk, hunching his shoulders against the winter wind.

Though they had exchanged small pleasantries in the law library, Calvin wasn't sure what to expect of his meeting with Mrs. Rabalais.

He knew she had lived on the farm for two decades in a small village called B-Line. The prison town, named for Camp B, which was established at the same site in the 1920s, was first developed in the '40s for the thirty-nine security officers charged with overseeing thirty-five hundred prisoners, a feat they managed by relying on unpaid incarcerated "convict guards." After leadership changes and court interventions brought an end to this practice in the 1970s, Angola's workforce quickly swelled to more than seven hundred, and B-Line was significantly expanded. There were not only residences but also a post office, baseball fields, a gas station, a snack bar, and a grocery store, all built by Angola's incarcerated. Families on B-Line, many of whom had lived and worked on the farm for generations, tended to hold firm ideas about how the prison should be run, some of which reflected the penitentiary's long-standing commitment to segregation and the use of force. Though originally from elsewhere, Mrs. Dora Rabalais had married into one of these families, and now her son was a corrections officer at Angola, too.

Yet in her role as director of Legal Programs, a position she had largely developed herself since the early '70s, Calvin understood that Mrs. Rabalais had done pioneering work by national standards. She oversaw the expansion of libraries and inmate counsel assignments to the prison's outer camps, spearheaded a certified training program for inmate counsels taught by outside lawyers, and worked to have inmate counsels recognized by state courts, allowing them to personally represent their clients in civil suits.

Norris once shared an anecdote about Mrs. Rabalais from the

early '80s, when the legislature established a new "commissioner's court." The court was created to hear legal actions filed by people in custody in Angola, aiming to reduce the number of cases that had to be handled by federal judges in Baton Rouge. Inmate counsels were permitted to serve as representation in the proceedings, which were to take place inside the prison at Camp F. However, the first time the inmate counsels were transported there from the Main Prison, they discovered that the guards intended to take oppressive measures, shackling them in leg irons, handcuffs, a waist chain, and a box on the cuffs that caused significant pain.

The counsels later told the prison newspaper, *The Angolite*, that the psychological toll and physical torment of being shackled hamstrung their ability to represent their clients. Indeed, the first counsel to appear in the new commissioner's court couldn't even jot down notes in his notebook. In response, Mrs. Rabalais asked security to remove his restraints, but they refused to do any more than unshackle his right hand. She sought a rule change from the higher-ups, but they wouldn't budge, either. So she told the counsels that they were not—and never would be—required to appear at Camp F if they didn't want to go through the ordeal. Empowered to say no, many did, and the administration was eventually forced to relent, Norris said.

Greeting Calvin in the conference room, Mrs. Rabalais had the presentation of a middle-school teacher, a manila folder beneath her arm and eyeglasses hanging from her neck. She was unsmiling, but he sensed a kindness in her face. He hoped he would make a good impression.

"You want to apply for the position of inmate counsel substitute?"

"Yes, ma'am."

"All right. The purpose of this meeting today is for me to get to know more about you." She took a seat and motioned for him to do the same. "I'm going to ask you some questions."

Calvin pressed his spine straight against the chair.

"Tell me what crime you were convicted of and your sentence."

"I was convicted of first-degree murder and I'm serving a life sentence."

"And what's your current job in the Main Prison?"

"I was assigned to the field, but the glare from the sun was hitting my cataracts and giving me blackouts. So I have an indoor duty status now—I clean the dorm. I recently began taking GED classes in the afternoons, too, to get my high school diploma," he added.

She marked up a printout in the manila folder as he spoke. He tried not to look at what she was writing.

"I see that you're in the law library an awful lot. Your name is in that logbook just about every day."

"Yes, ma'am, I have been trying to learn as much as I can."

Even though he wasn't an inmate counsel, by now Calvin was known for being "in the law" and focused on little else.

"I see that when you first arrived here you were put on lockdown in Camp D for disobedience," Mrs. Rabalais continued.

He felt a flush of embarrassment. "Yes, ma'am."

"Do you play dice or bet money?"

"No, I do not."

"No gambling of any kind?"

"No, ma'am."

"What about drugs. Do you smoke or drink?"

"No, ma'am."

She continued with questions like a nurse running through a

patient intake form. Norris and Checo Yancy, one of the other counsels, had warned Calvin to answer each one truthfully. Part of her
task was to assess the risk of others manipulating him.

"She's gonna interview the major over your camp, the security
that work in your dorm, the people who see you and watch what you
do every day," Checo explained. "She already knows the answers, she's
just asking to see if you're honest."

"Do you participate in homosexual activity?" Mrs. Rabalais asked.

"No, ma'am."

"All right." She closed the folder and put away her pen. "In a few
weeks, you'll be called up here again to take a written examination.
We'll see how you do after that."

"Thank you, Mrs. Rabalais."

He'd made it past the first hurdle, but in truth, he was hoping to
be back in the parish jail with a new trial before the exam was held.

Ten days before Christmas, however, and two years since he
lodged his appeal, Calvin received word from the Fourth Circuit
Court of Appeal.

The decision changed everything.

His appeal was denied.

THE STATE COURT OF APPEALS DECIDED CALVIN'S CASE IN A PARTIC-
ularly cruel way, analyzing his legal arguments under the Fifth
Amendment, even though he had argued under the Sixth. Despite
pointing out the court's error, his petition for rehearing was also denied. Since being found guilty, Calvin had clung to the hope that the
appellate court would rectify the jury's mistake, yet it dismissed his
claims with a callousness reminiscent of Judge Shea. Christmas was

already the most difficult time of year in the penitentiary; now it approached like a chasm. When Calvin was sixteen, his aunt Brunetta had pleaded with a juvenile judge to release him from detention, and the judge had agreed. Now a grim realization kept him awake at night: if Brunetta had let him serve his sentence, he would have been locked up at the time of David Yeager's murder and spared this nightmare. He sank into a deep, anxious depression and lingered there for weeks.

The Louisiana Supreme Court was his only way forward, though it wasn't even obligated to hear his case. He summoned the mental strength to file a writ early in the new year, then braced himself for another prolonged wait.

As his stay at the penitentiary seemed destined to last, Calvin grew more resolute in his ambition to become an inmate counsel. He wanted to be part of broader efforts to push for changes in the law.

In addition to the law library, Calvin had been spending more time in the regular library, immersing himself in novels and biographies he'd never encountered on the outside. Among his favorite discoveries were *Profiles in Courage* by John F. Kennedy, *The Count of Monte Cristo*, and *The Cider House Rules*. He was drawn to stories of individuals who held fast to their convictions in the face of immense pressure and persecution, inspired by their resilience. On tape, he listened to Martin Luther King Jr.'s "I Have a Dream" speech, riveted.

The exploration of how to live a moral life and withstand despair in the prison environment was not unique to him; it was a common topic among the men in the law library. They understood—as King often noted—that how they responded to their circumstances would shape not only their own lives but those of future generations. Calvin was coming to understand what Norris had told him from the beginning: Those who committed to a path of self-discipline and service were the ones who would succeed—not because it would hasten their release, but because it gave them a purpose to endure. Through their leadership, they would shatter stereotypes about what kids from the projects could accomplish; through their commitment to those less fortunate, they would refute the notion that poor people somehow deserved their fate. Even in confinement, they could lead lives that illuminated the potential society had overlooked.

In this spirit, a group of like-minded acquaintances formed a new club, the Angola Special Civics Project. The group aimed to mobilize the families of incarcerated people to advocate for legislation that would address Louisiana's increasingly Draconian sentencing regime. They would also invest in the broader community by organizing fund-raisers for outside causes such as sickle cell disease research. Calvin joined as a founding member, helping to research model legislation.

Within three years, the Special Civics Project had enlisted a legislator from New Orleans who committed to introducing a bill that would extend parole eligibility to everyone who had served twenty years and reached the age of forty-five. The group successfully organized outside support for the bill through allied organizations and voter education. Remarkably, the bill passed and was signed into law, with one notable carve out: people serving life sentences were excluded.

"We'll go back for more next year," Norris reassured the group. But they knew it would be an uphill battle.

Early in 1988, Calvin was summoned to the A-Building with three other candidates for the inmate counsel substitute position. Mrs. Rabalais was waiting in the conference room. She directed the men to separate tables and distributed papers among them.

"Norris and Checo tell me you're good at civil law," she said, placing a piece of paper facedown on Calvin's desk. "I'm sure you know *Spears v. McCotter*. You've got one hour to complete the test."

Calvin turned the questionnaire over, the hairs on his arms standing on end. Mrs. Rabalais was right—he was familiar with *Spears v. McCotter*. Ever since he first came across it, the case had irked him.

The United States Court of Appeals for the Fifth Circuit, which oversaw federal courts in Louisiana, Mississippi, and Texas, had been transformed in the 1980s by Ronald Reagan, who had also reshaped the US Supreme Court. Now considered the country's most conservative federal circuit court, the Fifth Circuit agreed in *Spears* that federal magistrates—who primarily handle administrative matters and preliminary proceedings for federal judges—had the authority to dismiss pro se petitioners' civil rights complaints as frivolous without submitting the question to a jury. The ruling underscored the limited and often cursory attention given to cases filed by pro se applicants, with the court's majority expressing frustration at "the myriad problems presented by prisoners' cases, the volume of which mounts daily."

The court's tone in *Spears* rankled Calvin. He found it disingenuous that the judges lamented the number of prisoner lawsuits without acknowledging the root cause: the unprecedented explosion in imprisonment rates. It came as no surprise that the court system was struggling to accommodate the downstream effects of tough-on-crime policies. Yet lawmakers, district attorneys, and judges conveniently shifted the blame to incarcerated people, accusing them of depleting resources by exercising their constitutional right to access the courts.

As he made his way back down the walk, he mulled over the lesson Joe Washington had taught him when he first read *The Brethren* in the parish jail: *We don't have rights; we only have what five justices say we have.*

Calvin feared that *Spears* was more than just a few conservative judges opining about their overloaded dockets; it read like a call to action—one being echoed by even more powerful national figures.

In 1984, US senator Strom Thurmond, a prominent Southern segregationist and chair of the Senate Judiciary Committee, had introduced legislation to set a one-year deadline for filing writs of habeas corpus in federal court, citing a "tidal wave" of prisoner cases. Anyone who filed after the deadline would be barred from having their case reviewed, regardless of the merits of their claims. The Department of Justice supported the measure, even though it was tracking data that showed the initial surge of habeas corpus writs in response to the Warren Court's decisions of the '60s had plateaued by the early '80s. Although Thurmond's bill didn't pass that year, it was clear he would try again amid a growing conservative effort to limit access to the courts. In state houses across the country, lawmakers were proposing new time limits and procedural barriers to allow prisoner appeals to be dismissed without meaningful review.

Newly appointed chief justice of the Supreme Court William Rehnquist proposed going even further. He argued that federal courts shouldn't review state criminal convictions at all. An ardent supporter of states' rights, Rehnquist had faced controversy during his confirmation hearings for a memo he wrote while clerking at the Supreme Court, which argued for upholding racial segregation in schools. He was also criticized for his role in allegedly promoting voter suppression efforts that targeted minorities. While he distanced himself from these controversies to win Senate approval, his views on restricting prisoner access to the federal courts were widely accepted in a climate dominated by tough-on-crime policies.

As Joe had warned, the Supreme Court justices who once protected the rights of indigent defendants were leaving the bench, replaced by jurists with views like Rehnquist's. Calvin suspected that *Spears* was a sign of things to come. Politicians and judges aimed to confine poor people in prisons, forcing them to serve their sentences in obscurity. And if silencing them meant shutting the courthouse doors, the federal courts seemed ready to play their part.

As Calvin walked, his mind returned to *The Cider House Rules*, a novel he'd come to hold dear. The story of Dr. Larch, who pursued justice for his female patients outside the bounds of the law, inspired him to want to do something about the predicament he and his peers were facing.

By the time he reached the dormitory, he was certain about one thing. Whether he was chosen to be an inmate counsel or not, he wasn't going to be a spectator on the sidelines as the battle for access to the courts waged. He would use the law to fight back.

Part 2

⫯⫯

They can put the chains on your body.
Never let them put the chains on your mind.

KUNTA KINTE,
ROOTS

1988

The visiting shed at the Main Prison bustled on Saturdays and Sundays. Given the prison's isolated location in the Tunica Hills, most family members had to travel at least three hours to reach the front gate—some, many more—making weekends the only practical time to come. Once through security, they boarded old school buses, stifling in summer and frigid in winter, and made the journey to the camps for their visits. In addition to seeing their own loved ones, visiting days were an opportunity for the men to meet one another's families and create new connections. Many romantic relationships began with an introduction in the visiting shed. Families would share food made by the inmate clubs and sold at concession stands, plates of fried catfish and soft-shell crab a welcome contrast to their institutional surroundings. Photographs were taken in front of ocean or mountain murals hand-painted by men at the prison and stored away in lockerboxes as precious keepsakes.

Mothers and girlfriends were the most faithful pilgrims. Having neither of these, Calvin was rarely called out. On the odd occasion he did receive visits, it was Mamie or Gail, with Ayana or a young cousin in tow.

Ayana's mother, Earline, had been battling a severe crack cocaine addiction for several years now, a fact Calvin learned from a friend in Angola whose brother was dating her. Both Gail and Mamie tried to look out for Ayana, who still lived with her mother as well as now a younger half brother and sister. It pained Calvin to see that, even in middle school, Ayana was already taking on the role of a parent. He knew the pressure it put a young person under to have to grow up so fast.

Mamie's family was also growing larger. She had a second son now—Dwayne, named after his father—and a daughter on the way. Mamie was devoted to her partner, but he suffered from drug addiction, too, and their relationship was tumultuous. Mamie never spoke to Calvin about it directly, but Gail let on here and there.

Calvin could see that the visits he received, sporadic as they were already, would probably peter out the longer he was incarcerated. He'd learned from an acquaintance at *The Angolite* that most guys stopped getting visits after their first five years at Angola; in fact, half the population never received a visit at all. The cost, time, and emotional toll were too much for many families to bear.

Knowing this, Calvin decided, perhaps unconsciously, to pull away first. He stopped making calls home and never asked his family to visit. Before long, their correspondence dwindled to the occasional letter.

Since Calvin wasn't called out for visits or club events very often,

Norris began leaving him in charge of the law library. While the counsels were occupied, Calvin manned the counter, signing people in and answering their questions. His helpful manner was often met with a surprised look that told Calvin how rarely his peers experienced even small kindnesses. With each person he assisted, his confidence grew, and he found that being useful to others helped distract him from his growing isolation.

One evening in the law library, Calvin heard his name. He looked up to see Alvin Abbott standing at the front counter.

"Alvin Alvin. What's goin' on?"

Alvin was only ever inches away from laughter or a grin, but tonight he wore a strange expression—something was amiss.

"You look like you've seen a ghost," said Calvin.

Alvin swallowed. "I did, brah. My own."

Calvin watched him, waiting.

"I was listening to public radio while I was on the yard this afternoon and this story came on about convicts. About how these dudes doing time would try to stay fit to preserve themselves for the outside world, hoping they'd get out one day."

Alvin moved his hand through his cropped hair.

"I heard that, and I look around, and I see all these dudes working their bodies into peak physical condition—and it hit me. I'm spending so much time making myself look good for the world, and I'm twenty-eight years from seeing it. I was nineteen when I was arrested, and I'll be fifty-two before I get out."

Calvin studied his friend, detecting a familiar panic. He recalled a conversation he'd overheard in the law library soon after he arrived at the Main Prison, where the Lifers Association—a prison club for those with life sentences—was meeting. One of its former presidents, Earl Clark, was approaching three decades in Angola; Calvin's first inkling that life in Louisiana really meant life.

That evening, Clark was joined in the library by four other men: Henry Hill, the head inmate counsel; Andrew Joseph, another old-timer; and two younger guys, Darrell Miles and Joe Stevenson. The group was asking Henry what potential legal or legislative challenges could be mounted against life-without-parole sentences. They lamented that more and more young men were coming through the gates of Angola without a hope of ever leaving. It was taking a psychological toll on the population.

"You hear about that fool hitting a dude up the side of the head with a lock in his pillowcase?" Darrell asked the group.

"He thought the guy stole his cigarettes," Joe scoffed.

"That dude's gonna be in Camp J for months," said Darrell. "These guys don't think they have nothin' to work toward anymore. They're losin' hope."

Calvin trained his eyes on his book at a nearby table, listening intently. His heart raced as he heard the group articulate thoughts he'd been wrestling with for months.

Since arriving at Angola, Calvin had recognized countless faces from the streets of New Orleans. So many people he had grown up with were now living their lives in prison. It almost made their incarceration seem inevitable. Even he, who had been determined to leave New Orleans, hadn't been able to escape Angola's clutches. There had to be a reason.

His mind returned to Kunta Kinte's journey in *Roots*. Since Black people's earliest encounter with America, he thought, their existence had been defined by their economic value only. Listening to the lifers, Calvin saw that a version of these old forces was still at work, ushering Black boys to Angola in droves.

After some time, he rose from his desk and wandered over to a stack of old copies of *The Angolite*. A decade earlier, the prison magazine had come under the leadership of a pioneering self-taught journalist, Wilbert Rideau. With the support of Warden C. Paul Phelps, Rideau, the first Black editor in chief of any prison newspaper in the United States, transformed *The Angolite* into a thriving quarterly newsmagazine that provided rigorous reporting on all aspects of incarcerated life. It was unique among prison publications for being uncensored by the administration, a hard-won commitment that Rideau fiercely defended for twenty-five years.

Calvin thumbed through the stack, scanning issues without knowing what he was searching for. When he saw an edition with an article on the front cover called "Life: No Rhyme, No Reason," he flipped it open.

The article began in much the same way as the conversation he'd just eavesdropped on, reporting that the number of people serving life sentences in Louisiana had ballooned more than fivefold in recent years, from 193 in 1972 to 1,084 by 1982.

Andrew Joseph was quoted discussing the disproportionate number of life sentences imposed on Black Louisianans compared with white defendants arrested for similar crimes: "Blacks today before a court of law are in much the same situation they were in during the days of the Ku Klux Klan," he told *The Angolite*. "The only difference is that today many of the racists wear black robes instead of white ones. We find that all that was accomplished during the civil rights era has been lost or drastically reduced."

The article explained that in the 1970s, Louisiana's legislature implemented a series of laws that drastically curtailed lifers' ability to go home. For more than fifty years, the Board of Pardons and the governor had routinely released people serving life sentences after ten years and six months, recognizing that this was enough time for a man to be punished and demonstrate his capacity to change. However, when the US Supreme Court imposed a temporary moratorium on the death penalty in 1972, Louisiana and many other states responded by lengthening sentences for a widening net of offenses. The Louisiana State Legislature made life without any possibility of parole the mandatory sentence for numerous crimes, including felony murder (a doctrine allowing someone to be charged with murder despite having no intent to kill or cause bodily harm) and drug offenses like heroin possession.

By 1984, Louisiana had become a national leader in the imposition of natural life sentences, imprisoning one third of the entire country's life-sentenced population. Hundreds of people at Angola who had been sentenced under the old laws and once expected to go home were now facing death in prison. Old Man Clark was one. When he was convicted, he thought he'd be released after little more than a decade. Now, he'd been in Angola for nearly thirty years.

This was the revelation suddenly hitting Alvin, as though he'd looked through a telescope to find a meteor headed straight for the prison. He might not be serving life, but his thirty-three-year sentence for robbery would have him wither away inside the penitentiary if he didn't take matters into his own hands.

His voice interrupted Calvin's thoughts.

"If you ain't busy, you think you could take a look at my case sometime?"

Alvin was rubbing his arm sheepishly, and Calvin knew that behind his question was the same terror that had spurred Calvin to plead with Big Dugger in the parish jail. If no one was coming to save him, how was he supposed to help himself?

"Are *you* prepared to look at your case?" Calvin shot back.

Alvin blinked. "I don't know nothin' about my case."

"If I'm going to look at your case, that means you've got to be up here with me," Calvin said. "At the law library. Pulling books. The whole works."

Alvin considered the deal. "I thought I could do all this time, Calvin. But I can't. I'll be an old man by the time I leave this place." He let out a small sigh. "Whatever you need me to do, I'll do it. I gotta find a way home."

ALVIN EYED THE STACK OF PAPERS ON THE DESK. HE HAD NEVER looked at his case. He hadn't read or studied much of anything since dropping out of school in the seventh grade.

"You can read, though, and you have your transcripts from your trial—that's better than ninety percent of people up here," said Calvin from a nearby seat. "Start with your court opinions."

Alvin obediently pulled out the appellate court's decision denying his direct appeal. It stated that he had been convicted of three counts of armed robbery for robbing three men at gunpoint with whom he'd been playing a dice game. He was to serve thirty-three years on each count, to run concurrently.

"Your lawyer filed a *State v. Martin* brief." Calvin shook his head. "That's when the lawyer turns the record of your trial over to the judges and asks them to identify legal issues 'cause he says he can't see any himself. No surprise you were denied."

"What's the point of having a lawyer if he can't see a legal issue?"

"That's why we've got to know our own cases, brah," Calvin replied. "So we can tell the lawyers what to raise, or raise it ourselves."

Alvin's trial had lasted only a couple of hours. His attorney didn't call any witnesses or offer any defense. Alvin was swiftly convicted and sentenced to twelve years in prison. Two days later, the prosecutors on the case returned to court and asked for Alvin to be "multiple billed" because he had a prior conviction for shoplifting. The multiple bill was a sentencing enhancement that the state could use to secure longer prison sentences for individuals with previous convictions. Unlike other district attorneys around the state who rarely imposed the enhancement, the Orleans Parish district attorney's office used multiple bills in almost every eligible case. The office was responsible for sending scores of young Black men to prison for decades longer than they would have otherwise served. In Alvin's case, the state requested his sentence be tripled, all because of a shoplifting conviction he'd received when he was eighteen.

Alvin's family scraped together money to pay a lawyer to handle his state post-conviction petition, but as was often the case, their best efforts had only been able to buy mediocre legal assistance.

"Maaaan . . . this dude only raised one assignment of error." Calvin dangled Alvin's post-conviction petition in front of him like a dirty sock. "We'll do better than that, I guarantee it," he added quickly, seeing the defeat on his friend's face.

Reading on, Calvin spotted something in the transcript of the sentencing hearing.

"Look at this."

Alvin followed his gaze.

"Your judge didn't want to give you all that time. Listen to what he said: 'This Court feels that this type of sentence is not called for under the law; that the twelve-year sentence imposed on the original conviction is one that more than meets with the facts of the case and the defendant's background, and one that would lead to his ultimate rehabilitation and re-entry into society.'

"Thirty-three years for robbing a dice game." Calvin tapped the transcript. "Keep an eye out for court decisions dealing with whether judges should have discretion to refuse the state's request for a multiple bill. Even if there's nothing out there now, a court of appeals might look at it down the road."

Alvin scribbled notes on a yellow legal pad he had bought from the commissary. A small marker of his new life as a man "in the law."

"All right. What else should I do, Calvin?"

"Keep reading."

Alvin scowled. "My head hurts, man."

"That's that ignorance, boy," Calvin teased. "It's fightin' to stay in there, but you forcin' it out."

IN MAY, MRS. RABALAIS SUMMONED CALVIN AND THREE OTHER IN-mate counsel applicants to the A-Building to announce her decision.

"This is a job that requires maturity and dedication—not just legal skill," she said, her expression stern. "Inmate counsels are given more responsibility and more freedom than many of the other inmates in this prison. Their positions must be approved not only by the warden but by the Department of Corrections in Baton Rouge. When the inmate counsels do their jobs well, they find they have my unwavering support. But if they do wrong, I don't hesitate to put them out. I can't afford to have anyone undermining this program."

She turned to Calvin.

"I'm particularly concerned about you. You're only twenty-five. I've been running this program for over a decade, and you're younger than anyone else who's held the position. That worries me for several reasons. People will want to use you for what you can get them. They will try to manipulate you to bring in contraband, drugs, you name it. I wouldn't put it past security to do the same." She eyed him carefully. "Nevertheless, I'm going to take a chance on you."

Calvin dipped his head. "Thank you, Mrs. Rabalais."

"Don't let me down, Calvin."

"I won't."

"WAKE UP, YOU'RE DONE," SAID THE TECHNICIAN, PLACING A COTTON ball in the crook of Calvin's arm. Calvin craned his neck to find the swab with his other hand. The vein throbbed. He lay back and waited for it to close over.

He always fell asleep when he was donating his plasma. From the moment his head touched the bench every Tuesday and Thursday afternoon, he was out.

Thousands of men lined up for plasma draws at the prison twice a week. In exchange for being jabbed with a horse-sized needle, they received $6.50 pay. It was a financial necessity for many, and a good deal for the administration, which pocketed more than a dollar per bleed.

The plasma building smelled of chlorine and sweat. Calvin eased his way down from the bench and gathered his law books, making space for the next man in line. He was off to meet Checo at the law library.

Legal Programs had a policy that new recruits worked under supervisors for at least six months before going out on their own. Checo and Henry Hill would supervise Calvin. The pair worked at Magnolia, a dorm designated for vulnerable individuals, as well as at disciplinary court at night. Calvin was to accompany them.

When he reached the law library in search of Checo, he saw Joe Pecker pulling books, this time with a freshly starched baseball cap perched on his head.

"How's it going down at the cellblocks?" Calvin asked.

"Been quiet lately. Gives me a chance to get more of these out in time for Valentine's Day." Joe Pecker pointed to the leather belt he was wearing. The prison held a rodeo for the general public once a year, and he had a spot at the hobby shop making leather goods to sell to the spectators.

"They're nice-looking."

"Want one?"

Calvin laughed. "Man, when I have a spare dollar you'll be the first to know."

Joe Pecker shrugged and turned back to the books.

Checo called out to Calvin from the back desks. "You ready?"

They were due for court in another part of the Education Building.

"Let me ask you something," Calvin said as they made their way down the hall.

"What's up?"

"A few guys been telling me to pass letters for them."

"At Magnolia?" Checo raised an eyebrow. Magnolia was the closed dormitory where residents weren't allowed to interact with those in general population.

"Yeah. I've been saying I can't but that seems to piss 'em off. What do you do in that situation?"

"That's gonna happen." Checo nodded. "Here's how you deal with it. Depending on where they want it delivered, accept the letter. Don't read it in their presence. But once you get out of sight, take a look inside and check there's no contraband in it. The guy who gave it to you is going to say it's legal mail or something to do with his case, whatever whatever. It ain't. And when you walk outside, security's gonna shake you down and find it. That'll get you locked up."

They paused their conversation as they passed a guard. "All right, sergeant."

Checo continued once they were alone again. "Now, security is okay with it as long as you don't bring it outside the building you're in. But here's the thing—you *want* to read the contents of those letters. It's how you can protect yourself. Most of the time they're to other guys—to their sweethearts—and if they know you know, they won't want to mess with you. Then you've always got something on 'em."

Calvin snorted. "This place is crazy, brah."

"Our job takes some negotiating." Checo shrugged. "You got the interests of security, the interests of your clients, and your own interests to balance—don't forget that, or you won't be in the job long enough to help nobody."

Calvin thought about this as Checo walked ahead into court.

At the door, he posted up to interview the men in line.

Walk-in Court, which they also called Night Court, dealt with minor disobediences. The hearings were quick and judgments swift. Calvin thought with a flicker of heat that Judge Shea would be well suited to it.

"Leroy Polk."

Calvin looked up from his notes to see a kid, barely eighteen and a bundle of nerves.

"I was just trying to get the mud off my hoe, it had been raining," he said.

Calvin nodded. "You'll be all right, man."

Behind him, Joe Pecker walked into the courtroom. He'd come to represent a friend, and his man was up.

"Major, he's trying his best." Calvin heard the familiar lines. "You won't see him again if you give him a chance."

Joe Pecker had the nickname "Two-and-Two" because he was an expert at getting the board to agree to sentences of two days in isolation and two days in the field on serious charges, or two days' loss of store and two days' extra duty for minor ones. He used breaks in proceedings to sell his leatherwork to guards and clients alike. He felt this softened up "the rank," the senior members of security who sat on the board.

Checo came to find Calvin.

"Your turn," he said, ushering Calvin into the room. "This ain't my night."

Rather than leatherwork, Checo relied on social finesse to manage disciplinary court. He chatted to security like they were old friends, lingering after the proceedings were adjourned to talk about football and to ask after their families. Though Calvin couldn't imagine ever approaching security with such familiarity, Checo assured him that he would see the benefits of working outside court procedure the longer he stayed around. "Make sure you go and see the major on duty before court starts so that you can see what mood he's in," Checo counseled. "If he's going on a hunting trip and wants to get home in a hurry, it's time to deal."

Calvin apologized to the kid he was interviewing and hurried into court. The next case on the docket was an aggravated disobedience charge. The major, ignorant and spiteful on his best day, was in a foul mood, and before Calvin knew it, he had doled out a mean sentence.

Calvin saw why Checo had tagged him in. Better to have the new guy bear the brunt, he thought wryly.

The next case was handled in the same abrupt manner. This time, Calvin stated his objection for the record.

"I won't have none of that objection stuff in my court," the major spat. "Next."

Calvin clamped his jaw shut. There was no use fighting him. He would save it for the appeal.

Two more cases passed the same way. Calvin shot Checo a glare for throwing him into the fire. The major called in the nervous kid from the hallway.

"Leroy Polk. You were written up for having an unauthorized metal tool in your possession while at work in the field."

Leroy nodded, hands clasped tight in front of him.

"What were you doing when you were discovered?"

Leroy looked thrown by the question. "Uh—I was using a piece of scrap metal I found on the ground," he stammered. "I was using it to get mud off my hoe 'cause—because the weather was bad—it had been storming and . . ."

The major clicked his tongue in disapproval. "This is a serious offense."

Calvin looked down at the disciplinary report. No, it wasn't. It was a minor rule violation. If they had thought Leroy intended to smuggle the tool through the gate to use as a shank, they would have placed him in administrative lockdown and sent him to Daytime Court.

The major directed his next comments to Calvin. "He was found holding a knife, which he would've tried to sneak into the compound if he wasn't discovered sooner."

"Major," Calvin tried, "I believe that the sergeant who wrote him up described it as a metal shard rather than a knife, and he acknowledged in the report that he wasn't hiding the tool or attempting to do anything else with it other than what he just described to you."

"I want a minute to review that." He waved Leroy and Calvin out of the room.

Back in the hallway, Leroy wrapped his arms over his head.

"This isn't going well," Calvin acknowledged. "But when he reads the report he should calm down."

"I did it so I could work faster," Leroy protested.

"I know."

Calvin understood why Leroy would have scrambled to clear mud from his hoe, to keep pace with the line.

When Calvin had first arrived at Camp D and been sent out into the fields, he'd had to learn how to use a ditch bank blade—a long-handled tool shaped like a hockey stick with a sharp metal blade at one end, used for cutting grass and foliage. Every morning, he and the other men from the working cellblocks were marched to a field. A prisoner at the line's front would initiate the cuts—one, two, three. Then the men worked their assigned cut until reaching the other side of the field, three or four hundred working in pairs. All the while, guards with rifles slung over their shoulders watched, shouting, "Don't walk out of the line!"

Calvin had been assigned to Hoggy Doggy's line, a corrections officer notorious for his backbreaking treatment of the field hands. "You got one week, dude," he threatened on Calvin's first day, meaning he had one week to learn the ditch bank blade and keep up with the line or he'd be written up for an aggravated work offense and thrown in the cells. Hoggy Doggy, who was from a rural parish near Angola, regarded prisoners from New Orleans with special contempt. "If you can't hack it, pack it. And if you fall, fall on your back," he added with a sickening grin, intimating what the other men on the line would do to Calvin if he fell on his front.

Despite his fear of lagging behind, Calvin struggled with the ditch bank blade. His cuts were slow and poorly positioned, and the sun's harsh glare in his eyes triggered brief blackouts. He was lucky not to injure himself. During those first weeks, his cell partner, Black Ice Angel, made a point of helping him. After finishing his own work, Black Ice Angel, who was openly gay, would refine Calvin's cuts, aware that other men vying for his affection would also pitch in. Without Black Ice Angel's intervention, Calvin would have been written up. He could only imagine the terror young Leroy had felt when his hoe got plugged with dirt.

The major called them back in.

"Based on the nature of the report, and your own statement that you did have the weapon in your hand, you are sentenced to Camp J," the major announced.

Calvin flinched. He heard Leroy suck in a breath as two guards came and put him in shackles.

"I'll file an appeal," Calvin whispered as the guards led him from the room.

He watched Leroy leave, aghast.

Camp J, established in the mid-1970s as a disciplinary camp, continued to serve that purpose despite official statements to the contrary. Its residents faced indefinite sentences and had to progress through various levels of classification before qualifying for a potential transfer. Those who returned to general population spoke of daily threats: acid-tipped darts, boiling water, and vile concoctions. Long-term detainees, dubbed Camp J warriors, were known for their resilience and survival instincts. Yet many spiraled into an existence consumed by who they could hurt before being hurt. The rank there was known to be cruel, condoning savage beatings and withholding necessities. The camp was marred by suicides, mysterious deaths, and frequent self-harm. It was the most hellish place in the penitentiary.

As soon as court was over for the night, Calvin headed to the law library to draft Leroy's appeal. Later, he lay awake in his cot, unable to block out the image of Leroy's terrified face.

He called Mrs. Rabalais from the dorm the next day. She listened patiently as he recounted the ordeal.

"Really, it's all because the major was having a bad night. He was being hard on everybody. But this kid got the worst of it."

"I'll review the disciplinary report and listen to the tapes," said

Mrs. Rabalais, referring to the recordings of the court proceedings. "Don't worry, Calvin."

Calvin hung up the phone. He was still racked with guilt. He needed to talk to someone.

He set off for Cell Block D.

One of the benefits of being an inmate counsel was having freedom to move to different parts of the camp with relative ease. As long as you didn't abuse the privilege, you could go most places without having to offer security an explanation.

Calvin reached the disciplinary unit where he'd served thirty days in the dungeon after his first write-up.

He found Joe Washington's cell.

"Hey, man."

"Is that Calvin?" Joe asked in mock surprise. "I don't recognize you with that lawyer swagger."

Calvin chuckled. He'd only seen Joe a couple of times since the parish jail, mostly because Joe was frequently in lockdown.

Sunlight struggled to pierce through the small windows across the tier, leaving Joe's cell dim and musty.

"So what you brought me, son? You got me some peppermints or what?"

"I ain't gonna bring you no contraband, you know that." Calvin frowned. "Don't be asking."

Joe's gnarled face flattened in disgust. "Oh, I see. They got you, boy. You been *broke*."

He'd always had a flair for the dramatic.

"So what you done this time?" Calvin asked.

"Refused to work."

Calvin gave a small chuckle. "Sounds right."

"I'll work if I want to work. I ain't behaving to get a carrot like some animal."

Joe had been convicted of aggravated rape, and he knew he was never getting out of prison. He was determined to live out his days on his own terms.

He stuck a peeper through the door bars to keep an eye on the tier.

"You got any suits going?" Calvin asked.

"You bet. I got a 1983 in federal court and three ARPs moving in state court." Joe moved his eyes to Calvin. "I see you're still here, then."

"Still here."

"How's the job?"

Calvin shrugged. "I'm doing Night Court right now. And I help with callouts in the law library. Last night I saw a guy go down for something he shouldn't have. It's been on my mind. This major, he just flipped out on this kid. Sent him to Camp J for nothin'. I was the one representing him so it's hard not to . . . I guess I feel responsible."

"Why are you responsible? You didn't ask to send nobody to J," Joe snapped.

Calvin fell quiet.

"Don't forget that's how this thing is set up." Joe shook his head. "We ain't the ones with the say-so. They are. That dude getting hauled off to J—that's the way they remind us that the rules don't apply to us. They call it disciplinary 'court,' they give us an 'Administrative Remedy Program'—it's the same as the judges. None of it means nothin' unless they decide it does. The fix is in."

"This is what I like about you, brah." Calvin smiled. "I can always count on you for a feel-good conversation."

"Ain't nothin' feel-good about this place." Joe leaned back against the wall. "The moment you think you're winning, that's when they take your legs right out from under you."

CALVIN TRIED TO SHAKE HIS ILL FEELINGS BY OCCUPYING HIMSELF with work. When he entered the cloistered dormitory of Magnolia that Friday, he was grateful for the distraction.

"Hi, sugar," he heard a sultry voice say as someone stepped up close beside him. The Magnolia residents often competed for his attention, seeing if they could win his loyalty and convince him to bring them contraband from the other dormitories. He insisted on being professional in return, but sometimes it was hard not to smile at their advances.

After a year at Angola, Calvin was coming to think differently about sexual relationships in the penitentiary. He noticed that most men who engaged in sexual activities with other men while incarcerated maintained silence about these experiences once released, adhering to an unspoken code. Calvin was learning that many aspects of life behind bars were situational, and more complex than he'd imagined. Like gambling and playing sports, however, any form of intimate relationship in the penitentiary could lead to competition and introduce a measure of danger. He would avoid them all.

He walked down the rows of beds one by one, pulling a small red wagon of books and papers behind him.

A young man near the front of the dorm leaned forward on his bed. "Say, Calvin, if they bring 'other crimes' evidence up in your trial, the court can't use the harmless error analysis to dismiss that, huh?"

Calvin detected an edge of frustration in his voice. He was probably in a disagreement with someone else in the dorm. Calvin knew the young man was wrong on the law but recalled the advice of Henry Hill, the head inmate lawyer: "Don't disagree with 'em straight off. Don't tell 'em they're wrong. Because you don't know if a guy is considered the lawyer on his tier. If you dispute what he says, you create enemies for yourself among his associates. Or maybe that interpretation of the law, wrong as it is, is his last hope. Wait until a quiet moment to introduce a case that will help him along. But don't crush him—especially not in front of other people."

Calvin met his young inquisitor's eye and feigned uncertainty.

"I dunno, brah, I'm gonna have to check on that for you," he said. "Let me pull some cases."

He continued down the aisle, stopping to hand out copies of requested legal materials at each bed.

"See you next week, honey," he heard someone say as he reached the door. Calvin gave a nod before slipping out.

Back on the walk, he thought about all the appeals he needed to write up from Night Court that afternoon. The disgruntled major had created plenty of work for him and Checo over the past week.

As he walked toward the law library, a familiar face caught his eye in the distance.

He squinted in disbelief. Yes, it was Leroy Polk.

Back from Camp J, he was chatting with an acquaintance on the yard, a basketball under one arm and the sun at his back.

Calvin felt a rush of gratitude. Mrs. Rabalais had kept her promise.

1989

At the end of the six-month training period, Calvin was ready to go out on his own. He took on new assignments at the hospital and the newly created mental health unit with Checo and another inmate counsel substitute named John Veller.

The hospital had two wards, each with sixty beds. The beds were arranged in rows out in the open, while isolation rooms lined the sides. Ward One was for short-term patients passing through. Ward Two was less hopeful; the elderly, the terminally ill, and those with permanent disabilities who were moved there seldom returned to general population.

Calvin's work took on a different tenor at the hospital. The bed-bound men didn't need a lawyer so much as a distraction from the chronic pain and boredom they lived with day in and day out. For the most part, Calvin spent his time on the wards chatting and telling jokes, doing very little legal work.

That changed when he came across Weasel.

Disciplinary court was held at the hospital just like it was in the camps. A senior member of security and a classifications officer decided whether a person had violated a rule and then chose the punishment. Inmate counsels represented the patients.

Calvin was scanning the court docket for the day when he spotted Weasel's name.

He'd met Weasel at Camp D when he first arrived at Angola.

The docket indicated Weasel was incapacitated, requiring the board to come to him. Calvin trailed the major and the classifications officer to an isolation room at the front of the ward. Entering, he took a sharp breath.

"Brian Patterson?" the major called.

Weasel's eyes were open, but he didn't respond. He lay still on the bed, three of his four limbs bound up in casts. His face was marred with bruising. The flesh above his cheekbone was swollen, pushing his eyelid closed. It looked as though he had been beaten half to death.

"Are you Brian Patterson?" the major repeated.

Weasel looked catatonic.

"At this time, I'm going to stand in for his rights," Calvin said as he stepped to the bedside.

Whenever a person's disciplinary offense could lead to criminal prosecution, such as a physical altercation between a prisoner and a guard, inmate counsels had to ensure their clients didn't make any statements that could be used against them in court.

The major nodded. The classifications officer read the disciplinary report out loud.

"The sergeant reports that he was bringing Patterson a tray of food at dinner when Patterson tried to hit him. After attempting to strike the sergeant with his cast, the sergeant fought the inmate off with the metal tray. The charge is attempted aggravated assault on security. How do you plead?"

"At this time, I am going to enter a plea of not guilty," Calvin replied.

"Okay, we'll confer," said the major, walking into the hall. The classifications officer followed, pulling the door closed behind him.

Alone in the room, Calvin studied Weasel's broken body.

He wasn't surprised that Weasel had gotten into a fight. Small guys like him had to stand up for themselves, or else they risked being put in bondage to someone else. Weasel had quickly learned to go on the offensive at any hint of disrespect; on defense, he would lose.

That was how he got his name. He was scrawny and tenacious, making up in guts what he lacked in brawn.

Whatever had laid him out this time, though, wasn't some ordinary fight.

The major and classifications officer returned.

"Brian Patterson, the board has found you guilty and sentenced you to two weeks' loss of store."

Given Weasel's state, the loss of store privileges wouldn't matter; the board was showing mercy.

After the disciplinary hearing, Calvin sought out Willie Harris, a relative of Weasel's, in the Main Prison. When he described Weasel's condition, Willie shook his head in disbelief.

"They need to know that people on the outside are watching," Calvin told him. "Someone over there is messing Weasel up."

Willie looked depleted.

"You should tell your people to call up here," Calvin urged.

He gave a reluctant nod. "Weasel's mom is going to take this so hard."

CALVIN MONITORED WEASEL CLOSELY, LOOKING FOR SIGNS OF LIFE whenever he made his rounds.

After more than a week, Weasel finally came to.

"Calvin!" He waved with his one good hand when he spotted the familiar face through the glass.

Calvin bowled through the door. "Weasel, it's good to see you! I've been waiting on you."

"I thought you was one of those sons of bitches coming to force meds down my throat," Weasel said with a scowl.

Calvin pulled up a plastic chair. "It's been a while since Camp D, man. I wondered what happened to you."

"They been messing me over."

"Where did this happen?"

"Camp J. Jimmy Johnson."

The name gave Calvin a chill. Major Johnson was universally feared in Angola. A Southern Baptist and self-described "disciplinarian," he wouldn't hesitate to beat a man unconscious over a sideways look. People said he had killed people back at Camp J, and there were whispers that some federal judges were trying to get the Department of Justice to bring charges against him. But if that was true, there was no sign yet.

"One day he came by my cell talking shit, so I spat on him," said Weasel. "He went and got his boys. They told me I was goin' to the dungeon, so I came to the front to get the cuffs on. Once I was tied up, that was it. They came in my cell, beatin' on me. I don't remember it all." He frowned. "But I woke up in here with a broken leg, broken ribs, my insides all messed up."

"He don't play," Calvin murmured.

Johnson's goons had been merciless.

"What about the thing in disciplinary court? That sergeant, the one who wrote you up, he's cool. He doesn't usually mess over people."

"I know," Weasel spoke in a whisper. "Johnson still sends his squad over here at night. After everyone else leaves, they come in my room and mess with me. I mistook the sergeant for one of 'em."

Weasel pointed to his tender cheekbone. He threw a limp hook with his free arm.

"All I can do is swing."

As if it wasn't enough that Johnson reigned over Camp J, he was in charge of the tactical team as well. The roving troop wandered the prison, searching cells and dormitories for contraband. They jumped at the chance to pull their batons and pepper spray. A guard once confessed to Calvin that he felt different during a rotation on the tac team. As soon as the uniform was on, he felt it changing him.

"In the morning, they go to the nurses and tell them I'm acting up. 'Weasel was throwing trays at us, Weasel was trying to get us when we weren't looking,'" he imitated. "So they start forcing medicine on me. Like I'm crazy or somethin'."

"They get a PEC for that?"

"Huh?"

"A physician's emergency certificate," Calvin explained. "Did a doctor authorize them doing that?"

"Yeah, the mental health people get the doctor to sign off. I never seen him, though."

Calvin wondered about possible legal actions.

"Will you call my mom for me?" Weasel asked. "I'll give you her number. Tell her I'm okay."

"Sure." Calvin took it down.

As more weeks passed, Weasel regained strength and movement in his body.

Then, one morning, Calvin found his room empty.

He spoke to one of the nurses at the back of the ward. "Ma'am, do you know what happened to Brian Patterson in Room One?"

"They took him to mental health," she replied.

Perplexed, Calvin hurried out of the hospital toward the mental health unit, the wheels of his red wagon clacking on the linoleum floor.

Though mental health was newly built, its design was identical to the cellblocks. He found Weasel holed up in isolation, eating from a plastic tray. When he saw Calvin at the door, his sleepy face filled with warmth.

"Hey."

"I heard they brought you down here. How's things?"

They gave each other a dap through the bars. Calvin handed him a couple of peppermint candies.

"Good. I'm glad to be out of there," he said, looking in the direction of the hospital. "But I don't know what I'm doing here. They brought me over the other night."

Calvin noticed Weasel's speech was a little slow.

"Willie Harris says hi," he said.

"How's he doing?"

"He's okay, he says your mom is worried about you."

Weasel's expression faltered, his eyes shifting away.

"Can I get you anything?"

"Nah, I'm straight," he replied.

Calvin was hesitant to leave. "I'll be back in a couple of days, all right?"

Weasel looked down at the candies in his palm, then began to slowly unravel one of the wrappers. "Thanks, Calvin."

A CLASS ACTION LAWSUIT CALLED *HEAD V. KING* HAD EXPOSED THE deplorable treatment of people with mental illness and intellectual disabilities at Angola. The suit was filed in 1984, and after fighting it for years, the administration agreed in 1989 to enter a federal consent decree with the plaintiffs, avoiding a trial.

As part of the consent decree, the prison agreed to house individuals with serious mental illness separately from general population and provide them with psychiatric treatment. Prior to the lawsuit, people with psychological disorders had mostly ended up in disciplinary cells in the outer camps, where they were confined alone twenty-three hours a day.

Even in the new mental health unit, residents remained housed in single-man cells, with many deprived of their one-hour break for days at a time. The prison labeled it "extended care" rather than extended lockdown, but Calvin could see no difference. On those occasions when the men were permitted to leave their cells to use the shower, they were shackled by their hands and feet.

The conditions in the unit were stark and unforgiving. Temperatures fluctuated wildly, noise bounced off the concrete walls day and night, lights were kept on at all times, and sunlight was shut out. Calvin was sure none of this helped the already precarious situation of the residents. It wasn't unusual for him to see the men engaged in self-harm when he walked past their cells, and suicides were common.

Old Augustine frequently rammed his skull against the bars of his cell until he fell, bloody and unconscious. The staff would chain him, spread-eagled, by wrists and ankles to a metal bunk, then cover him in "the Body Sheet," a ghastly contraption that strapped and buckled him to the point where he couldn't move at all. Then they covered his head with a football helmet, which seemed to Calvin to cause more pain. Sometimes, they left him strapped down for days, soiling himself and covered in flies, bellowing out old country and western songs, driving the other residents mad.

The inmate counsels had no formal training in assisting people with severe mental illness in this environment and had to learn on the job. If someone looked at Calvin with a cockeyed stare, he knew to keep his distance until the next time he made his rounds. Many of the men, however, craved human interaction so much that Calvin had to develop tactics to complete his rounds in a reasonable time. On days when he was in a hurry, he brought a pack of cigarettes and walked down the tier handing them out one by one, doubling back to offer each man a light.

He learned to pay attention to security, too. Not all the residents' injuries were self-inflicted. He doubted the guards had received any specialized training, and many seemed spiteful toward the men in their charge. Particularly on Monday mornings, unexplained black eyes appeared on the tiers after certain guards had been left unsupervised over the weekend.

Calvin noticed that many men on the unit displayed bizarre muscle spasms: eyes darting uncontrollably, lips twitching and smacking without reason. Troubled by what he saw, he sought out a man named Mwalimu, whom Calvin thought of as the Dalai Lama of Angola. Mwalimu had been paralyzed from the waist down by a bullet that was still lodged in his spine. FBI officers had shot Mwalimu, claiming he'd been involved in a bank robbery (a claim they would later withdraw once it became clear that Mwalimu was wrongfully convicted). As a result, he lived permanently on Ward Two at the hospital. Having been at Angola since 1977, and having seen some of its worst days, Mwalimu was a keen observer of prison life. There wasn't much he didn't understand about the place.

"Helldogs," Mwalimu replied when Calvin described the muscle contractions he saw on the unit. "An antipsychotic they make them take. If they don't use other meds to control the side effects of the Helldogs, or if they give them too much for too long, you'll start to see the muscles go."

Haldol, colloquially known as Helldogs, was developed in the 1950s and praised for its ability to sedate individuals experiencing emotional agitation or paranoia. However, concerns about its neurological side effects prompted caution. Many patients on the drug exhibited extrapyramidal symptoms resembling Parkinson's, with irreversible muscle tics and tremors that began in the face and spread throughout the upper body.

A cold dread settled over Calvin, remembering that when Weasel was still at the hospital, he had complained of being given antipsychotics for no reason.

"But these guys can't all be psychotic. Even if they were, what the drugs do to them looks horrible . . ."

Mwalimu nodded. "They're a blunt instrument. Sort of like a chemical lobotomy."

The next time he made his rounds, Calvin found Weasel propped against the wall in an odd position. Bug-eyes peered out from beneath his brow, darting around as if unable to find a center of gravity. Calvin sensed malice in their corners.

"Say, man, what's going on?" he asked gently.

In one swift motion, Weasel came at the bars and thrust something from his mouth. Calvin felt it land on the edge of his cheek and lifted his hand to his face. Warm spittle oozed between his fingers. Astonished, he looked back at Weasel, who snarled something under his breath and returned to the back of the cell.

Calvin hurried to the guards' station at the front of the tier.

"Do you know what's wrong with him?"

The sergeant glanced up briefly. "He's not eatin'. Thinks they've put poison in his food."

"Will you keep an eye on him?" Calvin pleaded. "Will you tell the people if he doesn't eat? Please, I want to make sure they know."

The sergeant nodded, looking startled at Calvin's tone.

Calvin returned to Weasel's cell and saw he was limp again.

He prickled with rage. His friend was deteriorating by the day, and he didn't know how to stop it.

IT TOOK A YEAR FOR THE LOUISIANA SUPREME COURT TO DECIDE whether to grant Calvin's writ application to review the Fourth Circuit's decision to deny his direct appeal. Toward the end of January 1989, he received the state supreme court's order in the mail.

His pulse raced as he ran his finger beneath the fold of the envelope.

Inside, he looked at the sheet of paper, his stomach swerving downward.

Denied.

Chief Justice Dixon, Justice Calogero and Justice Dennis would grant the writ.

The justices had denied his writ four to three. He'd lost the opportunity to have his case heard by a single vote.

The close defeat was crushing, and yet held out a sliver of hope. He'd won the favor of three justices. Perhaps he could sway one more to his side with an application for rehearing.

Ten days later, he filed a request to have his writ reconsidered.

The court declined.

Upon receiving the news, Calvin once again retreated into darkness, taking even longer to recover this time. The loss was total.

With his direct appeal over, he would have to challenge his conviction with new evidence. Direct appeals were limited to claims on the basis of the existing record, while applications for post-conviction relief required uncovering new facts that might have changed the jury's verdict if known. This could include evidence from the prosecution's file that wasn't shared with the defense, or important witnesses the defense failed to investigate. It was almost impossible for incarcerated individuals to discover new facts without outside help, since this required locating documents and speaking to witnesses. Post-conviction applications were heard by the original trial court, meaning Calvin would have to convince Judge Shea, the very judge who presided over his trial, compounding the challenge.

Eventually, he mustered the resolve to begin his post-conviction application and research potential claims. He spent weeks identifying his most persuasive arguments and figuring out how to support them with facts. During his research, he uncovered a critical issue: his judge had allowed newspaper articles into the jury room during deliberations. According to state law, this alone should entitle Calvin to a new trial. Given three Louisiana Supreme Court justices had suggested it deserved review, he would also include the claim he'd lost on direct appeal regarding his statement to the police. Finally, he would introduce a new claim that his attorneys had been ineffective for not requesting his initial police report and for failing to object to the admission of the Crimestoppers tip as hearsay.

Calvin was under no illusions about the inclination of judges, especially someone like Judge Shea, to reverse a conviction they had personally overseen. Still, knowing Louisiana law was unambiguous on the issue of written evidence going to the jury room, he was optimistic.

He filed his petition with Judge Shea in July 1989, anticipating another lengthy wait.

CALVIN WAS MAKING HIS ROUNDS ON THE MENTAL HEALTH UNIT ONE morning when he heard a strange cry coming from one of the cells. He looked inside to see Ron Moore standing over the toilet. Beads of sweat ran down the sides of his long, scarred face, and he was sobbing.

"Ron, are you all right?"

Calvin usually gave this man a wide berth—he wore a stare that demanded it—but today his cries drew Calvin close to the bars. A sour smell wafted. Ron was holding his penis over the steel toilet trying to urinate, green ivy creeping over his genitals.

Calvin dropped the handle of his red wagon and hurried to the social workers' office.

"Ms. Delta, can you help?" he asked the mental health director. "It's Ron. It looks like his private area has gangrene. I saw him going to the bathroom just now. I think he needs to go to the hospital."

Ms. Delta slid open the flap of an envelope with one of her poppy-red talons. "You know how Ron is," she said plainly. "He does it to himself. He keeps sticking staples up there so he can go to the hospital. He just wants a cigarette."

"Maybe so, but he's in real pain right now. He needs some help."

"The nurses hate it when we send him over there." She rolled her eyes. "We can't give him what he wants or he'll just keep doing it."

Though the social workers were charged with protecting the men in their care, Calvin often felt that their allegiance lay with the administration. There were rumors that some even had romantic relationships with correctional officers. He bit his tongue at Ms. Delta's response and left the room before he got himself a write-up.

Back at the cells, Ron was leaning against the bed. The big man had worn himself out.

"It's all right, dude, I'm gonna get some help."

Calvin moved to an adjacent cell.

"What's happening with him? Why would he do that to himself?"

"On weekends sometimes, the freemen pretend like Ron has a visit," Ron's neighbor answered. "He gets all dressed up, waits all day, even though nobody's comin'. Ron doesn't get visits, he's got no family. They just messin' with him. You know Ron, that's when he gets upset."

Calvin hurried to find Mwalimu.

"They got a guy in mental health with some kind of infection in his private parts." He paused, out of breath. "The freemen got him so upset he stuck something up there. When I told the social worker, she didn't want to do nothin'. I swear it's gangrene or something."

Mwalimu folded the newspaper he'd been reading. He leaned forward and met his young friend's eye.

"Calvin, you listen to me. You know these people. They won't do nothin' unless their hand is forced. You know what you have to do."

Calvin dropped his gaze.

What Mwalimu was suggesting was impossible. Filing lawsuits was easy in the parish jail because he had nothing to lose. But this was Angola. If he filed civil suits against the prison, they could retaliate and bury him in the cells. He might lose his job. He might lose access to the law library, his only chance of getting home.

But Mwalimu didn't budge.

"Do your job," he urged. "File on them."

RON SAT AT THE TABLE PICKING AT THE SKIN ON THE ENDS OF HIS fingers.

"You'll do good, man," Calvin reassured him.

They waited patiently at the A-Building for the court proceedings to begin. Calvin had prepared an emergency suit for Ron, and a federal magistrate would soon arrive to hear their case.

Upon spotting Judge Noland and her clerk entering the room, Calvin gave Ron an encouraging nod. Unlike some judges, she allowed inmate counsels to speak in court.

"If she asks you to talk, just repeat what I say," Calvin whispered.

The judge cleared her throat. "Counsel, you may proceed with your witnesses."

Calvin stood with a jolt, hardly believing what he was about to do.

"Warden Peabody."

Peabody, the deputy warden overseeing the mental health unit, sauntered from a seat at the back of the room to the conference table where the judge sat, not sparing Calvin a glance.

Despite his rank, Calvin questioned the warden as he would any other witness.

"Is there a reason that someone with Mr. Moore's issues would not be confined to a padded cell to prevent him from getting access to things he could use to hurt himself?"

"We don't have padded cells on the unit," Peabody snapped.

Calvin called the medical director next.

"Ron has received treatment for his infection," the director told the court.

"What about the staple that Ron inserted?" Calvin asked.

The witness glanced down at his papers, then turned to the judge.

"Mr. Moore has inserted a number of staples inside his genitals over time. These are large mattress staples." He held a forefinger and thumb two inches apart. "One of them has worked its way so far up his urethra that it would cause irreparable damage to his bladder to remove it. If we tried to take out the staple, Mr. Moore would have to live with a urostomy bag."

The judge's clerk shifted uncomfortably in her seat. Ron continued to examine his fingers.

"I'm going to wait to rule on the motion for an injunction," said Judge Noland. "For now, I will take this matter under advisement."

She called the proceedings to a close.

Calvin turned to Ron. "This is a good outcome for us. She's leaving the case open as a way of holding it over their heads. They'll be more likely to help you now, knowing that she can bring them back into court whenever she likes."

"They did take me to the hospital over the weekend," Ron said, smiling. "I got some cigarettes while I was there."

"That's good, dude." Calvin gave an exasperated laugh. "Now don't be doing any more of that painful shit to yourself."

WEASEL WAS BACK IN THE HOSPITAL AGAIN. CALVIN FOUND HIM RE-strained and sedated, with an IV in his hand and a tube down his throat. The nurses had been force-feeding him.

This marked the beginning of a cycle that Weasel endured for months. Calvin would find him with his tongue stuck to the side of his face, refusing to eat. Then he'd disappear to the hospital, where he was subjected to forced feeding and drugging. Calvin would file an Administrative Remedy Procedure against the administration, but as soon as the Helldogs wore off, the cycle would start all over again.

"Security's calling you a nuisance, brah," Checo warned. "Watch your back."

Up at the law library, Norris, who kept an eye on changing laws and statutes, showed Calvin a new US Supreme Court decision. "*Washington v. Harper*. It deals with forcibly medicating people with Helldogs."

In his brief to the court, Harper argued that the state violated his due process rights by administering the psychotropics without a judicial hearing. The majority of the Supreme Court ruled that Harper's rights were adequately protected because he was given a hearing by a special committee of trained mental health professionals. However, three out of the nine justices dissented in part, voicing serious concerns.

Buried in the footnotes of the justices' dissent, Calvin saw the harrowing words of Walter Harper himself, pleading unsuccessfully with the hearing committee not to medicate him against his will.

> Haldol paralyzed my right side of my body.
> You are burning me out of my life.
> You are burning me out of my freedom.

Calvin's throat tightened in anger. Weasel was a prisoner in his own body, just like Harper. Because of what the hospital had done to him, he was damned with the Helldogs and damned without them.

Yet Weasel had never received a hearing or had his medical records reviewed by a medical panel before being forcibly medicated. A lone doctor had authorized his treatment without examining him.

Calvin was sure Weasel ought to win relief under *Harper*. If the federal district court didn't agree, then he would take the case all the way to the US Supreme Court.

WHEN MRS. RABALAIS CALLED CALVIN TO THE A-BUILDING ONE MORN-ing, he could tell it wasn't good news.

"Now, Calvin, you know I don't interfere in what y'all do," she said in a low voice. "But these wardens are constantly complaining about you. Tell me what's been happening over there at mental health."

Evidently, Checo wasn't the only one having to protect him.

"The way security handles the guys is pitiful," Calvin explained. "Take Ron Moore—"

"Ron Moore," Mrs. Rabalais repeated. "Who is doing that suit?"

"I am," Calvin answered. "They're messing that man over so bad."

She tilted her head in recognition. "This is what's getting them so stirred up. When you file for discovery and all those interrogatories, you're asking for information that they don't want to give. You're calling wardens to court as witnesses for things that happened months ago—"

She stopped, examining his expression. Exhaustion had carved deep creases beneath his eyes.

"I can see this is taking a toll on you, Calvin. You need to take a couple of weeks off, all right? Starting today."

"If you want to move me from mental health to another assignment, you can go ahead and move me," Calvin replied, trying to keep the bitterness from his voice. Mrs. Rabalais looked taken aback.

"I'm not going to move you. That's not what this conversation is about," she said softly. "Listen, you haven't done anything wrong. On the contrary, you owe those men. You have a moral obligation to help them."

Calvin gave a small nod.

"It's just that in trying to help people, sometimes you can hurt them at the same time," she added.

As he followed her from the room, he wondered at the meaning of her words.

A FEW WEEKS LATER, CALVIN WAS CHECKING ON A CLIENT WITH A fresh bruise on his face when he heard his name.

He turned to see Lieutenant Heywood standing by his office door.

"I want a word with you."

The office was partitioned from the rest of the unit, with a glass window looking out over the tiers.

"Close the door," Heywood ordered.

Calvin pulled the door behind him, waiting for the click.

"I hear you've declared war on everybody over here," the lieutenant remarked, settling back in his chair. There was a challenge in his eye.

"I haven't declared war on nobody, Lieutenant," Calvin replied. "I've just been trying to get some help for these guys in here."

Heywood scoffed. "We're swimming in ARPs," he said, pushing a pile of papers forward on his desk. "Some may be genuine, but I'll bet a lot ain't."

Calvin tensed. The inmate counsels were instructed to only file complaints they believed had merit. Heywood was insinuating that Calvin was either pursuing frivolous suits or being duped by the men on the unit. He swallowed his anger.

"Can I speak freely, Lieutenant?"

Heywood raised a brow. "Go ahead."

"Neither the social workers nor security knows what to do with these guys over here."

Suddenly, Calvin didn't care if he was risking his job. He had to speak the truth.

"It seems like they have no training at all. They dope them up with all kinds of drugs and don't give 'em nothin' for the side effects. They taunt them like they children, messing with them for fun."

The lieutenant folded his arms tightly across his chest and didn't speak for what felt like an eternity.

"You're not wrong," he said finally.

Calvin wondered if he'd heard correctly.

"They dump these guys on us." Heywood sighed. "We do our best, but they need serious help, and my men ain't equipped for that."

He tapped a pen on the desk.

"If you was my best friend, I wouldn't tell you not to file," he admitted. "I'll tell you what. You go ahead and do what you need to do. But bear in mind, I don't speak for no one else."

Heywood returned his gaze to his desk, signaling the conversation was over.

Calvin lingered for a moment, hardly believing he was leaving the office unscathed. "All right, Lieutenant."

He found his red wagon of books and returned to the man with the bruised face.

WHILE MAKING HIS ROUNDS ONE AFTERNOON, CALVIN DISCOVERED A kid named Edward Butler in one of the cells. He knew Edward from administrative segregation at the Main Prison; the boy was often placed in isolation because he was young, slight, and vulnerable to attacks. But he'd never been on the mental health unit before. Calvin wondered if the horrors he'd suffered over the years were catching up to him.

"Hey, what's going on?" he asked gently.

"Calvin." Edward looked relieved. "I got a civil suit goin'. Can you help?"

He held some papers through the bars and Calvin scanned the filing. Edward had been attacked in the hospital bullpen and was seeking damages from the prison. Calvin couldn't believe they were still putting people like him in that room with the door closed.

Calvin tucked the papers into his wagon.

"I'm gonna help you," he said firmly. "That bullpen needs to go."

Up at the law library, Calvin discovered that Edward's suit was already moving to court, with a trial date soon to be scheduled. He didn't have much time to prepare.

On the day of trial, the judge called the court to order.

Calvin once again tried to take testimony from a hostile Warden Peabody, who refused to state how many beatings he had seen reported at the hospital bullpen. Next, he questioned the major overseeing the cellblocks, whose servile eyes flicked toward the doorway where Peabody had exited.

"I have no idea," the major answered.

"Your Honor." Calvin turned to the judge. "There's one last motion I'd like to make before we finish."

The judge looked uncertain. "Go on."

"It's a motion for you to view the bullpen."

The statement was met with an awkward silence.

"Ah—I don't think I can do that." The judge shook his head. "I wouldn't want to make myself a witness."

"It wouldn't make you a witness, Your Honor," Calvin insisted.

"Why don't you get with the sergeant there and draw me a diagram instead."

A guard walked over to Calvin's seat, and the pair began to scribble on a piece of paper. Minutes passed. Calvin made sure they wouldn't agree on a sketch.

Finally, the judge relented.

"Let's break for lunch. Y'all meet me at the hospital in thirty minutes."

Calvin flashed Edward a secret grin on his way out of the room.

Across the hall, he heard a hiss from one of the administration offices. "He's got a judge going down to the damn hospital!"

Around one o'clock, the group convened by the entrance to the bullpen.

"This is it?" The judge stepped cautiously over the threshold.

Though the staff had scrambled to clean it up, the stale stench of blood and sweat still wafted. Security watched with venom as Calvin pointed out the setup.

"Here's where the freeman who opens the door stands," he said. "And here's the hallway where general population come and go for the doctor. But look: nobody can monitor what goes on inside here while they're opening and closing the gates and shaking people down. There's no direct line of sight into the room."

The longer the judge absorbed the scene, the tighter his features became.

"When one guy knows how to get out of his handcuffs, the others are sitting ducks."

The sergeant mumbled in objection but the layout was plain to see.

The judge gave a nod, then signaled he was ready to go back to the A-Building.

Edward likely wouldn't win the lawsuit, but Calvin was confident the administration would hesitate before closing the bullpen door again.

The final nail in the coffin came a few months after Edward's trial. Henry Montrell, who was confined in Camp J, had the life nearly beaten out of him in the bullpen while waiting his turn to see the doctor. Soon afterward, an inmate building crew was dispatched to construct single-person holding cells near the entrance to the dentist's office. From then on, anyone brought from the cellblocks to visit the doctor was held in an individual cell. The bullpen was repurposed into an office.

CALVIN'S DAYS WORKING ON THE MENTAL HEALTH UNIT WERE NUM-bered. Senior security treated him with open hostility after Edward's trial, and one assistant warden accused him outright of trying to run them into the ground with legal work.

He was the only inmate counsel regularly taking the administra-tion to court, which boosted his popularity among the population but made him increasingly vulnerable in the prison. Legal Programs wasn't immune to the competition and power struggles that affected the rest of the penitentiary, and some of the inmate counsels grum-bled that Calvin was making them look bad. Checo promised to fend off his detractors as best he could, but he could only keep them at bay for so long.

Word came from Mrs. Rabalais that the interim warden of An-gola, Larry Smith, wanted to meet with Calvin and the other inmate counsels from the mental health unit.

Smith was a rarity in the Department of Corrections, having climbed the ranks to be appointed Angola's first Black warden with-out the help of nepotism or political patronage. Still in his thirties, he was known for his no-nonsense approach and sense of fairness.

The warden entered the room with a lieutenant colonel in tow.

To everyone's surprise, he asked his associate to leave before clos-ing the door. The departing officer shot the counsels a filthy look on his way out.

"Look, if you ever repeat this, I will always deny it," said Smith, turning to the counsels. "This meeting never took place."

They nodded.

"Now. What the fuck is going on over at mental health? I'm getting sued and sued—and who the fuck is C.F.D.?"

Heat rose in Calvin's cheeks. "That's me, Warden."

"Well, tell me what is going on over there so I can understand why you're clogging up my desk with all these suits."

Calvin glanced at Checo, who gave him a nod of encouragement.

"There's a number of problems on the unit, Warden. A big one is that there ain't nothing for the guys to do. They're stuck with no televisions, no programming, no nothing. It would make anyone crazy. They cut themselves, eat dookie. If they defecate on themselves, nobody cleans it up."

Smith's nose crinkled in disgust.

"The guards aren't trained, either. They agitate them and pick fights for fun," Checo added.

"At night and on weekends, when the social workers aren't around, they beat them," Calvin said.

He paused, waiting to see if this last accusation would anger Smith, but his expression remained even.

"The drugs are terrible, too," Calvin continued. "They force Helldogs on the guys and it gives 'em seizures. Their tongues stretch up the sides of their faces."

He made a smearing action up his cheek.

"I get they're hard to deal with, that they provoke security and all that. But that's the point. They've got mental issues. And these people don't know how to look after them."

"You could come see for yourself," Checo suggested.

Smith thought about this. "When?"

"When they're feeding up, so you can see that cold, nasty food."

A few days later, the warden entered the unit with an entourage. Calvin was waiting in the lobby area for disciplinary court with a client named Howard, who was sitting on the floor, shaking.

"Get up, man," he motioned, reaching down. "There's someone here that I want to see you."

The security surrounding the warden noticed Calvin maneuvering the stammering man into Smith's line of sight and shifted to block his view. Calvin nudged Howard to move over, and Smith noticed.

"What's wrong with him?" he asked.

"They gave him Helldogs," Calvin replied. "They don't give him medicine for the side effects because they think it's funny to see him shake like this."

The warden lifted his gaze to the office where disciplinary court was being held. He pushed his way through the door.

"What's going on with that man?" Smith pointed at Howard.

"He's faking," replied one of the rank.

"Send him over to the hospital!" Smith erupted. "I've been working mental health for this department long enough to know that *nobody could fake that shake.*"

He strode angrily out of the office to the food cart where trays were being held for lunch delivery. He bent down to inspect their contents, then stood up with a look of revulsion and left the unit as abruptly as he'd come.

After Smith's visit, things on the unit changed rapidly. More social workers appeared, televisions were installed on two of the tiers, and a new captain and a new major were brought in.

For the first time, the residents were allowed to come out of their cells in groups of three or four for counseling sessions. They were given small jobs to do on the tiers, like rolling cigarettes donated by the Inmate Welfare Fund for people who couldn't afford their own. The new captain came in on weekends to monitor the conditions, and occasionally he served the men ice cream.

One afternoon, a party was held in the lobby. For the first time, everyone on the unit was permitted out of their cells at once. Calvin, Checo, and John Veller helped serve the food, and editors from *The Angolite* came to take pictures for a story. They couldn't believe the transformation taking place.

"Look," said Checo happily. "We've made real changes over here."

Calvin nodded. "Things are getting better—for now. But if they don't put these protocols in writing, who's to say they can't just revert back? You know they still leave the guys in four-point restraints for days, pissing and shitting on themselves. Soon as there are staff shortages, it'll get worse again."

Checo shook his head. "We're at a party and you're already thinking about what lawsuits to file next," he chuckled. "Remember to appreciate your wins along the way, Calvin. We're running a marathon, not a sprint."

CALVIN HADN'T MADE IT ONTO THE YARD IN MONTHS. AFTER A LONG night in the law library, he was eager to go for a jog and lose himself in the vast green expanse.

It wasn't just the turmoil on the mental health unit weighing him down; a recent order from Judge Shea denying his post-conviction application gnawed at him.

In a curt tone, the judge had summarily dismissed each of Calvin's claims for lacking merit, without giving reasons. Now, Calvin would have to prepare another writ to the state court of appeals and convince himself once more that he could prevail.

From a young age, Calvin had experienced episodes of numbing fog that would bring on an unyielding urge to sleep during periods of intense stress. He could sense he was descending into one of these slumps now. He'd managed to keep up with his cases and make his rounds, but it felt like he was going through the motions, his fatigue intensifying each day. Instead of working in the law library, he found himself napping on his cot most afternoons and retiring to bed early at night. He worried how long it would take to find his way out.

Hopefully, exercise would help. Jogging the yard was the closest feeling to freedom in the penitentiary. Calvin picked up speed on his second lap. He felt the wind whip his ears and the sensation made him run faster. He relished the lactic acid building in his legs, the force of it grounding him to the earth.

He ran the yard five times, covering almost as many miles. Then he slowed to cool down and climbed the steps to the walk.

Floyd Webb was waiting for him.

"How's things, Calvin?"

Floyd had previously served as an inmate counsel before leaving Legal Programs to become a writer for *The Angolite*. Calvin valued that Floyd, unlike some of the other white inmate counsels, treated him as an equal and didn't condescend.

"All right," he replied. "What's going on, brah?"

"My feature on life sentences is coming out this issue; thanks for your help with the case law updates. Say, I heard you been making friends over at mental health."

Calvin shot Floyd a grin.

"You know about that new position opening up at death row? I figured you might be looking for a change." Floyd nodded in the direction of the mental health unit. "You keep bothering those people, sooner or later they'll find a knife under your bed."

Calvin nodded. He knew Floyd was right, but he wasn't ready to concede.

"Think about it," Floyd said.

THE NEXT TIME CALVIN MADE HIS ROUNDS, RON'S CELL WAS EMPTY.

He dropped the handle of his wagon and hurried to the front of the tier.

"Where is Moore?"

The guard on duty gestured toward the exit. "They moved him to Hawk."

Calvin recoiled. Hawk was a disciplinary cellblock in Camp D. "Hawk? Why?"

The guard responded with a shrug.

Mrs. Rabalais's words sprang to mind. *Sometimes by helping people, you can hurt them.*

He hurried to the social workers' office, thinking he might be able to enlist their help. Ron would be vulnerable and completely alone in Hawk. He would be locked down in his cell with no one to calm him or get him a cigarette. Who knew what he'd do to himself?

But he paused at the door. He'd been filing complaints against Ms. Delta and the other social workers with the state board of social work for neglecting their ethical duties on the unit. By now, they probably hated him as much as security did.

Beads of sweat gathered on his brow. What could he do? He'd made enemies of everyone.

He returned to the law library and emptied his wagon, dumping the books onto his desk in a heap. Then he sank into a chair, resting his head in his hands.

When he became an inmate counsel, he hadn't realized what it truly meant to represent the people he was locked up with. Joe Washington had been right: the administration would never let him forget who kept the keys.

He sat there for some time, watching the sun dip low on the horizon. Finally, he pulled a piece of paper from his notepad.

It was clear what he had to do—there was no way around it now. But he wouldn't send the note to Mrs. Rabalais today.

He didn't want them to know so soon that they had won.

1991

A string of important new decisions had recently been issued by higher courts, and so on an August evening, Calvin and Alvin Abbott were working to decipher their implications.

They were joined in the law library by a larger band of collaborators, trusted friends from New Orleans who helped each other with their cases, whom Calvin referred to as his "law crew": Spencer Lewis, Sweet Tooth, Joe Warner, and Tip.

In the first decision, *Cage v. Louisiana*, the US Supreme Court had determined that Orleans Parish judges had been using a faulty, unconstitutional jury instruction to define "reasonable doubt." The court held that the instruction effectively lowered the state's burden of proof, allowing juries to convict people and judges to sentence them to life in prison even if the state had not proven their guilt beyond a reasonable doubt. The Louisiana Supreme Court had permitted the *Cage* instruction for years, meaning hundreds of felony convictions out of Orleans Parish were tainted.

The second decision addressed inadequate legal representation for indigent defendants on appeal. In *Lofton v. Whitley*, a court-appointed attorney filed a two-sentence brief for his client, Larry Lofton, who was serving life without parole at Angola. The lawyer's brief stated that he hadn't identified any legal claims to raise in Larry's case. The federal Fifth Circuit Court of Appeals concluded that such gravely deficient representation was tantamount to no representation and ordered Lofton a new appeal. Many defendants from New Orleans, including Alvin and Calvin, had received similar treatment and could now ask for a new appeal under the ruling. Though Calvin's lawyer had included one legal argument in his brief, the claim was already barred by Supreme Court precedent, effectively leaving him with no appeal at all.

Last, in May 1991, the Louisiana Supreme Court issued *State v. Desdunes*, a case where a trial judge in New Orleans had imposed an illegal sentence on a defendant by failing to specify whether he was eligible for parole or not. At the time, Orleans Parish judges were routinely making this mistake due to a misunderstanding of the law governing sentences for armed robbery. *Desdunes* meant hundreds of people would need to have their sentences reviewed. Among Calvin's law crew, everyone except him had been convicted of armed robbery and could potentially benefit from the decision.

The group sat poring over their transcripts together.

"I never even noticed that my judge didn't say nothin' about whether I was eligible for parole," said Joe Warner.

Calvin nodded. "When you go to court and he sees your conduct record, he'll see that you've mentally matured since the offense. He might be willing to cut down your sentence. Just be prepared to speak to him yourself, don't leave it up to your lawyer."

"What if the judge doesn't want us to speak, though?" asked Tip.

"Ask nicely but be firm. If you don't speak up for yourself, you know what will happen. Judge Shea will point to whichever lawyer is in the room . . ." Calvin rose from his seat and put a scowl on his face, then started waving a finger. "*Stand for him,*" he imitated, pointing at Joe. Then he turned to Tip. "Now—I'm giving you fifty years. *Get out of my courtroom.*"

He dropped back into his seat, shaking with laughter.

"Man, how you learn all this stuff, Calvin?" Spencer wiped his eyes, still grinning.

"I made so many mistakes when I started out with civil cases in the parish," Calvin assured him. "One time I went to court and said, 'Your Honor, you haven't ruled on my motion in lime.' The judge asked the court reporter, 'What's this man talking about?' And she says, 'He means a motion in limine.'"

He gave another belly laugh. "The judge denied me right there and then."

As their banter subsided, Calvin noticed Alvin retreating into an uneasy silence.

These days, his best friend spent as much time in the law library as the inmate counsels, researching and helping other callouts with their cases—finding purpose in the law. Calvin took immense satisfaction in witnessing Alvin's transformation.

He watched him now, waiting for him to say what was on his mind.

Alvin shifted in his seat. "I got a question. On some level, all of us have come to accept our situation. We know why we're here. I might not think my sentence is fair, or my appeal was handled right, but I did my crime. So I got to make lemonade out of lemons." He turned to Calvin. "But you? You're innocent."

It was a strange word to hear in the penitentiary. Justice wasn't tied to innocence or guilt the way it was on the outside. Everyone understood that a fair trial depended on access and impartiality—privileges reserved for the wealthy. Those convicted of something they didn't do were unlikely to talk about it beyond their closest confidants. Calvin's law crew were the few he'd ever spoken to about his case.

"I just don't understand how you accept your situation," said Alvin. "How you make this work for you without losing your mind."

Calvin paused, considering his response. In truth, though he had learned much from his mentors and the books he'd read since arriving at Angola, the question still weighed on him daily. He was always searching for stories of people who'd survived traumatic events, hoping to find the wisdom to keep going.

"The way I see it," he said, "we all came from the same place, had to navigate the same terrible stuff, did what our young minds thought we had to do to survive—and paid the price. I shouldn't be in here for murder. You shouldn't be in here doing thirty-three years for robbing a dice game when you were nineteen. We both should've gotten a real lawyer, or better yet, some help when we was kids." He paused, thinking. "You know what's different between me and you? Not our convictions. Our sentences. Every day that passes, you're a day less in here. Every day for me is the same day." He tapped the table. "The *same* day. So the best I can do for myself is to be careful never to deceive myself. If other guys want to spend their time shooting dice or playing football, that's good, go do it. But me? The only way I'm getting out of here is if I get good at the law. That's the reality of my situation. If I concern myself with anything other than my freedom, I ain't never goin' home."

Alvin and the others murmured in understanding. Though they would never say it, Calvin knew they didn't want him to see them waste their potential. After working side by side for months, the law crew had come to feel a responsibility not just to themselves but to each other.

"Do you think we'd be in a better position if we hired someone to represent us on these claims?" Joe asked thoughtfully. "I have a little money saved."

"It might be worth it to get a lawyer that knows your judge." Calvin nodded. "We could try Joe Rome or Ron Rakosky—sometimes Rakosky's willing to wait until you're home to collect on his fees."

"We could pool our money to make sure everyone's covered," Alvin suggested.

The group had helped one another send money home to their children on birthdays and holidays, but they'd never made this serious a commitment before.

Spencer didn't hesitate. "I'm in."

"Me too." Tip nodded.

"I'll write to Joe," said Calvin.

AUNT BRUNETTA, WHO WAS IN HER LATE FORTIES, DIED THAT SPRING after suffering heart complications from varicose veins. While sifting through her belongings, Calvin's family stumbled upon a photograph of Tiny Duncan with Mamie when she was an infant. Mamie sent the photo to Calvin at Angola.

In the dormitory, Calvin bent over the photograph of his mother, studying it intently.

She was wearing a white shift dress, her hair styled in short waves. Eyeshadow, rendered silver by the sepia tone of the Polaroid, brightened her lids. She lay on her side, her daughter nestled in her arms. The obvious affection between them struck Calvin, as did the haunting reality of their impending separation. At the time the photo was taken, his mother was on the run from Herbert Owens, camped out in a relative's dingy spare room with two infant children, a cancer diagnosis on the horizon, and no salvation in sight. The longer he contemplated the scene, the more the sadness of it overshadowed his excitement at receiving the photograph. He tucked it away in his lockerbox and didn't retrieve it for some time.

THE ATMOSPHERE IN THE LAW LIBRARY WAS CHARGED WITH HOPE. The new legal decisions coming down from the courts fostered camaraderie among the callouts and reinvigorated people's belief that the law could work in their favor.

Calvin's law crew pooled their resources to hire the lawyers they wanted to represent them on their *Desdunes* claims. As predicted, when they returned to court for resentencing, each man's positive conduct record was rewarded with a reduced sentence to time served. Tip was the first to go home, followed by Joe Warner, then Spencer.

Others in the prison began to win *Lofton* claims and receive new direct appeals. Now able to present evidence of a *Cage* violation or evidence contained in their newly discovered police reports, some had their convictions overturned and were released.

When the broader population noticed that people were going home, the callout slots for the law library filled up, and night after night, it was packed with individuals seeking help.

For those with a potential *Cage* claim, their first challenge was securing their trial transcripts to prove that their judge had used the erroneous jury instruction. Burl, an expert in criminal law, was quickly inundated with requests to locate transcripts and draft petitions. Calvin, who usually assisted the callouts with civil law, stepped in to help meet the demand.

He remembered the template he'd used to streamline requests for police reports a few years earlier and spoke to Broom, his friend from the parish jail, about creating a similar template for the *Cage* motions. They strategized how to gather case information and produce petitions for the population quickly. Calvin posted flyers in each camp instructing people to send him their cases. He also helped Gerald Bosworth, a former civil attorney serving a life sentence for murder, to get the word out by doing research for a lengthy memorandum Bosworth was preparing for *The Angolite*. Each night, Calvin returned to the dorm to find a stack of letters stuffed under his pillow. In the months to come, he and the others working on the project produced more than three hundred *Cage* petitions.

One morning on his way to Classifications, Calvin ran into Big Dugger, who had been moved to the Main Prison from the parish jail after the Louisiana Supreme Court remanded his case. His death sentence had been reduced to life without parole.

Calvin spotted him at the entrance to the Education Building. "Hey, what's going on?"

"Look here, if it ain't my lawyer." Big Dugger smiled.

Calvin was eager to assist Big Dugger with his legal work in any way he could.

"I want to get with you about your case," he said. "You heard about this jury issue in *Cage*?"

"You know I don't understand that law stuff." Big Dugger shook his head. "That's why I came looking for you."

"I'm sure this case could help you, brah, they used the wrong jury instruction in Section G all the time." Calvin lifted a package that was wedged under his arm. "I gotta get to Classifications. Why don't you come by the law library tonight?"

That evening, Calvin heard a booming voice at the entrance to the law library. "Anybody seen my lawyer?"

He waved Big Dugger up the back to the desks where he was working.

"What's goin' on, Dog?" Big Dugger pulled a chair over. "You hookin' me up with one of your motions?"

"First, we gotta get your transcript from Judge Shea. And ideally, a copy of your lawyer's objection to the jury instruction," Calvin explained.

The humor drained from Big Dugger's face. "You know my lawyer didn't file nothin'."

"Yeah, but the Indigent Defender Board was filing these motions all the time back then; there's a chance they got your lawyer to file one, too. I'm gonna send a request to the clerk of court and see what I get back. Either way, I think we should file a post-conviction," Calvin advised. "If you could win a remand to Shea's court, a lawyer might get appointed to your case and get your records for you."

"Are we talkin', like, a new trial?"

"Yes, especially if we can find the objection. Shea might deny us, but if he does, we'll go to federal court," Calvin insisted.

Big Dugger's smile returned. "All right, Dog. I do what you tell me to do."

When their meeting ended, Calvin remained in the law library to work on Big Dugger's petition. Sometime later, a familiar voice interrupted him.

"You still doin' them *Cage* things?"

Calvin looked up to see a young man he recognized from the parish jail.

"Yeah, didn't you write to me? I remember doing your motion but you never let me know if you wanted it filed."

"I filed my own motion," the young man replied. "But I got denied. I need you to hook me up on my appeal."

Calvin looked at him quizzically. "Sure. Just put it here." He tapped the edge of his desk.

When he'd finished with Big Dugger's petition, he turned his attention to the young man's motion. He noticed it bore the signature of one of the white inmate counsels, yet looked identical to his own *Cage* template.

"Damn!" he exclaimed, pushing the paper away.

Checo looked up from a nearby table. "What's up?"

"We don't think nothin' of each other, do we? Or ourselves, for that matter. This dude don't trust *one of his kind* to do the job, so he gets a white guy to do it. That guy used what I wrote word for word, and probably charged a whole carton of cigarettes, too."

Checo shrugged. "Look at it this way, brah. You go shopping for a car: you want the five-thousand-dollar car or you want the fifty-thousand-dollar car?"

Calvin crossed his arms. "The fifty-thousand-dollar car."

"Right. Don't take it personal. When we offer them help for free, what are their crazy minds gonna tell them? Find a guy who's gonna make them pay."

"But it pisses me off that these dudes think the only ones smart enough to do their legal work are the white counsels," Calvin replied.

Checo nodded in understanding. "Just ignore it and keep doin' what you do."

Calvin returned to his work, periodically glancing at the plagiarized motion.

When his temper finally cooled, he flipped to a fresh page on his legal pad and began drafting the young man's appeal.

"CALVIN, THERE'S ONLY ONE PERSON I WANT YOU TO WORRY ABOUT when you start up there on death row next week," Mrs. Rabalais instructed at the next inmate counsel staff meeting. "Henry Montrell, on CCR. He's got more civil suits going than you do."

Chuckles floated up from around the table.

Calvin recognized Montrell's name. He was the last man to take a beating in the hospital bullpen before the administration finally closed it down.

"It's going to be a full-time job helping him, at least for a while," Mrs. Rabalais warned.

"Glad to do it, Mrs. Rabalais."

Calvin would be joining Lane Nelson, Ed Smith, and Keith Elliot as an inmate counsel at death row. A recent lawsuit resulting in a consent decree had prompted the prison to increase the number of inmate counsels assigned to the unit.

"It's not only me who expects the four of you to do your best," Mrs. Rabalais reminded them. "You have a federal judge looking over your shoulder, too."

Calvin regretted leaving the mental health unit, but at least he could still be of use on death row. He felt an affinity for the men there, having narrowly escaped the same fate at his own trial.

He was also assigned to the Closed Cell Restricted (CCR) unit, which was used to hold people in long-term isolation. Among them were Robert King, Herman Wallace, who went by "Hooks," and Albert Woodfox—soon to be known as the Angola 3. Hooks and Woodfox had been confined in isolation since 1972, King since 1973.

Both death row and CCR were in the same building, near the front gate of the penitentiary. Their design mirrored the cellblocks in the Main Prison: a row of concrete pens lining the wall, each equipped with a bed, a sink, a toilet, a small table, and a stool fixed to the floor. Measuring six by nine feet, the cells were enclosed with barred doors. There were no windows, only slim openings on the opposite side of the tiers for sunlight and air to filter through. Residents of death row and CCR were allowed a mere hour outside their cells each day—and even then, it depended on the shift whether security would actually give them a turn. During the hour, they could only shower, walk the tier, fetch hot water or cigarettes, or sit by another cell to play checkers through the bars, and all while shackled.

The inmate counsels had a dedicated office in the building, with one computer to share. Per the federal consent decree, they'd had to qualify for the position by undergoing a written exam and interviews with the American Civil Liberties Union to ensure that they could provide meaningful legal assistance.

Calvin would begin his new role by shadowing Ed Smith.

His arrival on death row was strangely joyful. Many of the forty men housed there were friends from his days in the parish jail. They were excited to catch up on lost time, and he spent much of his first weeks chatting at the cell bars.

On CCR, he soon met Woodfox, Hooks, and King, and was immediately impressed. Like Norris and Checo at the law library, the men used their influence on CCR to educate younger guys and help them find mental reprieve from the confines of their cells. Calvin saw Woodfox and Hooks offering literacy, civics, and political education to men on the tiers, much like Slim Jenkins had done for him in the parish jail. King, a skilled jailhouse lawyer, assisted with people's cases and was working on a suit to secure more yard time for those on the unit.

Calvin took lessons from the men as he figured out how to be effective on CCR. In order to assist Henry Montrell with his lawsuits, he first needed to learn how to earn his trust.

Ed showed Calvin to Henry's cell. Calvin extended a hand through the bars, but the man inside didn't look up.

"I'm one of the inmate lawyers. You want any cases or law books today?"

Henry shook his head. "And I don't need no pawns of the state helping me, neither."

Calvin accepted the rebuff without protest. He knew Henry had spent considerable time at Camp J before ending up on CCR, and Ed had warned of his deep-seated paranoia. To build any form of rapport, patience would be key.

Henry's civil suits detailed episode after episode of excessive force by security. In the most recent incident, the tactical team had come through the tiers scouring for contraband. When Henry refused to vacate his cell, they assaulted him within sight of the other cells to ensure the rest of the tier complied. Reading these allegations, Calvin felt a wave of disgust, recalling that the same team had come to the hospital in the middle of the night to terrorize Weasel.

It wasn't just the tactical team's calculated violence that earned them such hatred from the population; it was also their profound disrespect. When they conducted searches, they ripped and threw just about every possession a man had, regardless of whether they expected to find anything illicit. The guys had so few possessions to begin with that the act of randomly upending them was a calculated, needless cruelty, and Calvin despised it. He would gladly help Henry with his suits.

Death row and CCR were a mile from the Main Prison, which meant the inmate counsels had to arrange their own transportation to work. Calvin began his day at four in the morning to ensure he had time to locate a guard with available space in his truck. Returning at the day's end proved even more challenging. Often, Calvin wouldn't find his way back to his cot until past midnight, having spent sixteen hours at his job. He made up for this by sneaking under his desk some afternoons for a discreet nap. Once, a lieutenant in search of a pen took a seat at Calvin's desk, oblivious to his presence underneath. Calvin was jolted awake by an exclamation of "What the hell?" when the lieutenant's boots found his back. Fortunately, the lieutenant only laughed.

Within a few months of making rounds on CCR, Calvin had come to value Woodfox, Hooks, and King as trusted friends. Though security kept them housed on separate tiers, the captain of CCR gave Calvin permission to pass notes for them so they could communicate. He sought their advice on legal strategies, and they ran civil law questions by him, knowing that was his area of expertise.

Frequently, he discussed with them the immense difficulties involved in helping guys at the prison obtain their records. Reviewing files was the first step in providing meaningful representation, yet the numerous barriers to accessing them made Calvin's job nearly impossible. Attorneys assigned to handle criminal appeals did not provide their clients with copies of their transcripts or pleadings. In post-conviction cases, petitioners were left to fend for themselves unless their families could afford to hire a lawyer. No nonprofits had the funding to meet the needs of those serving life sentences, and any government funding for post-conviction representation was reserved for individuals on death row. The only attorney Calvin came in regular contact with was Keith Nordyke, assigned to monitor conditions at Angola as part of the ongoing consent decree stemming from the landmark 1971 lawsuit. Keith was generous with his time and expertise, providing guidance to the inmate counsels during his regular visits to the law library, but solving the records issue was beyond his scope or capacity.

"It's impossible to prepare claims that don't look frivolous if you can't provide the evidence that supports them," Calvin pointed out to Woodfox one day on his rounds. "But even in cases where I'm sure the state has suppressed witness statements, I can barely get the guy's trial transcripts, let alone his police reports or DA file."

Woodfox listened with a sympathetic ear, having been stonewalled in his own case.

"It's a problem for just about everyone up here."

He went quiet, thinking.

"I wonder if we could start an organization; find somebody on the street that would copy documents for us."

"I've considered that," said Calvin, "but who's got the time and money to do it? Our families don't have either."

"The person could charge for their time, and we could pool resources to cover the cost," Woodfox suggested. "I probably have family that would do it for a reasonable fee. Nothing crazy, just for the gas and the hours involved in copying the records."

"Maybe the guys would be allowed to draw from their prison savings accounts if the money was for document retrieval?" Calvin wondered.

Each month, a portion of an individual's wages at the prison was deposited into his savings account, but only certain expenditures, like educational courses or court costs for filing lawsuits, were permitted to be paid from it.

"I think there's a strong argument for that." Woodfox nodded. "I bet we could make something happen, at least for the guys out of Orleans. Give me a week to ask around."

True to his word, by the end of the month, Woodfox had found a sister-in-law willing to take on the project for a small fee. Calvin sent her the names of people who needed records, and she sent back packets of documents in return. After some months, she was no longer available, and the operation dried up. Still, the men were happy to have advanced a good number of cases in the meantime, and returned to problem-solving by other means.

Though Calvin was supposed to be helping Henry Montrell with his civil suits, he quickly spotted a compelling legal issue in Henry's criminal case.

Henry and his uncle had been convicted of armed robbery in New Orleans, each receiving a fifty-year sentence. Calvin saw that the trial judge had failed to specify that they were ineligible for parole, meaning Henry could potentially file a motion to correct the illegal sentence under *Desdunes*. Given Calvin's prior successes with *Desdunes* motions, he was confident in the strategy. Yet he hesitated to suggest it directly, fearing Henry might reject it out of suspicion.

In time, Calvin formulated a plan: if he could persuade Henry's uncle to file a *Desdunes* motion first, Henry might witness his uncle's progress and be motivated to follow suit.

At the next inmate counsel staff meeting, Calvin shared his idea.

"Mrs. Rabalais, I think I can get Henry out of prison."

"You mean you could actually get Henry home?" Mrs. Rabalais looked at him over her glasses.

"Yeah."

"If you get Henry Montrell out, you can have two weeks off."

Henry's uncle had a different outlook on doing time than his nephew. He had long abandoned his legal case and resigned himself to the daily grind of prison life, knowing he would likely never go home.

When Calvin told him that a recent court ruling might offer another shot at freedom, the uncle's face lit up.

He quickly gathered whatever documents he had and brought them to Calvin, who helped him file the *Desdunes* motion.

Weeks later, he found Calvin at the law library, a judge's order in his hands.

"They gave me a hearing!"

"We got 'em!" Calvin replied. "You're going home, I know it, brah. Get your program certificates together so that when you go back to court, you can show your judge you've rehabilitated."

Sure enough, when Henry's uncle went to court, the judge found that his sentence was illegal and resentenced him to time served. He was immediately released.

Calvin quietly delivered the motion he'd prepared for Henry's uncle, along with a copy of the judge's order granting relief, to Henry's cell. But Henry never mentioned the motion, leaving Calvin unsure whether he planned to file it.

One afternoon, security called the inmate counsel office, instructing Calvin to come over to CCR.

"Montrell is outta here," a sergeant declared when he arrived. "They've already processed his order of release."

Moments later, Calvin found Henry coming down the hall.

"Appreciate you, man," Henry said simply, but Calvin could tell how much it meant. He was going home.

"Good luck out there," he replied.

Henry gave him a dap and headed down the stairs.

Calvin watched him climb into the transport van before turning to a guard. "Can I make a phone call?"

The sergeant dialed for him.

"Rabalais speaking."

"It's Calvin," he said, grinning. "I am calling to inform you that Henry Montrell is gone."

Mrs. Rabalais paused, absorbing the news. "Calvin, are you kidding me? Henry Montrell?"

"Henry is going home. To-day."

She chuckled in disbelief. "Looks like I owe you two weeks off."

"I might be too busy for that, Mrs. Rabalais."

"I bet you are," she said warmly. "Well done, Calvin."

———

AFTER HIS REINTRODUCTION TO *SPEARS* DURING HIS INMATE COUN-
sel exam, Calvin stayed on high alert for any federal court rulings or
legislation aimed at restricting access to the courts. Under Chief
Justice Rehnquist, the Supreme Court had recently issued opinions
denying a constitutional right to counsel in state post-conviction cases,
which—while not changing the status quo in Louisiana—further
confirmed the court's new direction. Calvin and Norris did their best
to check for new legal decisions and legislative bills, but with updates
often arriving to the prison months late, staying current was a constant struggle.

Early in 1991, Calvin discovered a bill passed the previous summer by Louisiana lawmakers amending the state's post-conviction
statute. His eyes quickly zeroed in on the words under a heading labeled "Time Limitations":

> No application for post-conviction relief, including applica-
> tions which seek an out-of-time appeal, shall be considered
> if it is filed more than three years after the judgment of con-
> viction and sentence has become final.

He read the legislation a second time before rushing to the nearest phone.

"Mrs. Rabalais, I've just come across a new law that's gonna hurt
everybody up here."

"What's wrong, Calvin?"

He took a moment to steady his voice. "The legislature's imposing a time bar in state post-conviction proceedings. They're giving

us three years from the time our direct appeal was denied to file our post. If we're already past that window, which most of us are, we've only got *one* year to file from the date that the bill became law. The clock started ticking six months ago. In other words, we've got six months to help the entire prison population file an application for post-conviction relief."

"Tell me the name of the new law," Mrs. Rabalais pressed. "What's the filing deadline?"

"It's Article 930.8 in the Criminal Code of Procedure. The deadline is October 1, 1991."

The line went silent.

"I'll call the inmate counsels together right away," she said.

AS NEWS OF ARTICLE 930.8 SPREAD THROUGHOUT THE PRISON, SO DID the beginnings of a panic. Calvin littered the desks of the law library with copies of the new law. The editors of *The Angolite* hurried to report on 930.8 in their next issue—the first publication in the state to do so. It was a constant topic of discussion among the inmate counsels.

"The judges, the lawyers, no one noticed the bill pass the legislature," said one at a staff meeting. "The Baton Rouge *Advocate* is only just writing about it now."

"They can't pass a law that would cut us out like that," Burl declared to murmurs of agreement. "And they definitely can't limit our ability to raise our claims in federal habeas—the state has no authority over the federal courts. If they want to impose a deadline in state court, then we can just skip state post-conviction and file our issues directly with the feds."

At this, Calvin stiffened. "You're assuming the federal courts won't defer to the state regulation—what makes you think they won't? They've been waiting for this. Federal courts don't want to hear from us no more. It's right there in *Spears v. McCotter.*"

The others stared at him. He had never publicly challenged Burl before.

"That's different, *Spears* is civil law," said Burl.

"The problem is the same to them, whether it's civil or criminal," Calvin shot back. "Too many filings from people in prison. They've been working up to this for the past ten years."

"Seems like even the lawyers on the outside are interpreting this 930.8 thing different ways," another counsel offered diplomatically. "One guy told me his lawyer thinks that the state can't stop the federal courts from looking at our claims, even if we're barred in state court. But another dude from Baton Rouge told me his lawyer said the opposite."

"I think we have to treat this as a worst-case scenario," Calvin insisted. "The law says we have until October first to file our post-conviction or our claims will be barred. I don't see why we wouldn't file by that date."

"How could we possibly do that?" Burl asked.

"All right," cut in Mrs. Rabalais. "I want you all to go away and do more research. Think about the best use of resources. Let's revisit this in a week."

The meeting disbanded and the counsels wandered off in huddles of two and three. Calvin stayed behind to do more research at the law library.

Alvin had been waiting in the hallway to learn the outcome of the discussion. He found Calvin at his desk. "So, what do you think we should do?"

"Get ready to file," Calvin replied. "I'm going to get petitions together for every guy whose case I'm handling, no matter what the others decide. And I'm going to file my own. Anyone who puts their trust in the federal courts to come through for us on this—"

"Is that what they were saying?" Alvin nodded toward the meeting room.

"I understand people not wanting to believe it." Calvin sighed. "But if we stick our heads in the sand, we'll pay the price. We always say 'the federal courts, the federal courts,' but we've got to understand those days are over. The pendulum has swung."

Later that week, Calvin typed a sober letter to Mrs. Rabalais to request her help in soliciting support from local law schools.

> The thought of not having an application timely filed has created a state of panic among the inmates here at Angola. The inmate counsels are assisting as many inmates with quality work as they can, but it will be impossible to assist a very large number of desperate inmates who cannot afford the assistance of outside legal help. The recent decisions in *Cage v. Louisiana*, 111 S.Ct. 328 (1990) and *State v. West*, 568 So.2d 1019 (La. 1990) have only seriously complicated a seemingly already hopeless situation.

The next time Mrs. Rabalais saw Calvin at the Education Building, she pulled him aside.

"I've tried to get outside assistance," she said, shaking her head. "But it doesn't sound like we can count on the law schools."

Calvin reported this to Checo at the law library.

"You know who we should speak to about this?" asked Checo. "Bosworth."

With his background as a practicing lawyer, Bosworth was a prominent inmate counsel and maintained a close relationship with the new head warden, John Whitley, who had replaced Larry Smith.

Checo and Calvin tracked him down in *The Angolite*'s offices.

"We want to speak with you about this post-conviction thing," Checo said.

"What about it?" he asked.

"Do you know if anyone has spoken to Keith Nordyke yet?"

Nordyke had been at the law library just recently on one of his monitoring visits.

"He said he's only just heard about it himself, that the law went through the legislature without anyone noticing," Bosworth said.

"If we're going to get any of these petitions in on time, we're going to need to figure something out that helps a lot of people at once," said Checo. "There aren't nearly enough of us to work up a post for each person."

"You're not wrong," Bosworth agreed. "Perhaps we could file for an extension of time?"

"There's no authority in the statute for a judge to grant it," Calvin replied.

"Research it further and see if you can come up with one," Bosworth suggested. "In the meantime, I'll go see Warden Whitley."

CALVIN HAD PLEDGED TO DRAFT AND SUBMIT APPLICATIONS FOR AT least twenty clients before the deadline. He was also committed to helping the guys on his rounds. As October loomed, finding time for his own petition became increasingly challenging.

After Judge Shea dismissed Calvin's post-conviction application, his writ to the appellate court was also denied. Now he was waiting to hear whether the Louisiana Supreme Court would review the lower court's decision.

Since the new statute barred repeated post-conviction applications, Calvin's next petition would need to anticipate any issues he might want to raise in future litigation. Yet without his court and police records, he still lacked evidence to support his claims. Ironically, the new law, meant to deter frivolous petitions, instead compelled them by imposing a deadline that forced people to file before they were ready. He could only do his best.

Gerald Bosworth, Keith Nordyke, and Nordyke's law partner, June Denlinger, formulated a strategy to challenge the new law's constitutionality by filing civil lawsuits in both state and federal courts. Their primary contention was that the one-year deadline unjustly denied defendants meaningful access to the courts. While Calvin lent his research skills to Bosworth and Nordyke, he maintained his focus on filing petitions, suspecting that any court ruling might not materialize until well after the October deadline had passed.

Meanwhile, Warden Whitley agreed to assist Legal Programs in their effort to help the population. After brainstorming with Bosworth and Nordyke, he solidified a plan. One Saturday afternoon, a month prior to the deadline, Nordyke, Bosworth, and Norris Henderson convened in the prison radio studio, located in the A-Building. As they readied themselves to broadcast their message, inmate counsels dispersed throughout the prison, taking positions in each dormitory and cellblock.

At 4 p.m., the entire prison went into lockdown. Regular activities ceased, and the population was instructed to wait by their beds for a special broadcast from Warden Whitley. After calling for people's attention and introducing his guests, Whitley handed the microphone to Nordyke. The attorney explained the new law, emphasizing the serious consequences of missing the filing deadline for both state and federal appeals.

Henderson and Bosworth, figures of trust within the prison community, took the mic next. They outlined the strategy they had devised for the timely filing of everyone's post-conviction petitions and offered step-by-step instructions for filling out the forms. The workers at the prison print shop had labored day and night to produce five thousand blank applications for the inmate counsels to distribute throughout the prison. Applicants were assured that the inmate counsels would help them file the post-conviction petitions on time, along with requests for a 180-day extension to supplement them with facts and evidence. Questions were taken via the guards' telephones so that people's concerns could be addressed over the air.

For the next four hours, the inmate counsels helped individuals across the prison complete their forms. Dorm partners stepped in to assist their illiterate peers, making sure every page was filled out. By the end of the effort, they had gathered over two thousand petitions.

The radio program was rebroadcast two more times that weekend, leading to additional last-minute submissions. The inmate counsels worked sixteen-hour days to supplement each one with relevant arguments and issues, while *The Angolite* shut down its operations to donate its typewriters to the effort. Keith Nordyke secured outside computer and printer donations for the law library, while Warden Whitley simplified the usual indigent postage procedure to expedite the mailouts. As a safeguard, the inmate counsels compiled a comprehensive list of everyone they had assisted, and the Classifications department authenticated it with a notary.

Calvin managed to write claims to populate the applications of all his longtime clients: Ron, Weasel, Edward, Catkiller, Alvin, Big Dugger, and others. For anyone he couldn't help at CCR, he prepared an affidavit for them to file in court:

> Calvin Duncan, Prison Number 109136, after being duly sworn, deposed and says that he is an Inmate Counsel Substitute at the Louisiana State Penitentiary and that he has been unable to accept any more cases due to the high number he is already working on, and other job requirements.

In the final week of September, a terrifying realization hit Calvin. While worrying about everyone else's cases, he had overlooked a crucial detail in his own: he had meant to supplement his petition with a *Lofton* claim. To make matters worse, he was sure *Lofton* was his best issue.

With special clearance from security, Calvin spent the night in the law library, all the while berating himself for neglecting his own case. The next day, he sent off a supplement, praying it would reach the court in time.

By October 1, the inmate counsels were confident they had extended help to everyone in the prison who required it, marking an exceptional accomplishment.

"The spirit of cooperation that developed between inmates, and between inmates and security, was unheard of in the long history of Angola," observed *The Angolite*. "Nothing like it had ever happened before."

———

"WHAT DO YOU DO IF SOMEONE ASKS YOU FOR HELP BUT YOU CAN SEE he's already missed his deadline?" Alvin asked, eyes trained on the page in front of him.

He and Calvin were working alone, the law library desolate now that 930.8 had gone into effect. The earlier optimism surrounding *Lofton, Cage,* and *Desdunes* had faded as the consequences of the new procedural bar took hold. The courts had mostly denied requests for extensions of time, and as a result, they were also denying people's post-conviction petitions. Calvin testified in Keith Nordyke's civil case over the law's constitutionality, but the litigation was unsuccessful. He remained proud of their efforts to file for everybody—the most they were able to do under the circumstances—but there was no denying the law had dimmed their chances of meaningful post-conviction review.

Calvin pursed his lips at Alvin's question. "My policy is, if I can see he's in a ditch, I let him know he's in a ditch. Nine out of ten times, he's gonna disagree with me. If he is adamant that he's in a fine position, then I leave him where he is."

Alvin looked uncertain. "But you always say our job is to give people hope."

"If there's even a one percent chance of success, I make sure they know it. But I never tell them a lie."

"So what's the alternative for that guy? If we don't do it, some lockerbox lawyer is gonna tell him he don't have to worry, then take his cigarettes and leave him deeper in the hole."

Calvin shrugged. "It's a bad situation. If I take his case, and he has that mindset that I should be able to do something for him, he's gonna feel like I messed him over when he gets that denial, and he's not gonna understand why I spent all my time on the procedural bar without paying attention to the merits of his claims. He doesn't understand that the merits are irrelevant to me at this point, because they're irrelevant to the court until we overcome that bar."

Alvin looked back down at the papers. "I just wish we could do something for all these guys, Calvin."

"I know, brah." Calvin nodded grimly. "It's gonna be a massacre."

IN DECEMBER 1991, THE LOUISIANA SUPREME COURT ISSUED A FAVOR-able ruling clarifying that DA files were subject to public records requests once a conviction and sentence were final. The decision was a much-needed bright spot in the aftermath of 930.8.

Calvin responded by immediately lodging a request. He was surprised to receive a swift response from the Orleans Parish DA's office, but his optimism withered when he read their letter. The custodian of records claimed he had no right to a copy of his file, referencing case law that the state supreme court had just overruled.

Calvin drafted a writ of mandamus to compel the DA's office to hand over the records, highlighting the state's wrong understanding of the law. He filed it in civil court, the same route he'd taken to get his police report five years earlier, hoping it would work again.

The court sided with Calvin, ordering the DA's office to copy its file. But the office refused to respond. After a frustrating eight-week wait, Calvin resorted to filing another writ of mandamus, this time with the appellate court, to compel the civil judge to enforce his earlier order. The appellate court informed Calvin that the district court had lost his petition, and asked him to submit it again.

Exasperated, Calvin searched for help outside the prison walls. Though anyone from the public was entitled to approach the DA's office for his file, he hesitated to burden Mamie or Aunt Gail. Instead, he turned to Tiny Man, an old-timer in his dorm, knowing that Tiny Man's wife, Rosemary, would likely want to help. After Calvin had met Rosemary in the visiting shed years earlier, she and Tiny Man had come to regard him as family.

Rosemary was quick to honor his request. She promptly visited the DA's office, secured the copies, and sent them to the prison.

When the packet arrived, Calvin raced to the law library to pore over the contents. He'd been working to discover what was in his DA file for almost a decade.

The first few documents looked familiar—his original police report and a few pretrial motions. However, as he delved deeper, he came across something new: a typed statement from the eyewitness, Kristie Emberling, taken six days after the crime. In it, she referred to the shooter as "the fat guy" eight separate times.

Calvin turned to another new document, a lengthy investigative police report written by Detective Marco Demma. The report described familiar events leading up to Calvin's arrest: the Crimestoppers reenactment that aired in February 1982, the tip from an unidentified male caller who said that "a negro male by the name of Calvin Duncan" committed the crime, the search Detective Demma ran on the police computer system that turned up Calvin's mugshot and juvenile arrest for shoplifting, and the photographic lineup he showed Kristie.

Kristie's response to the photo array, however, caught Calvin's attention.

According to Demma's notes, he showed the array to Kristie at 11:15 in the morning. Her testimony at a pretrial hearing, however, was that the identification was made around midnight—Kristie recalled sitting in Demma's car with a light on. The report went on to say that Kristie looked through the photographs, and upon reaching the mugshot of Calvin, she stated, "This is the one who shot David." But when Demma asked if she was positive, Kristie looked at the photograph again and said she wasn't sure, and that she was very scared. The report continued:

> Dets. Demma and Curole, feeling that Kristie Emberling was not completely positive in identifying Calvin Duncan as the subject who fatally shot David Yeager, departed [her home] enroute back to the Homicide Office to further the investigation.

Half an hour later, Demma wrote, Kristie called him at the police station to say she was positive, but feared the suspect might try to kill her if he found out she had identified him.

It was the first Calvin had heard of Kristie hesitating over her identification.

He quickly skimmed the remainder of the report, hunting for more inconsistencies. When describing the investigation in Oregon, Demma wrote that Lieutenant Reed, not Detective Peterson, had been his point person—also contrary to what he had told the jury.

Calvin's mind swirled with the same questions that had haunted him since his arrest: Why did the police seem so intent on pinning the murder on him? Was there pressure to solve the crime because of its proximity to the French Quarter? Was it because of who the victim was? Or did they just need a win to deflect attention from the city's high rate of unsolved murders?

He turned to the final document in the packet—a brief memorandum penned by the prosecutor, Bruce Whittaker, before trial. In the memo, Whittaker urged that Calvin be offered a plea to the lesser charge of second-degree murder. Calvin was floored.

Among Whittaker's reasons were Kristie's initial hesitation in making an identification, and—new to Calvin—the fact that soon after he was indicted, Lieutenant Reed apparently faced his own indictment on federal wiretapping charges. According to the memo, Reed had been fired from his job and sentenced to five years of felony probation.

Calvin had always wondered why the prosecution portrayed Detective Peterson as his interrogator instead of Reed. The answer was astonishing: if Reed had testified, the jury would have learned that he had been convicted of a federal crime.

"I recommend reduction for the following reasons," Whittaker wrote in the memorandum:

1) The case stands or falls on the identification by one witness—Kristie Emberling. At the time of the offense, Emberling was 15 years old. In the original photo lineup, she made a tentative identification. Although she states the tentativeness was due to her understandable fear, the fact remains that the identification was seriously damaged for trial.

2) Reed's inextricable involvement in all statements and his subsequent conviction would present serious problems in a jury trial. In response to a defense discovery request, the State informed the defense that none of its witnesses had a conviction record. In light of our continuing duty, such answer is no longer sufficient.

3) The admissions by the defendant, although suggestive, do not bind him firmly to the scene of the crime. The timing and detail of the videotape and news article could suggest to a jury that Duncan gleaned his knowledge from media accounts, not personal experience.

4) The issue of race, always present in interracial crime, is here an integral part of the case. In all statements by the defendant, the race of the victim and witness was emphasized by his claim of "persecution." Detective Curole told me that race permeated Duncan's discussions with the police. A strong race "angle" is unavoidable.

In light of all the circumstances surrounding this troubling case, it is my request and recommendation that we agree to the proposed plea to second-degree murder.

Calvin stared at the final sentence.

This troubling case . . .

The prosecutors knew that their evidence against him was unreliable: that the eyewitness had hesitated over his identification, that the sheriff's deputy who interrogated him was corrupt. Yet instead of offering him a plea, the DA's office had omitted all of this from their presentation to the jury. They'd even asked the jurors to sentence him to death.

Calvin noticed one final document in the envelope: a short, hand-written note.

> There are presently no leads as to the identity of the second perpetrator. Obviously, it would be very difficult to convict the defendant on the evidence that exists presently. I felt that he should at least be indicted in order to have him arrested and possibly obtain a statement. . . . If, however, no further evidence can be developed and the ID cannot be firmed up, let me know and we'll do whatever is necessary.

There was no signature on the note, but judging by the comments, it was written by a prosecutor early in the investigation.

Calvin burned with rage. The state had indicted him as a means of gathering evidence, upended his life to extract statements from him in custody, and then falsely imputed "guilty knowledge" to those statements, knowing they needed to firm up their case.

We'll do whatever is necessary.

The weekend after Rosemary mailed the DA file, she called Calvin to the visiting shed during a visit with Tiny Man.

"Thank you for everything," Calvin told her as he sat down at their table. "Those police reports are helping me understand so many things I have been wondering about all this time."

"Good." Rose looked around, then leaned forward. "There was more in the file."

Calvin frowned, not understanding.

"I saw a transcript from the girl's testimony to the grand jury, but the man at the DA's office wouldn't let me copy it," she explained. "That girl said she wasn't sure about her identification of you."

"What do you mean?"

"She says she had to think about it for a week or so after the police showed her your photo."

Adrenaline surged through him. Maybe the identification was even weaker than he thought. "I need to get that testimony; that's proof of my innocence. Why'd they say you couldn't have it?"

"I don't know. The man just came up on me and said I couldn't copy it. I felt like I couldn't disagree with him."

"That's all right," Calvin reassured her. "I'll find a way."

The following week, he wrote to a Baton Rouge attorney who was helping some of the men at the prison prepare their pardon applications. He asked if she would request Kristie's grand jury testimony the next time she traveled to New Orleans.

"I'd be glad to help after all you do for the men incarcerated there," she replied.

The attorney soon mailed him a copy of the transcript, and Calvin saw that Rose was right. Kristie's account to the grand jury, in which she again described the shooter as fat, was markedly different from what Demma had written in his report.

> **Q** *Now, Kristie, when you looked at these pictures, did [Detective Demma] ask you if you could identify the guy who shot David Yeager?*
>
> **A** Yes, sir.
>
> **Q** *And what did you tell him the first time you looked at the pictures?*

A I told him at first I wasn't sure. Then I called him back and told him "yes."

Q *And then when did you call him back?*

A I don't know. It could have been a week or so after.

The prosecutor tried to massage the timing, asking, "Perhaps it was more like a few days?" However, Kristie indicated twice more that she wasn't sure when she called Demma back. The exchange continued:

Q *Alright, Kristie, do you know—can you explain what made you change your feelings about this from being not sure that this is the guy to being sure that it is the guy?*

A Uh, I kept focusing back on the night—you know, on the guy. And I just kept it up and kept it up, you know.

Q *You kept trying to think about that night after you saw the pictures.*

A I kept going back to the guy's face and looking at it, you know. And that's when I decided that was the guy.

Calvin considered what she had said. Nothing about fear, only uncertainty.

I kept going back to the guy's face and looking at it.

I wonder if they left her with my picture, he thought.

At trial, Kristie's account aligned much more closely with Detective Demma's. She testified that she had called the detective back within half an hour of viewing Calvin's photograph. Clearly, this transcript threw that testimony into doubt.

Calvin removed his glasses and rubbed the bridge of his nose. He should have felt relief at having evidence of the state's deceit in his hands, but he was too angry.

Even as the prosecution acknowledged the weaknesses in their case against him, they displayed no concern for the possibility of targeting the wrong person. Their sole focus seemed to be on gathering just enough evidence to secure a conviction.

After reviewing countless other cases, Calvin had no illusions that criminal prosecutions were noble searches for the truth. Yet the revelations from his DA file stunned him. He thought of all the days—*years*—that he'd sat in the parish jail, naively hoping that the police and prosecution would realize their mistake. But here was the plain and awful truth: from the moment they had the name Calvin Duncan, they didn't much care if he was guilty or not.

1994

Calvin unpacked a fresh box of chalk and wiped down the blackboard at the front of the classroom, sizing up the expectant faces from the corner of his eye.

He had started the law class months earlier at the suggestion of a club leader whose members wanted a better grasp of the law. It was easier to seek forgiveness than permission to launch a new initiative—a legacy of the prison's segregated past, where leadership roles were reserved for favored prisoners. So Calvin began without informing security, and as the class grew and continued, it gained tacit approval, becoming a fixture of Saturday afternoon programming at the Main Prison.

"Welcome back," he told Buff, one of his regular students who had just returned from a stint in Camp J, where he'd been forced to file his post-conviction application without access to the law library. Despite the constraints, Buff had crafted an impressive brief. As

Calvin turned to address the rest of the students, he wondered if he had a future inmate counsel on his hands.

"Today we're talking about what happens when we win the chance to go back to court."

He summoned his preacher voice—deep and emphatic.

"The day is coming when you will win the right to an evidentiary hearing or a resentencing in your case. Whether it's tomorrow or ten years from now, when that day arrives, you must be prepared. You will be appointed a lawyer—a momentous occasion. What you may not have considered, though, is that for that overworked, underpaid lawyer, your case might be just another drop in the bucket."

He watched as unease rippled through the room. Then he turned and wrote *Tucker v. Day* on the blackboard.

"When my friend Raymond Tucker won a resentencing, he wasn't appointed a lawyer until the very moment he was brought before his judge. The lawyer didn't consult with Raymond, had no knowledge of his case, and didn't speak once during his hearing.

"I wish I could tell you that what Raymond dealt with is unique, but there are plenty of judges who will get a lawyer to stand for you with no preparation. And you'll find those lawyers are usually just going through the motions. A lot of them have lost hope.

"That's where you come in. You know your case, so it's up to you to educate your lawyer. You can give him the issues, give him the strategy, give him hope that he can win your case. And if he doesn't listen, talk past him directly to the court! We have a constitutional right to participate in our own defense, and your case is your life. Don't ever let it rest in someone else's hands."

He paused to see if the class was following and noticed several unfamiliar faces, likely transfers from Elayn Hunt Correctional Center. He pivoted to give the newcomers an orientation.

"So, how do we prepare to advocate for ourselves with counsel or in front of a judge? You probably heard that once you arrive at Angola, us inmate counsels are going to help you give your case back so you can go home. That's what they told me in the parish jail, too. You might have even heard that this class is a fast track to getting us to work on your case. It's true that we'll do our best for you, and that if you come to class, you are likely to get more help. But here's what you need to know: we can only help you as much as you're willing to help yourself."

He wandered down the aisle.

"Every single one of us in here is up against impossible odds. We are trying to learn the law without an education. I'm uneducated, you're uneducated: we're trying to figure it out together. So let's set some rules: No criticizing people. No making each other feel like we asked a stupid question. Let's let everybody be heard. And one last thing: Don't ask a question you don't want the answer to. *Especially* about your case. Because we're gonna be straight about things in here, whether you like what you hear or not."

He surveyed the room.

"Raise your hand if you've ever read the Constitution of the United States."

A few hands shot up. Aware that most of his students couldn't read, Calvin was careful who he called on.

"AC, tell me what the Fourteenth Amendment says."

A man with thick-rimmed glasses twirled a lead pencil between his fingers. "No state will deprive any person of life, liberty, or property, without due process of law, or deny anyone the equal protection of the law."

"Thank you. And when was the Fourteenth Amendment adopted?"

"After the Civil War."

Calvin nodded. "Some of us know that the Fourteenth Amendment is what gave us, Blacks, citizenship and equal protection under the law for the first time. But I wonder if anyone knows what it did for the Bill of Rights?"

He looked out at a sea of blank faces.

"The Supreme Court used the Fourteenth Amendment to force the states to adopt the Bill of Rights. What is the Bill of Rights, AC?"

"The first ten amendments to the Constitution."

"Yes. The rules the government must abide by: giving people the right to a fair trial, the right to be free from cruel and unusual punishment, the right to an attorney, and so on. Now, think back to when you was a kid. Your mom gave you money to walk to the corner store and buy her some milk. If you were lucky, maybe she gave you a few extra cents to buy you a bag of CheeWees. But when you got home, she made you share the CheeWees with your sisters. Did you like having to share them? Or did you want to keep them all for yourself? That's how the Southern states feel about the Bill of Rights. When the Supreme Court made them apply the Constitution to us, guess how they felt?"

"Pissed off," one of the newcomers answered.

"Correct. The South never bought into the Fourteenth Amendment 'cause they didn't want those rights to apply to us. There's a doctrine called states' rights that says the federal government shouldn't have the power to interfere with what the states decide to do. And a lot of the states still believe that. When the court is watching, they'll hand a few rights over to us—Blacks, prisoners, poor people—but only for a period of time. As soon as the court looks the other way, they take back whatever they can."

A young man raised his hand with a scowl.

"Yes?" Calvin asked, returning to the podium at the front of the room.

"Look, you know those white people ain't never gonna let us out. You know that, man. So what's the point of coming here and acting like we can do somethin' about our situation?"

At this, another hand shot up. "I've been tryin' to get my records. Why we can't get the inmate lawyers in here to help us with that?"

"Shit . . . we can't even get our families to help us," one of the regulars grumbled.

Calvin nodded. "These are good points and I'm glad you raised them. I've got some thoughts about that."

He waited for their murmurs to die down, then squared up at the class, his tone sharpening.

"First of all, don't bring your families into this. 'Cause guess what? We weren't hangin' around our families before we came to prison. Some of us stole from our families. Some of us never contributed anything to our family's table. So don't play on your families.

"Second, what are *you* doing to get your records? You could go in the hobby shop, sand lumber for a guy, save up your money, and file for them. I don't see you doin' that.

"And the gentleman that says white folks ain't gonna let us out of here—those complaints are common and you'll notice that each one is predicated on what the white man wants." He scanned the room.

"White people are not concerned about us in this class. This class is about what we're doing for ourselves and each other, understood?"

"Now you gone an' cranked up this ol' fool," groaned an old-timer from the back.

"Yeah, I'm loose now!" Calvin called out. "When you come into this class, you come in with the attitude of David. The attitude of someone who is ready to take on Goliath. We all have a story. We all came from messed-up backgrounds. We went to bed hungry, our parents were on drugs. Shit, if I told you my story, you'd be cryin' just to hear it. But when you come to this class, you come with an attitude of bettering yourself so that you can help yourself." He jabbed a finger toward the door. "And so you can go out there and help somebody else."

The class looked back at him in stunned silence.

"If you don't have that attitude, then please do me a favor. Stay down the walk and play jacks, play checkers, play with your paper dolls—do whatever unserious people do. This class is for people who want to learn."

Calvin let his words hang in the quiet. He scanned the students' faces, sensing the fear beneath their complaints.

"I can guarantee that most of you have winning issues in your cases. I know this because I know Louisiana is trying to keep your rights from you. That's why I don't want to hear none of this shit about 'it's never going to work for me.' The Constitution is on your side, and your job is to keep raising your issues until the courts get it right. Will I be the hero of my own life?"

The regulars had heard the line a hundred times.

"Or will that station be held by somebody else?" Buff finished.

"Homework for next week is to read *Gitlow v. New York*." Calvin pointed to a pile of handouts on his desk. "Come to class ready to dissect it."

AT A MEETING OF THE INMATE COUNSELS, MRS. RABALAIS ANNOUNCED that Tulane Law School had gathered a collection of used textbooks for donation to Angola's law library. They needed to be collected and she was looking for volunteers. Calvin and Ed Smith raised their hands.

It wasn't only the prospect of a day outside the penitentiary that appealed to Calvin, but also the thought of returning to the law library with a vanload of books.

On the morning of the journey, he was happy to learn that Slim Rogers had been assigned to transport them to New Orleans. Slim was good-natured, and, reporting to Mrs. Rabalais, he knew to treat the inmate counsels with respect. Contrary to policy, he chose not to handcuff Ed and Calvin—the first time Calvin had traveled unshackled outside a courtroom, prison, or jail since the day he was taken from Timber Lake years ago.

The van left Angola before sunrise and arrived in the city around 9 a.m. At Claiborne Avenue, Calvin felt a prickle of excitement at seeing Uptown and Tulane University. He had never visited the campus before he went to prison. Once, as a child, he tried to go to the public pool at nearby Audubon Park with some family members, but they were turned away—a rejection Calvin understood was because of the color of their skin. With no other reason to venture beyond Canal Street for much of his early life, he never did.

As they walked through the grand campus, he noticed the smooth pavement, manicured grass squares, and stone arches. Ironically, something about the red brick and enclosed courtyards reminded him of the Iberville projects, but that thought vanished when the law school came into view.

Entering the law library was like entering the Sistine Chapel. Calvin slowed to take it in: the muffled scrape of chairs, students engrossed in their work, the ancient, sour smell of the legal reporters. Thousands of books gazed down at him from ceiling-high bookshelves, more than he'd ever seen in one place. He imagined laying an armful out at one of the center tables and pulling up a leather chair.

If I were a student here, he mused, you'd never catch me outside the law library. And the thought burrowed deep, like a seed rooting in soil, that he would be a law student one day. When all of this was over, he would go to law school.

A librarian directed him and Ed to the books they should load into the van.

As they began making trips to the storage room, Calvin noticed the library staff and passing students subtly averting their gaze. Even though they moved freely and wore T-shirts and jeans, somehow, there was no hiding that they were convicts.

On Calvin's third trip to the van, he met Todd, the building supervisor and the only other Black person he'd seen on campus that morning. With a hospitable gesture, Todd offered his help with the books, and Calvin gladly accepted. As they worked, their conversation flowed easily, with Calvin asking Todd questions about the law school.

As they loaded the final books into the van, Calvin surveyed them with anticipation, knowing these were the same resources used by the students he had just seen in the library.

Todd extended a handshake. "What are you looking forward to most about being on the outside today?"

Calvin didn't miss a beat. "Stopping at McDonald's on the way back."

Todd grinned as he walked off. "Enjoy your Big Mac."

MONTHS AFTER FILING HIS POST-CONVICTION APPLICATION, ALVIN Abbott received thrilling news: the Fourth Circuit Court of Appeal had granted him a new appeal under *Lofton,* and a local university legal clinic had been appointed to represent him.

Calvin was in the law library when an angry Alvin burst through the door, waving a copy of the appeal that the clinic had submitted.

"I know I shouldn't be surprised. But you're not going to believe what these dudes did."

Calvin scanned the brief. "Isn't this . . . ?"

"The same claim that the court dismissed on my first post-conviction? Damn right it is. This lawyer has gone and raised the exact same issue that the Louisiana Supreme Court already knocked down in my case five years ago."

Calvin shook his head. "I don't know what to say, Al."

"This dude didn't even read the record!" Alvin's tone drew stares from the callouts working nearby. "He only files *one claim,* and this is what he files. Asshole!"

He turned on his heel and headed back to the exit.

"We've still got your supplement to file," Calvin called out. "You've got good issues."

But Alvin was already out the door.

He didn't return to the law library for months, and Calvin didn't push him. Instead, he quietly finished the supplemental brief they had drafted together and made sure Alvin mailed it in.

When the Fourth Circuit issued its opinion some months later, Alvin found Calvin in the law library to read it over.

As predicted, the appellate judges quickly disposed of the legal clinic's brief, dismissing the claim as repetitive.

"You can tell the judges are pissed off that they even have to respond to this," said Alvin.

Calvin skipped to the next page. "Let's see what they say about our pro se claims."

The court's shift in tone was immediate.

The judges recognized that neither Alvin's lawyer nor his judge had informed him of the potential ramifications of pleading guilty to his earlier shoplifting charge. Specifically, they hadn't mentioned that he could be subjected to the habitual offender law. Had he known, Alvin might have chosen to go to trial instead of accepting the plea.

"Accordingly," the court declared, "sentence is vacated and the case is remanded for a new multiple bill hearing."

Alvin broke into a grin. "I got another hearing!"

"We got 'em now," said Calvin. "Now we bring *Dorthey*."

While Alvin's appeal had been pending at the Fourth Circuit, the Louisiana Supreme Court had issued a pivotal ruling in a case called *State v. Dorthey*. The decision emphasized that if a trial judge felt a mandatory punishment amounted to "nothing more than 'the purposeful imposition of pain and suffering' and was 'grossly out of proportion to the severity of the crime,'" the judge had a duty to reduce the sentence to one that wasn't constitutionally excessive.

Calvin was sure that *Dorthey* could help Alvin. At sentencing, his trial judge had expressed anger at being forced to render such a punitive sentence, remarking:

> This Court rues its position in meting out this type of sentence. However, the Court feels that it has no alternative, when the District Attorney's office persists in filing a multiple bill under these circumstances. This Court feels that this sentence is cruel and unusual . . . but that the Court has no other alternative but to impose it.

"Once your judge sees *Dorthey*, he's going to want to reduce your sentence," said Calvin. "But we should have a lawyer there to make sure the hearing goes smoothly."

Calvin suggested Laurie White, a young attorney with a practice in New Orleans. She had introduced herself to Calvin after admiring the legal memorandums he'd written to assist her clients. In recent years, Laurie had taken on several cases of people serving life without parole, bringing newfound hope to Angola.

Alvin had diligently saved his wages and plasma donation payments for such a time as this. He emptied his account to cover Laurie's retainer, and Calvin pitched in to make up the difference.

On the morning of his court appearance, Alvin waited impatiently for the docket to clear and the bailiff to call his name. As he moved from the jury box to the defense table, Laurie greeted him with a reassuring smile.

She rose to face the judge, who was ready to deliver his remarks.

"When I first sentenced the defendant many years ago now, I indicated at that time that I felt that the sentence was appropriate at twelve years," said the judge. "I have felt for many years that many of the sentences that were imposed under the multiple bill statute were excessive."

Alvin stole a glance at the prosecutor, who was listening with strained forbearance.

"The question now, as far as I'm concerned, is whether there is a basis for the defendant's sentence to be below the mandated minimum of thirty-three years. With the defendant's past record, seventeen and a half years would be the guideline sentence without consideration of any multiple bill. Let me say, the fact that this is where the sentencing guidelines bring us doesn't mean *any* of these long sentences make any measurable contribution to acceptable goals of punishment, and certainly almost all of these sentences amount to the purposeful imposition of pain and suffering. But I can't find that it is grossly out of proportion to the severity of the crime. And for that reason, I think that the appropriate sentence here should be—and is—as follows."

Alvin drew an anxious breath.

"It is the sentence of this court that the defendant be committed to the Louisiana State Department of Corrections at hard labor for a term of seventeen years and six months without the benefit of parole, but with credit for time served."

The prosecutor shot to her feet to lodge an objection. Laurie White counter-objected that the new sentence was too long. But Alvin wasn't listening. He was too busy counting.

In seven more years, he would be going home.

CALVIN WATCHED WITH INTEREST AS THE FILM CREW SET UP THEIR cameras and lights outside his office at death row. It wasn't the novelty of a movie being made at Angola—that wasn't unusual—but the possibilities this particular film, *Dead Man Walking*, presented. When he read Sister Helen Prejean's book the year before, he was deeply moved by her portrayal of Louisiana's death penalty horrors. Like Sr. Helen, Calvin believed that capital punishment wouldn't survive if the public saw executions up close. Even correctional officers like John Rabalais—Mrs. Rabalais's late husband, who had managed the death house during the events in the book—seemed uneasy about their roles. Now the film would bring the grim reality of the death penalty into people's living rooms. If the public could meet the men Calvin worked with and understand the trauma and deprivations they endured as children, surely they would put an end to capital punishment.

Not far from Calvin's window, the actress Susan Sarandon walked the concrete path from the security gate to the entrance of death row. Her brows were knitted, her lips pressed into a hard line. Occasionally, Calvin glanced up from his work to see her repeating the walk, perfecting Sr. Helen's resolute stride, take after take. Hours later, she was still at it, and he marveled at how any human drama could endure such a painstaking process. Perhaps her determination to get it right was her small act of defiance against an indifferent system.

IN SPITE OF CALVIN'S OPTIMISM, CHANGE WAS STILL FAR OFF.

As the 1990s wore on, the Democratic Party, reeling from historic losses in the 1994 midterms and under pressure from Republicans branding them "soft on crime," had endorsed harsher criminal justice policies. In 1996, President Bill Clinton, seeking to bolster his law-and-order bona fides ahead of the presidential election, signed sweeping federal laws that expedited appeals in both capital and non-capital cases and shielded prisons from accountability for civil rights abuses.

The first of the new statutes was the Prison Litigation Reform Act (PLRA), designed to curtail the federal courts' ability to hear prisoners' civil rights complaints. Historically, federal courts had taken a hands-off approach to regulating state prisons, until the civil rights era ushered in a wave of new constitutional safeguards, expanding protections under the Civil Rights Act of 1871. In the 1970s and '80s, federal courts finally began addressing the rampant, systemic abuses prevalent in state prisons. By 1988, an astounding forty states had come under some form of federal consent decree—a stark rebuke of the notion that states should be left to manage their prisons without oversight. Even Angola's head warden acknowledged in 1976 that "progress in the last five years has not been made by correctional administrators, but by federal court orders resulting from suits filed by inmates."

These federal interventions provoked the ire of many state officials. By 1995, as incarceration rates continued to soar, prisoner civil rights filings comprised a fifth of the federal civil docket. That year, four state attorneys general published a letter in *The New York Times* mocking prisoner lawsuits they characterized as frivolous. The widely read piece was a product of a targeted campaign by the National Association of Attorneys General to spark a backlash against challenges to conditions of confinement—one that proved successful. The PLRA passed Congress the following year with bipartisan support, imposing an impossible maze of burdens and restrictions that blocked most plaintiffs from reaching federal court, no matter how troubling their allegations.

The second piece of legislation, the Antiterrorism and Effective Death Penalty Act (AEDPA), dealt another devastating blow to state prisoners. In the aftermath of the Oklahoma City bombing, the new statute promised to accelerate appeals and—in capital cases—executions. By this time, the Supreme Court, under Chief Justice Rehnquist, had already played a major role in restricting habeas corpus review. AEDPA, which Rehnquist strongly supported, would go further by increasing deference to state courts, limiting successive petitions, and imposing a one-year deadline on habeas corpus applications, affecting capital and noncapital defendants alike. Many prominent Democrats, including President Clinton's own legal counsel, criticized the bill's broad scope. Despite widespread concerns about its constitutionality, Clinton plowed ahead, signing AEDPA into law on April 24, 1996.

It wasn't until more than a month later, when a local death penalty attorney, Nick Trenticosta, came to Angola, that Calvin and the other inmate counsels first heard about the law. In a legal seminar at the A-Building, Trenticosta explained that the new procedural rules would make it far more difficult to have one's legal claims considered by federal courts. Like Article 930.8, the one-year deadline would affect the entire prison population at once.

News of AEDPA quickly circulated through the prison. Controversy and discord ensued. Some inmate counsels felt the Supreme Court would rule the law unconstitutional. Others took the position that the federal statute couldn't take precedence over state rules, and therefore, they still had three years to file in post-conviction before their federal one-year clock would run. Calvin disagreed. He thought everyone needed to file their state post-conviction petitions within one year. If they didn't, their window to file in federal court would close, rendering their claims unreviewable.

"A deadline is a deadline," he told his law class. "I'm not gonna gamble with my own case, and I wouldn't gamble with yours."

Mrs. Rabalais found Calvin at the law library to discuss the matter. "Will you walk with me back to the A-Building? I want to hear more about this new law."

As they made their way down the walk, Calvin explained that AEDPA set a one-year time limitation for state prisoners to file their federal habeas petitions. Since they couldn't file a claim in federal court that they hadn't first exhausted in state court, AEDPA necessitated that they file their state post-conviction applications within one year as well. Even worse, the new law required federal courts to defer to state court rulings with few exceptions, making it much harder for federal courts to overturn unconstitutional convictions on review.

"We have the same situation now that we had with 930.8," Calvin concluded. "This law is intended to wipe us out, and a lot of us will get hit once the April 1997 deadline passes."

They stopped at the entrance to the A-Building.

"I'll call a meeting with the inmate counsels if you think it will help," said Mrs. Rabalais. "I'm sure you can work together to meet the deadline like you did with 930.8."

She pointed out that they were in a better position to manage a big push this time around.

Calvin shook his head. "The problem is, we're not going to agree on a strategy, Mrs. Rabalais."

"Why?"

"We can't get on the same page."

Her face fell in disappointment.

"May I take two weeks off my rounds to work on my case?" he asked as she passed through the gate.

"Of course, Calvin."

Unlike in the lead-up to the 930.8 deadline, the population's panic over AEDPA steadily dissipated. Conflicting perspectives on how to interpret the law made it too discouraging and difficult to navigate. Even some of the inmate counsels shrugged when the subject came up, saying, "It's in God's hands."

Calvin wouldn't hear it. He continued sounding the alarm at legal seminars and in articles for *The Angolite*. But the lack of any consensus among the inmate counsels rendered his efforts futile. As April crept closer, many of Calvin's associates—even longtime friends—distanced themselves from him. It felt as if nobody wanted to confront the looming crisis.

Calvin couldn't bear the thought of watching people get cut off from the courts as he had after 930.8. He thought about the harried faces of the callouts who had come looking for him when they realized they were time barred. All he'd been able to do was give them an honest assessment of their predicament. It was too late to help.

He couldn't go through it again. He wanted to escape, to retreat to some quiet place where he could focus on his clients' cases and his own.

Perhaps he would go to Camp F.

Camp F was an outer camp reserved for those with trusty status, a classification that granted access to better jobs and more freedom of movement. The age of its residents skewed older, toward men who had already served decades at the prison. To many, Camp F was considered a sleepy outpost, like moving from the city to the country. Which was precisely what made it appealing to Calvin.

"I can't watch them get their brains bashed out in court," he confided in Alvin as they walked the yard one morning. "I don't know how I'm going to get all my work done as it is."

They watched a group of guys playing basketball, oblivious to the danger.

"I get it. People are too spooked or confused to know what to do," Alvin commiserated. "They're losing hope. They're gonna hate it when they realize you're gone, though, and they're stuck with the Lawyer of Last Resort."

Calvin cocked his head. "Who's that?"

"Me!" Alvin laughed.

Later that week, after his request for a transfer came across her desk, Mrs. Rabalais called Calvin to her office.

"Are they forcing you to go to F, Calvin?"

"No, Mrs. Rabalais, I want to go," he replied.

She studied him. For more than a decade, the Main Prison law library had been the center of Calvin's world. It was the place where he'd built his career at Angola.

"What about your law class?" she asked.

"I cleared it with security. They're gonna let me come over to teach on Saturdays. The rest of my job will stay the same."

She freed him from her gaze. "All right. I just wanted to know that this is what you really want."

Calvin nodded. "I assure you, Mrs. Rabalais, it is."

Part 3

Simply because we were licked a hundred years before
we started is no reason for us not to try to win.

ATTICUS FINCH, *TO KILL A MOCKINGBIRD*

1997

After serving more than thirty years on the bench, Judge Shea announced his retirement. His seat would be taken over by a former prosecutor named Julian Parker. The news made its way to Angola via the New Orleans *Times-Picayune*. Calvin, Big Dugger, and others from Shea's section huddled around the newspaper on the walk.

"What do you think it means for us?" Big Dugger asked.

"Hard to say," Calvin replied. "Laurie White says Parker is tough but fair. He was a prosecutor most of his career, though. He's the one that put Tommy Cage on death row."

In recognition of Calvin's advocacy for others, Laurie had offered to represent him pro bono. Within weeks, she'd convinced Judge Shea to grant him a new appeal—something Calvin had been trying to accomplish for two years. Despite his optimism at having legal representation, the state appellate court denied his appeal, acknowledging that while the state had withheld favorable evidence, it wasn't enough to warrant a new trial. Now he was entitled to seek post-conviction relief again, this time before Judge Parker.

"He's gotta be better than Shea. I read that Shea did six jury trials in a single day," said Big Dugger.

"Well, at least he's one of us," another man offered.

"Yeah, but he's one of them *passe blancs*—dude's even got blue eyes."

They hunched closer, peering at the new judge's photograph.

Calvin shrugged. "None of that means nothin' until we see how he deals with us from the bench."

Laurie White offered to continue representing Calvin in post-conviction. He was hopeful that her involvement would give him an edge. She and Julian Parker had previously worked together at the DA's office when Laurie was a prosecutor there.

Once Judge Parker took the bench, Laurie approached him to review Calvin's post-conviction application. To Calvin's delight, the judge agreed that his claims merited an evidentiary hearing. A court date was set for February 1998.

Calvin left Angola for New Orleans with two security officers as the sun was rising. Alone in the back of the van, he lay across the seats. It would take close to three hours to reach Tulane and Broad, and the rock of the van would quickly put him to sleep.

When they reached the causeway, thirty miles outside the city, the hum of traffic on the bridge stirred Calvin from his nap. He sat up, taking in the view of Lake Pontchartrain, where storm clouds gathered on the horizon. Sun rays sliced through the clouds, sending staggered beams across the ash-blue water. The sight pulled his thoughts back to Timber Lake and to the old ritual of readying himself for court in the parish jail—certain each time that he was about to be returned to Mount Hood. It was worrying how distant those memories felt now, as though they belonged to someone else.

The van pulled into Tulane and Broad just as raindrops began slapping the roof. The guards slid the door open, and Calvin looked past two flights of granite stairs to a set of towering bronze doors.

The courthouse was considered a neoclassical masterpiece when it first opened in 1931. Six decades later, it was hard to see anything attractive in the hulking limestone structure. Relentless seasons of sun and rain, compounded by the human misery inside, had disfigured it.

Calvin was led into a dimly lit marble lobby. He heard the hallway upstairs teeming with people, but Section G was tucked away on the first floor under the stairs, easily missed.

Once inside, he was taken to the jury box to wait until his case was called. After twelve years, the courtroom looked the same as the day he was tried there. Lacquered wood panels, brass embellishments, and a giant seal of the State of Louisiana behind the judge's seat: "Union, Justice, Confidence."

A line of Black men entered the court in single file, chained together at the ankles, wearing orange jumpsuits. The clink of their shackles summoned the nursery rhymes of his youth, sending a shiver down Calvin's spine.

Judge Parker, a round-faced man with a graying mustache, peered down at the room with narrowed eyes. He seemed at ease on the bench, alternating between gruff outbursts and winding lectures, as though channeling the spirit of his predecessor. Calvin became uneasy watching the judge conduct a plea colloquy with a young man pleading guilty to armed robbery.

"Don't say 'Yeah,'" Parker bellowed, "say 'Yes, sir.' *Do you hear me?*"

Bewildered, the kid nodded back. "Yes, sir."

"I'm sentencing you to sixty years at hard labor without benefit of probation or parole."

The young man kept his eyes forward, confusion plain on his face.

Calvin's stomach turned. This poor kid likely understood a sixty-year sentence no better than Calvin had grasped life without parole at his age. By the time reality set in, his appeal deadlines would probably have already passed.

With the docket finished for the day and the courtroom emptied, Calvin was directed to sit at the counsel table next to Laurie White.

She greeted him with a pat on the shoulder. "Ready?"

"Yes, ma'am."

Laurie and the prosecutor stated their names for the record and gave the judge a procedural history of the case.

Parker flipped through a stack of court files before finally looking up.

"All right. Let's start taking some testimony."

Laurie's first witness was Calvin's former trial attorney, Numa Bertel. Calvin barely recognized him, he'd spent so little time with the man.

Laurie's task was to demonstrate that Calvin's lawyers had objected to Judge Shea's use of the *Cage* jury instruction. Under the law, if a lawyer failed to object to a legal error during trial, the defendant couldn't litigate that error on appeal—one of many reasons why the quality of a person's trial lawyer could permanently alter their fate.

Bertel confirmed that his cocounsel, Phil Johnson, had filed a written objection to the reasonable doubt instruction for Calvin. They did so in every case where it was proposed, he said.

Satisfied, Laurie moved on to the issue of newspaper articles going back to the jury room.

Bertel and his cocounsel had presented two newspaper articles about David Yeager's murder as evidence. One, published shortly after the murder, described the shooter as short, fat, with a mustache and beard—details that could only have come from the police. Yet these physical characteristics conflicted with the descriptions given by Kristie Emberling and Detective Demma during the trial. During deliberations, the jury requested to see these newspaper articles. The Louisiana Supreme Court had made it clear that jurors could not view written evidence during deliberations without the consent of both parties, as they might be tempted to give the written material more weight than witness testimony or other evidence. Yet over Bertel's objection, Judge Shea provided Calvin's jury with the articles.

Calvin had long believed this was his strongest issue. Under the law, a structural error like this one (or the *Cage* instruction) required a new trial without the defendant needing to prove the error affected the outcome of the case. Structural errors, such as the denial of the right to counsel or a public trial, were so fundamental, they were presumed to undermine the trial's integrity. In contrast, for a claim of prosecutorial misconduct, Calvin had to show that the withheld evidence would have undermined confidence in the jury's verdict. Such errors could be dismissed by judges as "harmless," meaning they weren't damaging enough to warrant a new trial.

The prosecutor rose to his feet. "There's no objection in the record. The defense didn't object," he complained.

Laurie walked over to Bertel and handed him a document. "I'm going to show you what's marked as Exhibit Three. It's entitled 'Judgment,' and there's a signature on the second page."

Laurie and Calvin had discovered the written order while they were preparing for Calvin's appeal.

"Does that judgment pertain to the case and the newspaper article I'm questioning you about?" Laurie asked Bertel.

"Yes, it indicates that both the state and the defense objected."

"And that judgment also is clear that the judge felt it was within his discretion to allow those documents to go back to the jury?"

"Correct."

"You don't question this judgment's authenticity as being Judge Shea's?"

Bertel shook his head. "No. As a matter of fact, I recognize his signature."

The signed order was unequivocal proof that Judge Shea had violated the statute.

Judge Parker rocked back in his chair, listening as Laurie summed up her arguments.

"According to the minute entry, the state objected to the written materials being sent back to the jury, but the defendant did not—but the minute entry is wrong. This judgment from Judge Shea, written in 1989, says both the state *and defense* objected to the materials going into the jury room."

"How do I know that judgment is correct?" Parker quizzed her. "How do I know that that judgment is authentic?"

Laurie hesitated. "Judge, you can look in the record."

"All right. I mean, if the minute entry is wrong, how do we know the judgment is not wrong?"

"Well . . . because you have a judge's signature on a judgment."

"I wouldn't know Judge Shea's signature if it was painted in six-foot letters across the back wall of the courtroom," Parker scoffed. "But go ahead. I'm listening."

Laurie snuck Calvin a wide-eyed glance. If a court couldn't rely on the authenticity of a judge's signed order, what could it rely on?

She explained that the Fourth Circuit Court of Appeal had overlooked Shea's written judgment in the record when it denied Calvin's out-of-time appeal.

"The Fourth Circuit missed it?" Parker asked.

"Yes, Judge," said Laurie. "There's not been a single case in which written evidence went into the jury room that the appellate courts have not reversed."

Parker nodded.

After Laurie outlined her other claims, the judge instructed both parties to submit supplementary memorandums within thirty days.

"Let's look at having another hearing. How about May seventh?" he suggested. "I'm going to rule that day."

"Thank you, Judge." Laurie leaned over to Calvin. "I think he's going to rule our way."

Back in his dorm at Angola, for the first time in years, Calvin allowed himself to dream of going home. Time and the prison walls had done their work to distance him from his family; the pain of their separation had transformed over time into a dull, persistent ache that he could suppress but never escape. Now he let his imagination wander to what his days on the outside might be like—caring for Aunt Gail in her old age, helping Mamie with her kids, and visiting Ayana, who planned to join the navy after high school.

He hadn't seen Ayana in years and hoped she knew he still thought of her daily. Tyrone Smith, a friend who had left Angola some time ago, passed her a few dollars whenever Calvin asked. Still, Calvin knew she was shouldering heavy responsibilities as she entered adulthood and wished he could do more than send money now and then.

Lying on his cot, his thoughts drifted to his sister, wondering what her life was like now. His last attempt to reach her had ended abruptly when a young cousin answered the phone, saying the family "didn't know any Calvin." That was years ago. When he left for the West Coast at eighteen, he never imagined it would be their final goodbye while he was still free. She had been his sole responsibility after their mother disappeared, and now he spent his days defending others, unable to defend her. He wondered if she felt abandoned.

As evening settled over the dormitory, an old memory of Mamie visited him.

It was nighttime, and they were young—maybe nine or ten—sharing a narrow mattress on the floor of the Clouet Street house. Their skin was slick from the summer heat, and they were hiding, most likely from the cousins.

In the dark, Mamie whispered Calvin's name, propping herself up on one elbow.

He rolled over sleepily. "What?"

"Let's fan each other."

She spread her fingers wide and began wafting them above his face. "One. Two. Three . . ."

Calvin kept his eyes closed, trying not to laugh as she pushed the humid air back and forth.

At the count of twenty, she stopped.

"Your turn," she chirped, dropping onto her back.

Calvin obliged her, his movements noncommittal. She peeked

open an eye and, catching him looking at her, promptly shut it with a giggle.

"Thirty-three, thirty-four . . ."

He saw her jaw go slack and her head gently tilt to the side.

"Thirty-nine."

Calvin stopped waving and lay back down, pleased that he had helped her fall sleep.

The recollection, small shard that it was, remained the happiest memory of his sister he had.

ANOTHER ENCOURAGING UPDATE CAME FROM JUDGE PARKER'S COURT: he had awarded Lionel, Calvin's friend and fellow inmate counsel, a new trial based on his lawyer's failure to present evidence that Lionel was insane at the time of his crime. It was a promising sign that the new judge was willing to correct past mistakes.

When Judge Parker failed to rule on Calvin's post-conviction application by May 7, Calvin took the delay in stride. By the end of June, with still no response, Laurie visited the court to request a new date. While there, she spotted Parker's law clerk leaving his chambers.

She wrote to Calvin,

> Great news, I heard from the judge's law clerk that it is her recommendation that your petition be granted! She is preparing and submitting a written judgment to the judge to edit and sign off on. Hopefully, he will follow her recommendation. It sounds like she feels the (1) jury charge, and (2) papers into the jury room are the winners. Keep your fingers crossed—I'm so excited. Laurie.

It was the break Calvin had been waiting for. Given that he had already served over fifteen years, the state would likely dismiss the charges, knowing they couldn't win a conviction against him a second time. He waited anxiously for Judge Parker's ruling to arrive in the mail.

Two weeks later, a damning news story broke. Six months earlier, a lawyer named Pinkston had told Judge Parker that his client—who was also his stepson—had received a four-year sentence for manslaughter. Pinkston claimed a clerk in another court section had mistakenly recorded the sentence as twenty-one years and asked Parker to correct the minute entry. Unaware the claim was false, Parker did as he was asked, leading to the stepson's release. When the state discovered the error, a warrant was issued, and police found him attending classes at Southern University. The fiasco ignited a media firestorm.

Calvin wasn't surprised to see Pinkston's name embroiled in controversy. As an inmate counsel, he'd been called on for help in numerous cases where Pinkston had either missed an essential deadline or neglected to file anything at all. Many families had scraped money together to hire him, only to be abandoned. Years later, he would be disbarred.

Amid this latest uproar, Judge Parker defended himself as a victim of Pinkston's deceit. He said he thought he was merely rectifying a typographical error in the minute entry after a previous judge had lawfully revised the sentence.

Yet there were concerns that there might be more to the story. An investigation was underway to examine whether other defendants had been prematurely released by judges at Tulane and Broad in exchange for financial kickbacks. The Judiciary Commission was being asked to examine Judge Parker's actions, while Pinkston was under scrutiny by the Office of Disciplinary Counsel.

Three days after the story broke, Calvin received another update from Laurie.

> I have not gotten the ruling from Judge Parker. I am a bit concerned because of recent developments and accusations swirling. . . . He has had two investigative reports on the news the last couple of nights. . . . I will be extremely deflated if the judge does not rule in our favor because of the political problems around him. I know this will be extremely distressing for you but please hang on. I'll let you know as soon as I speak with his law clerk, but in the meantime, he has fired his minute clerk, who is now being accused of receiving bribes and is alleging that Judge Parker improperly terminated him. Stay tuned.

Laurie was right to be concerned. Eight weeks later, Calvin received a copy of Parker's ruling. In it, he denied all of Calvin's post-conviction claims, providing little reasoning for his decision.

In the Main Prison visiting room, Laurie's eyes blazed with anger. "We had it," she said, shoving the single-page ruling away. "I can't believe this."

Calvin shook his head. "I don't expect none of us to get play outta that dude now."

"No judge wants to look like a crook or a fool," Laurie agreed. "We'll appeal the decision. And I want to get a proper investigation done in your case—it's just going to take me some time."

"I know you run your practice on your own. You have a lot of people depending on you."

"I'm going to continue helping you, Calvin," she insisted.

He could see that she was crushed.

"You should get back to New Orleans." He stood up. "It's getting late and it's starting to rain."

They walked to the front of the A-Building.

"I appreciate everything you've done for me," he said as they parted.

"Don't give up," Laurie replied. "I'm with you all the way."

IN THE DESPAIR THAT FOLLOWED, A PERSISTENT QUESTION PREOC-cupied Calvin: How did humans endure these kinds of ordeals without losing their sanity? In the library, he sought out accounts of Holocaust survivors and soldiers who had narrowly escaped death, noticing how, amid their suffering, they often saw the line between reality and their imagination blur. He studied Viktor Frankl's *Man's Search for Meaning,* and took to heart Frankl's observation that those who clung to a future purpose were more likely to survive.

Lately, Calvin's confidence in his memories had begun to wane. When he thought of Timber Lake, the place he'd been trying to get back to all these years, doubt crept in. Had he really seen those mountains? Was the Columbia River truly that vast? Was the landscape, which seemed to grow more beautiful in his mind each year, even real? He hadn't spoken about Mount Hood since the parish jail, when Catkiller mocked him for trying to describe its profound quiet, insisting that such a place couldn't exist. Now, over a decade later, Calvin wondered if Catkiller's scorn had been justified.

He thought of Kunta Kinte in *Roots* longing for his homeland, and wondered if his memories of Mount Hood, like The Gambia, were just dreams from long ago. It was a disorienting and terrifying thought that led to more unsettling questions. Had he concocted other fanciful notions to comfort himself? Was becoming a skilled prison lawyer enough to secure his freedom? Could he really hope to overturn his conviction?

These worries deepened his depression, making it impossible to work on his case. For weeks, he wandered through the prison like a ghost.

Then, one afternoon while walking the yard, a realization struck him: He was missing Frankl's point. What did it matter if his memories were true or not when he was stuck in this interminable present? Angola had taught him never to dismiss anyone's dreams. The outside world—real or imagined—was all a man here had.

He vowed to endure this latest setback by clinging even tighter to Mount Hood. He would see it again or die trying. There was no other hope.

He turned once more to his case.

Despite Laurie's desire to help, Calvin knew the demands of an investigation would outstrip her available resources. She ran a small civil practice with no investigators, and he didn't want to burden her after all she'd already done. He decided to save her assistance for when he needed a lawyer in court.

Now that he was facing federal court, he had to prepare all claims for his habeas petition at once or risk being barred by AEDPA in the future. Yet to comply with AEDPA's deadline, he wouldn't have enough time to uncover all the evidence needed to support his claims. He would have to focus his efforts. His top priority was tracking down

Kristie Emberling and unraveling the truth behind her identification. He even questioned whether the woman who testified at his trial was really Kristie. Given the inconsistencies in her statements, the idea that the prosecution might have paid someone to pose as a witness and tell the story they wanted no longer seemed far-fetched. After all, who would know the difference?

He'd already saved funds to hire an investigator. The challenge was to find a competent one who would agree to help him.

He began his search by writing to an investigator who had worked on a friend's case on death row.

> My police report shows that several individuals gave descriptions of the perpetrators fleeing the scene, but were not called by the prosecutor at trial. After obtaining some information from the D.A. file, I learned that the girl that testified against me told the police that she was not sure about her identification of me. I need someone to interview the witness who testified against me, and the witnesses who weren't brought to my trial. I don't have much money, but I am willing to pay. With your help, I'll have a good chance on proving my innocence.

"I was very moved by your letter," the investigator responded, "and I wish that I could help you. But I'm afraid I only work on capital cases."

Perverse as it sounded, there were times when Calvin found himself wishing he'd been sentenced to death—and this was one of them. He had seen friends led away to execution and didn't mean to downplay the gravity of their plight. But to have someone stand up for you was a rare and sacred thing, something most men in Angola had never experienced. Not to mention the obvious fact that having a skilled lawyer drastically improved your odds: 40 percent of capital cases were overturned in federal court once specialized legal teams had time to uncover constitutional violations and litigate them. In noncapital cases, where there was no right to counsel, reversal rates in federal court were as low as one in one hundred before AEDPA, and fewer than one in three hundred after.

Calvin decided to try a different tack. He reached out to an attorney whose clients he had assisted over the years, asking if the lawyer would simply hire an investigator on his behalf. Calvin had already prepared a memorandum detailing the work that needed to be done. The attorney wouldn't need to allocate any resources for oversight; they'd simply handle Calvin's payments to the investigator. To his dismay, however, the lawyer never replied.

With one year to file his habeas petition in federal court, Calvin's desperation grew.

On a Saturday afternoon in the law library, he compiled a list of names, jotting down every attorney and law firm he knew. He found their contact information in the Yellow Pages, determined to write to each one until he received a favorable response.

He started with Ron Rakosky, the attorney who had represented his law crew years ago. After one of the men reneged on a payment arrangement with Rakosky, the lawyer had refused to continue working with them.

"Before you throw this letter away, PLEASE give me a minute," Calvin wrote. "I will not be a burden. All I need is a lawyer."

Rakosky didn't reply.

Next, Calvin tried an attorney he had previously recruited to represent one of his clients at the US Supreme Court after helping the man win a cert petition. The attorney responded with a warning:

> If you are going to go to the trouble of hiring an investigator, you need to see that the investigation is done properly—you probably will not get a second chance. You must have an attorney who represents you to coordinate the presentation of facts to the court.

Calvin's stomach dropped at the next line:

> I cannot act as that attorney as my present workload will not permit me. I appreciate you contacting me, and frankly, I am flattered, because I know first-hand your knowledge of the law, and your currency with all significant appellate decisions. I wish you luck in your efforts.

Trying not to get discouraged, Calvin wrote to an appellate attorney whose work he greatly respected. But the attorney also declined. "If you have money, I'm sure you don't need a lawyer to act as an intermediary."

After all the years he'd spent corresponding with these lawyers and assisting their clients, surely one would step forward.

The silence was deafening.

He turned to the Louisiana Legal Directory, hoping for blind luck, but that proved useless, too. He tried elected officials, hoping the US attorney for New Orleans or a Louisiana senator might be moved by his story and willing to help.

When that came to nothing, he tried civil rights organizations outside of Louisiana: Amnesty International, the Synagogue Council of America, the National Urban League, the NAACP, the Jewish Peace Fellowship, the Center for Nonviolent Social Change, the Center for Constitutional Rights, the ACLU of Illinois, Human Rights Watch, the NAACP Legal Defense Fund, and the Equal Justice Initiative. Any place that he'd seen advocate on behalf of incarcerated people, he tried. And with each letter, his tone grew increasingly desperate.

> I just need a lawyer willing to assist me in hiring an investigator. I have prepared a memo so you will not have to spend hours on my case getting familiar with it. Please write me back and express that you are willing to assist me.
>
> Please, please help me.

In little more than two weeks, Calvin had mailed off thirty-seven letters. Barely a trickle came in reply, and among them, none offered the help he needed.

1998

The fallout from AEDPA took years to fully reveal itself. By the late 1990s, it had gained a reputation as one of the worst-drafted pieces of legislation ever passed by Congress. Each one of its endlessly vague and complex clauses had to be litigated to determine their meaning. To complicate matters, circuit courts often reached conflicting conclusions. In case after case, the US Supreme Court was asked to clarify the law. When the court chose to remain silent, it invariably hurt defendants in Louisiana, since the Fifth Circuit tended to apply the strictest-possible reading of the statute. When the Supreme Court did weigh in, it often took a position analogous to the Fifth Circuit's, perceiving the litigation as a proxy battle over capital punishment. The result was that federal judges had their hands tied, rarely able to address the merits of claims raised by state prisoners, over 90 percent of whom were unrepresented. Men serving life at Angola were being shut out of federal court left and right.

These obstacles were exacerbated by the lackluster performance of many lawyers appointed to handle direct appeals in Louisiana. The systemic incompetence that had caused the federal court of appeals to issue the *Lofton* decision back in 1991 eventually compelled the creation of a state-funded office dedicated to criminal appeals. The intention was for this office to house attorneys with specialized expertise, ensuring competent representation for those unable to afford private counsel. When the Louisiana Appellate Project (LAP) came into existence in 1996, it kindled hope among indigent defendants across the state. However, it wasn't long before Calvin realized that the organization wouldn't bring about the change they hoped for.

LAP attorneys perpetuated many of the same problems as their predecessors. Calvin observed that they routinely overlooked viable claims in their briefs, neglected to inform their clients about the outcome of their appeals, and failed to provide them with copies of their records for post-conviction. They also waived the right to present their clients' claims at oral argument. They recycled old briefs, in some cases forgetting to swap out a previous client's name. In a quarter of cases that crossed Calvin's desk, LAP attorneys told the courts they could find no legal errors in the record at all. Yet when Calvin reviewed these cases, he frequently identified significant legal issues, even winning some in post-conviction that LAP had neglected on appeal.

What baffled Calvin most, especially considering the constraints of AEDPA, was that LAP attorneys wouldn't file writ applications to the state supreme court after their clients' appeals were denied. Filing a writ, which entailed little more than attaching a cover sheet to a copy of the direct appeal, would have properly exhausted their clients' claims, preserving them for federal court. It would have delayed the start of their one-year clock. Yet LAP wouldn't do it, nor would they inform their clients to undertake this step on their own. Calvin found it unconscionable that a practicing attorney would abandon their clients in this manner.

He decided to address Jim Looney, LAP's director, about the issue directly. When Looney came to Angola for an inmate counsel training, Calvin pulled him aside. Why would LAP lawyers refuse to mail their clients copies of appeal decisions and fail to file writ applications with the state supreme court?

Looney didn't sugarcoat his response.

"Because it would be a waste of time."

This stopped Calvin short. It was one thing for conservative judges to assert that prisoner complaints were meritless; it was another for the head of a *defense* organization to take such a position. Calvin had won enough of the cases LAP had ignored to know how wrong Looney was. Unable to contain his outrage, he turned away, worried he might say something he would regret. Perhaps it was cynical, but he wondered whether the state had chosen Looney to run LAP precisely because he was so contemptuous of his clients.

"What reason does he give for why his lawyers can't be more diligent about this?" Laurie asked when Calvin relayed the story during one of her visits.

"He said it's not worth it," he replied.

Laurie's eyes flashed. "That's despicable."

"I know. I'm thinking of filing a public records request to ask what exactly those LAP lawyers spend their time on," Calvin said.

"Why don't you? I'd be curious to know the answer myself."

Calvin drafted a public information request asking LAP for a list of attorneys who contracted with the project. He asked about their hourly fees, how much time they spent on each case, what they filed, and the organization's policies on requesting oral arguments, seeking review from the Louisiana Supreme Court, and providing clients with their records. Per the statute, he gave LAP three days to respond.

Jim Looney replied that he wasn't obligated to provide Calvin with the information he'd requested because Calvin was incarcerated.

"You are not a 'person' as defined in the statute," Looney wrote, referencing the Public Records Act. "R.S. 44:31.1 specifically excludes from the definition of 'person' anyone who is in custody for a felony."

The barb was well aimed and hit its mark. Calvin's jaw clenched as he stared at the words on the page. Right there, in black and white, was the prejudice he had witnessed for nearly two decades from a legal system that thumbed its nose at poor people. And now, even worse, this prejudice was directed at him by a defense attorney.

You are not a person.

Calvin shared Looney's letter with a few lawyers he knew were concerned about LAP's negligence, but didn't dare pass it to Laurie White, knowing it would infuriate her. So when he learned she had somehow obtained a copy and responded to the Louisiana Indigent Defender Assistance Board, he was surprised—and moved.

> [LAP's] response is disappointing and disturbing, especially from a group that contracts with your public agency and that has as its mission to serve and represent indigent convicted felons. I personally find the LAP response to this public record request inappropriate and unprofessional.
>
> Calvin Duncan is most assuredly a "person." He has been my client, a friend, and a very knowledgeable and talented,

self-taught inmate counsel substitute who helps less fortunate inmates with their *pro se* pleadings. He works extremely hard, under difficult circumstances, to help inmates who do not have access to legal representation.

I would ask that LAP and LIDAB reconsider its position and respond to the public records request which I now submit to you for action.

Despite Laurie's efforts, Looney never responded to Calvin, nor did he produce the materials Calvin had requested under the Public Records Act. LAP continued on in the same manner, and the inmate counsels were left to pick up the pieces as best they could.

THAT SAME YEAR, 1998, CALVIN RECEIVED AN UNEXPECTED CALLOUT for an attorney visit. At the A-Building, he was greeted by a woman in her thirties, formally dressed in a suit. Her blue eyes were friendly.

"Katherine Mattes," she introduced herself.

Calvin followed her into the legal visiting room.

Katherine explained that she had recently moved to New Orleans from San Diego and was working with a small civil rights firm. Her boss had asked her to research a way around the procedural bar rules for a federal constitutional claim with clear merit.

When she struggled to find helpful case law, she sought advice from Denny LeBoeuf, a prominent capital defense attorney, who told her: "I bet the only person who knows that is Calvin Duncan."

Katherine asked for Calvin's number.

"You can't call him," Denny replied. "He's in Angola."

Calvin chuckled as Katherine relayed the story.

"So that's why I'm here," she said. "I hope you don't mind me asking. I'm looking for a way to get our client's claim into court. It's a very old case but he would prevail if not for the procedural bar. Are you aware of any decisions that would support the argument that ineffective assistance of counsel in post-conviction should create an exception?"

"Ineffective assistance of counsel? No. You should look at *Coleman v. Thompson*, 501 U.S. 722, 1991," he replied. "The defendant was on death row in Virginia and they denied him federal review because his lawyer filed his state post-conviction petition three days late. *Coleman* says you can't claim constitutionally ineffective assistance of counsel because there is no constitutional right to an attorney in state post-conviction. You will have to meet one of the exceptions in the statute."

Katherine scribbled the citation down, her eyes widening. "May I ask, how did you first learn the law?"

He recounted his experiences in Orleans Parish Prison, sharing how he had always wanted an education, particularly since it had been denied to him from an early age.

"What did you study in college?" he asked her.

"I was a philosophy major."

"Oh, I'm reading Immanuel Kant—the categorical imperative. Did you study him?"

Katherine's surprise returned. "I did."

"I'd like to go to law school one day."

"Did you ever think of going to college?"

Calvin thought about how to answer her. "Did you ever watch that TV show *Dallas*, about the rich family?"

"Sure."

"Did you ever think that you could live like they live?"

Her answer came slowly. "No."

"To me, going to college was like you thinking you could be one of those people in *Dallas*."

Katherine's lips drew into a line. She nodded in understanding.

Calvin liked her. She wasn't like most other lawyers—she listened.

"I can send you a memo explaining some of the ways to overcome procedural bars, if you like."

She accepted gratefully. "It's been a remarkable experience meeting you, Calvin. I hope we can stay in touch."

They stood and shook hands.

"I'd like that," he said.

SOON AFTER THE ENACTMENT OF AEDPA, THE LOUISIANA SUPREME Court, which had trended increasingly conservative throughout the '90s, ruled that all sentencing issues had to be raised on direct appeal rather than in post-conviction proceedings.

The decision would hamstring the inmate counsels' ability to assist people. Sentencing issues were the few legal claims they could litigate from within the prison, since those didn't require outside investigation. With LAP's attorneys already overlooking viable issues on direct appeal, the inmate counsels would be powerless to stop vital sentencing claims from going by the boards.

"All our sentencing issues are out the window," Alvin despaired as he and Calvin walked the yard.

Alvin had recently followed Calvin to Camp F after being made a Class A trusty.

"Illegal sentence under *Desdunes* is gone, multiple bill issues are gone, constructive denial of counsel is gone . . ."

Calvin gave a heavy sigh. "Between this and AEDPA, they have shut us out of the courts. From now on, our job is to help people avoid procedural bars and that's *it*."

IN THE FACE OF THIS BLEAK REALITY, CALVIN FURTHER CHANNELED his efforts into teaching.

Four years into his law class, a core group of students had found their way under his wing. Though he wasn't drawn to leading prison clubs like Norris and Checo were, he poured himself into his class without reservation. He rewarded his most committed students with time and attention, and though he was careful never to play favorites, his mentees knew who they were.

Among them was Buff, who had filed his post-conviction petition from Camp J and had an insatiable hunger for learning the law. Calvin had been observing him and was glad to see he hadn't strayed from his path.

Another was Groovy Lou, whose mild demeanor hid a fierce determination. The law hadn't come easily to Lou—he struggled for two years before the concepts finally clicked. Now confident in himself, he was often the last to leave class, always eager to extend the discussion.

Calvin had developed a system of small groups that would research and workshop cases before presenting them to the larger group. In a mock oral argument, they would face off with Calvin, who played judge, questioning them like they were presenting to the state supreme court.

Today, Groovy Lou's group was up. Calvin was pleased to see the twenty-two-year-old, who had been sentenced as a child to life without parole, standing at the front of the room with ease. Calvin had read the group's brief before class: it was a case involving a defendant who confessed, and the question on appeal was whether the incriminating statement should have been excluded from evidence. The brief was strong, and though Calvin couldn't think of a single time he had "granted" anyone's petition at the end of one of these workshops, Lou clearly thought it was his day.

Lou opened with an overview of the procedural rules, knowing Calvin would require this before hearing any arguments on the merits.

"The application was timely filed on April 23, 1997, within one year of the case becoming final."

He moved on to his main issue.

Lou's argument was that the defendant's statement should have been excluded from trial because it was taken in violation of his Sixth Amendment right to counsel.

"The confession was made to the detective after the defendant had already been arraigned and appointed a lawyer," Lou explained. "Under *Michigan v. Jackson*, even if he waived his Miranda rights, the right to counsel still attaches."

"Let me ask you this," Calvin interrupted. "If the court wants to analyze the claim under the Fifth Amendment, what is your argument?"

Lou explained that the defendant had a blood-alcohol reading of 0.2. Therefore, even though he had been given a Miranda warning, his choice to give a statement didn't constitute a knowing and intelligent waiver of his rights.

"Can the court dismiss it as harmless error?" Calvin asked.

"Yes, it is a procedural rather than a constructive error," Lou replied.

"And that's according to the Fifth or the Sixth Amendment?"

"The Fifth."

"And the Sixth?"

"Procedural . . ."

Lou had studied both standards of review, but the more questions Calvin fired at him, the more he second-guessed himself.

"So are you arguing that the court should analyze the claim under the Fifth Amendment or the Sixth Amendment?" Calvin asked pointedly.

Lou took a moment to think. "The Fifth," he decided.

"Petition denied," Calvin declared.

"Damn." Lou punched the air. "I had it, man."

Buff slapped his back as he resumed his seat. "So close, Groovy Lou."

"Somebody tell me what went wrong," Calvin asked.

An old-timer raised his hand. "The Sixth is the easier standard."

Calvin nodded. "A violation of the right to counsel is a heavier burden for the state to overcome. Lou was arguing it correctly until I made him analyze the claim under the Fifth Amendment. The lesson? Don't let anyone, not even a judge, pull you off course. Believe in your argument, even if no one else does."

An older man whom Calvin had recently helped with an appeal poked his head into the classroom, revealing a box of donuts under one arm.

"Appreciate you, brah."

Calvin shook his head. "You know I can't accept those. We worked on your case together."

The gift-giver shrugged and gave Calvin a dap, continuing on his way. The class looked longingly after the donuts.

"For a man who ain't religious, he sure is disciplined," Lou grumbled to Buff.

Later that afternoon, when the class was filing out, Calvin asked Buff to stay behind. He'd given him an assignment: identify the line of cases dealing with ineffective assistance of counsel and read through them to see how the law had changed over time. There were dozens, spanning decades.

"How's your research coming?" he asked.

Buff shook his head. "Honestly, I don't know what I'm supposed to take from these cases. The courts are all over the place. Their decisions about how to apply *Strickland* are totally inconsistent."

"That's what I wanted you to notice," Calvin said. "The case law on ineffective assistance is all messed up. It's important to see that even the courts don't really understand it."

Buff tilted his head back in mock exasperation. "Man, you know how many hours I could've saved if you'd just told me that?"

Calvin smiled, impressed by Buff's analytical skills. With a little more training, he would make a talented inmate counsel.

Eventually, a position opened up at Camp F, and Calvin asked Buff if he wanted to be recommended.

Buff didn't hesitate. "Yes, Calvin. I really do."

"You've done well for yourself," Calvin told him. "I'm proud of you for getting this far. Just promise me one thing," he added with a wry smile. "Don't make the mistake I made and spend all your time helping the population. Remember to save yourself."

THERE WERE CERTAIN CASES CALVIN WAS DETERMINED TO LITIGATE to the bitter end. Big Dugger's was one.

Luckily, he had reached Big Dugger early enough to secure his records and preserve his *Cage* issue in state court, ensuring a smooth transition into federal court without any procedural bars. Though the federal district court had recently denied Big Dugger, Calvin thought there was a chance that the Fifth Circuit Court of Appeals would rule in his favor. No principle in English law was more foundational than the requirement to prove a criminal defendant's guilt beyond a reasonable doubt. Big Dugger's jury had been misled about that standard's meaning, and the only remedy was a new, fair trial.

As a first step, Calvin needed to convince the Fifth Circuit to review Big Dugger's case. Big Dugger was entitled to a full appeal only if he first obtained a certificate of appealability (COA). To win a COA, he had to persuade the court that his claims had "arguable merit." As a pro se petitioner, the odds of winning a COA were infinitesimally small, an enormous camel passing through the eye of a needle.

"The statistical probability is slim, but the case law is strong for us. You've got the perfect issue," Calvin told his friend.

"Whatever you say." Big Dugger mirrored his optimism. "I'm riding with you."

While Calvin was preparing the COA, Big Dugger suffered a major heart attack. He was transported to a hospital in Baton Rouge and didn't return to Angola for over two weeks. The damage to his heart was severe. Calvin found him recuperating on the hospital ward.

"I'm telling you, man, I died," Big Dugger exclaimed. "They got me to Earl K. Long and I went belly-up, right there on the operating table. I died, Calvin! And the only thing I could think about was you, man."

He pointed a chunky finger at Calvin's chest, spittle spraying from his lips.

"I came back to life because you're going to get me out of prison. I saw it while I was dead."

Calvin blinked, overwhelmed by a sudden urge to laugh. "Big Dugger, the next time you die, you stay dead. You hear me?"

Big Dugger's earnest expression dissolved, and the men's cackles filled the ward.

"Don't come back, Big Dugger," Calvin said, laughing harder. "Don't come back!"

For a while, it seemed Big Dugger's brush with death had indeed courted luck. Against all odds, the Fifth Circuit granted Calvin's request for a certificate of appealability. He and Big Dugger celebrated in the law library with their feet up on the desks.

Whether *Cage* should be applied retroactively—to convictions finalized before the Supreme Court declared the jury instruction unconstitutional—remained an open question. Most federal circuit courts agreed it should, but the Supreme Court had yet to provide clarity. Predictably, the Fifth Circuit took the most restrictive stance, ruling that any conviction finalized before *Cage* wasn't eligible for relief. Still, Calvin held on to a glimmer of hope: perhaps there was a reason the Fifth Circuit had granted Big Dugger's COA. Maybe it would reconsider its position.

When the court eventually ruled, the result was devastating. While it acknowledged that Big Dugger's case plunged it back into "increasingly familiar yet persistently thorny terrain," and noted inconsistencies in its own prior rulings, the court concluded that AEDPA barred it from granting Big Dugger relief.

Back in the law library, Calvin and Big Dugger absorbed the opinion.

"I know the Fifth Circuit is wrong," Calvin said. "We need to appeal this decision. The US Supreme Court only grants certiorari in two percent of cases a year, but yours ought to be one of those cases."

Big Dugger had grown frailer since his heart attack, but Calvin's encouragement lifted his spirits. "You've brought me this far," he declared. "If anyone can get the Supreme Court to look at my case, it's you, Dog."

A Texas attorney, David Schenck, certain as Calvin was that the Fifth Circuit had erred, asked to represent Big Dugger before the Supreme Court. The two joined forces to work up Big Dugger's petition for certiorari. In the meantime, in a twist of fate, the Supreme Court took up the retroactivity issue in another case out of Angola—that of Melvin Tyler. Calvin had helped Tyler with his cert petition and knew he faced more hurdles than Big Dugger, having already been through federal habeas once before.

The court rejected Tyler's petition in a narrowly divided 5–4 decision. Still, Calvin believed Big Dugger's case, which was in a different procedural posture, could succeed.

The court took additional time to consider it, raising Calvin's hopes. In the end, though, it was another difficult loss—the court declined to hear Big Dugger's petition.

Calvin found Big Dugger on the walk, his wide frame resting heavily against the wire.

"I'm sorry, brah," he said.

Big Dugger gave him a dap. "You've been with me since I had the death penalty, and you've always helped me on my case," he said. "You've never let me down."

Calvin would keep looking until he found a way to get Big Dugger back into court. "Just hold on, all right? You had an unconstitutional trial. We'll find a way to fix it."

But fate had other plans.

After being transferred to another prison, Big Dugger's heart gave out for good. He was only fifty-seven years old.

When Calvin got word of his passing, he was flattened by sorrow.

1999

On the morning of his thirty-sixth birthday, Calvin woke early from a bad dream.

The dream had begun peacefully: He was perched on a boulder at the edge of a familiar river, surrounded by forest. The midday sun shone overhead, and birds called out from the canopy. He felt the smoothness of the rock beneath his feet, worn by wind and rain. As he stretched out his arms, a spray from below dotted his skin with flecks of frothy water.

The sound of the river conjured the other boys, and suddenly they were there with him, bodies banging against one another as they ran. Sweaty with competition despite the cold, they launched off rocks into the water, their giant splashes followed by an ungraceful sloshing as they scrambled back to the bank. Laughter echoed through the trees.

Calvin wriggled his toes closer to the edge of the boulder. It was his turn to jump. His insides churned at the thought of the frigid water, knowing the current would pull him under and his nose and ears would sting from cold.

He had to stay beneath the surface longer than the others if he was going to win the game. Readying himself, he looked up to check that his friends were watching.

But they'd vanished as quickly as they'd come.

He searched the edge of the bank, thinking they'd moved down-river. But when he listened, the forest had fallen silent.

Suddenly, night didn't seem far off. The sky was turning black.

He knew it wasn't safe to be out after dark. He wanted to get back to the campus, but the others were still nowhere to be seen.

Finally, he spotted a movement in the distance. A bobbing head.

It was the boys, farther downriver than they ought to be. They were still thrashing in the water, but he realized now it was out of desperation, not fun. Their arms were reaching for something to hold on to, but the force of the water was too great. They were speed-ing away fast.

He looked behind him and saw that the trees had threaded to-gether like a wall. He wasn't sure how to find his way back to the road on his own. He thought about jumping in the water to follow the oth-ers, but terror fixed him to the rock.

Calvin woke from the dream with a start, and a chill lingered in his chest, making it impossible to return to sleep. As he waited for dawn, he struggled to push aside the growing fear that Mount Hood might betray him; that his hope might slip away.

Later that morning, he hurried through his rounds on death row and CCR, hoping to get back to Camp F so he could take a nap before chow.

He stopped at the sally port to ask Mrs. Pat, the corrections officer who manned the gate, to call him a ride. Tutu, an old-timer tasked with keeping the sally port clean, announced Calvin's arrival with a grin.

"Mrs. Pat, your boyfriend's here."

"Oh good," Mrs. Pat deadpanned.

Tutu liked to tease that Calvin was sweet on Mrs. Pat, and, to be honest, Calvin did hold a fondness for her. It wasn't exactly romantic, more like a youthful flirtation that added some lightness to his day. She was one of the rare free people in the penitentiary who understood that a sense of humor made life more tolerable for all.

Rather than picking up the phone, Mrs. Pat got up from her seat and moved to a cabinet at the back of the guard shack.

She returned with a cake inscribed with the words "Happy Birthday" and set it down on the table.

It took Calvin a moment to realize it was for him. It wasn't only his first birthday cake in prison—it was the first birthday cake he'd ever received.

His throat went dry. "Thank you, Mrs. Pat."

Tutu and a couple of the other trusties who worked at the front gate gathered around to share slices, their backs obstructing the view from the guard tower. It was against the rules for a free person to give someone in custody a gift.

When their bellies were full, Calvin took the rest of the cake to Camp F to share with Alvin and his other friends.

Mrs. Pat's gesture was a rare kindness after so many years locked away, and one he would not soon forget.

———

IN THE EARLY MORNING HOURS OF NOVEMBER 6, 2000, ALVIN ABBOTT was roused in his cot by the sergeant manning his dorm.

"Pack your shit. You're headed out."

Alvin scowled and rubbed his eyes. "What do you mean?"

"You're out of here. They're taking you to a halfway house."

"Are you joking?"

The sergeant cocked his head. "Do I look like I'm joking? Get your shit."

Alvin bolted upright. The dorm was still except for the whir of the overhead fans. He grunted in disbelief. He still had a year of his sentence left to serve. Nobody had ever hinted that he might go to a halfway house.

He'd barely had time to fill a sack with the contents of his locker-box when the dorm sergeant was back to collect him.

His dorm partners began to wake with the noise. "What's going on, Al?"

"They're moving me." He trailed the sergeant out of the dorm, no time to say goodbye.

Word spread quickly throughout the camp.

"Ya boy is leavin'," someone told Calvin as he made his way to the shower.

"Who?"

"Al. They got him up front. They're processing him out."

Calvin got in the first truck he could wave down headed for the front gate.

He found Alvin sitting in one of the CCR holding cells, a free-standing cage.

Alvin leapt to his feet. "Calvin! I didn't think I was gonna see you. I'm so glad you made it."

They dapped through the bars.

"They didn't tell you this was the plan?"

"They didn't tell me nothin'. I feel so bad. I got to leave my work. I got to leave you guys. I can't even take my cases. All those guys I promised to help . . . I thought I would have time to get everything ready."

Alvin bent his head. Calvin felt the sting, too; he was about to lose his closest friend.

Despite Alvin's self-proclaimed title as the Lawyer of Last Resort, he had become an expert in his own right. His caseload was as demanding as the inmate counsels', and his commitment to his clients just as strong. Over the years, his sharp understanding of multiple-bill and search-and-seizure case law had helped secure the release of several individuals. Many depended on him.

Calvin gently tapped the cage door. "Don't worry about the guys, I'll take care of your cases."

Alvin looked up at him, lost. "What am I gonna do out there?" he asked.

Improbable as it seemed, Calvin understood why Alvin was losing his bearings at the very moment he was approaching freedom.

It reminded him of his old friend Kenny Mills. Years ago, Calvin had written a motion to correct Kenny's illegal sentence, convinced it would free him. But Kenny never left the prison. When Calvin asked why, Kenny lied, claiming he had returned the motion for edits. Calvin knew this wasn't true but said nothing. Eventually, Kenny confessed: he had kept the motion in his lockerbox because he was scared it would work. He wasn't ready to leave.

Each person had to find their own way of coping with an unending sentence: some found the torture of it too much to bear and resorted to suicide; others embraced Angola as their world. Even for someone like Alvin, who had fought to get out at every opportunity, the front gate, after this many years, represented a frightening precipice. At Angola, he had a clear purpose. In the outside world, he would be starting over.

"Just make sure you don't go and get yourself in bondage right away," Calvin warned. "I know your girl is waiting for you. But everyone's going to want something from you, Al. Take your time. You got to make a way for yourself. You hear what I'm saying?"

Alvin broke into a grin. "I hear what you sayin', brah, but I can't wait to get in bondage. I been down sixteen years!"

Calvin was relieved to see him laugh.

"Damn. You the only one I got to say goodbye to, Calvin." Alvin turned somber again. "I've grown up with these guys, you know?"

"I know."

"I'm not ready to leave."

They fell silent. Calvin contemplated life at Angola without his dearest friend.

"They gonna make you go," he said eventually. "But you'll be okay, Al. You gonna make it out there."

They gripped hands through the bars a final time.

THAT EVENING, BACK IN THE DORMITORY, CALVIN LONGED FOR THE day to end. Despair was closing in from all sides.

Alvin was gone. He was facing long odds in the courts. He'd lived in Angola longer than he'd lived in the free world. He hadn't felt this hopeless in a long while.

Sitting on the edge of his bed, he stared at his lockerbox, debating whether he had the energy to work. Maybe he'd read *To Kill a Mockingbird* instead; the story of Boo Radley and Atticus Finch always reenergized him.

When he opened the lid to retrieve it, he was met with a sea of white papers and mustard-colored envelopes. Neatly stacked, they filled every inch of space. Calvin paused, reflecting on the thousands of pages of legal work, many yellowing with age. Handwritten memorandums and lists of citations were sorted by subject; newspaper articles referenced landmark legal decisions; there was even an old advertisement for a hack investigator proposing to review DA and police files "for a low, low price." The paperwork reached back beyond his days on the mental health unit, a physical representation of his sprawling legal career.

Skimming the files, he pulled out one for Carlos Poree, a gentle, older man from the mental health unit he remembered with fondness. The Louisiana Supreme Court had outlined clear grounds for relief in his case, but Poree, suffering from schizophrenia, had no way of knowing to file. Forgotten by the system and without access to counsel, he languished in an isolated cell until Calvin discovered him. After Calvin prepared a petition, Poree's conviction was vacated, and he was transferred to a forensic facility, where proper treatment alleviated his symptoms. Over Calvin's objections, Poree still sent twenty dollars each year on his birthday.

Lawyers on the outside could never grasp what it was like to represent the people you lived with—to witness your clients in front of the television at night or lying under a sheet in the dark, their glassy stares absorbing a recent court denial. Their victories and losses became yours, their fates intertwined with your own. Each man dangled above the same floodwaters, one defeat away from drowning.

Digging deeper into his lockerbox, Calvin felt something smooth against his thumb. He shifted a binder and uncovered an old shoe.

He breathed in the faint smell of leather and searched for the other one, holding them up to the dim light of the dormitory. He hadn't worn them since they arrived in the mail back in 1987, a time when he thought freedom was only months away.

He had waited for good news then—and with each subsequent appeal—like an apostle waiting for the Second Coming.

It occurred to him now that every one of Jesus's disciples had died waiting for hope to arrive.

He placed the shoes back in the lockerbox and covered them over.

A NEW FACE APPEARED IN CALVIN'S LAW CLASS.

"Dwight LaBran." The young man introduced himself once the rest of the class had left. "I've got a little girl," he said, his expression despondent. "Her mom is livin' with your cousin. He doesn't want me calling up there but I need to talk to my daughter. I haven't spoken to her in months."

Calvin's chest tightened—he hadn't seen his own daughter, Ayana, in years.

"I'll call and try to talk him around," he offered. "I saw you paying close attention in class. What's going on with your case? Do you know where you're at in court?"

"I just had my motion for a new trial denied."

"Your lawyer filed that?"

"No, I did."

Calvin was impressed. Few people had the wherewithal to pre-pare and file a motion for new trial in the parish jail.

Dwight explained that he was convicted of murdering a young man while riding in the back seat of his car. Although Dwight had a solid alibi—he was eating dinner at a restaurant across town with his family when the crime occurred—the jury still found him guilty based on the testimony of a single eyewitness.

Calvin remembered his own cousins being torn apart by the prosecution on cross-examination at trial.

"I think the state's witness was the one that did the murder," Dwight explained. "I just don't know how to prove it."

Calvin noticed deep rings around his eyes, the trauma of the trial still fresh.

"Have you got any of your records?"

"No, I don't know how to get ahold of them."

Calvin looked at the clock on the wall. "I'm gonna be up here at the law library on Tuesday. You want help on your case, come see me then."

Calvin and Dwight began meeting regularly. Calvin instructed Dwight's mother on how to retrieve court records, and she uncov-ered evidence from Dwight's file showing that the state's key witness had testified under an alias. Dwight was convinced that the witness had framed him.

Based on this new evidence, Calvin and Dwight submitted an-other motion for a new trial. Again, the judge denied it, but when they appealed the decision, the higher court remanded the case for an evidentiary hearing.

Calvin tried to obtain a copy of Dwight's DA file before the hearing, confident that it would contain more favorable evidence. However, without an outside lawyer or investigator to push it, the DA's office ignored his requests.

At the evidentiary hearing, the prosecutor told the court that she was unaware her star witness had testified under a fake surname. She assured the judge that the witness had no outstanding warrants at the time of Dwight's trial, and, therefore, no incentive to lie about his involvement in the murder. The court denied the motion for a new trial for the third time, and the appellate courts affirmed the denial. Dwight had one year to file a post-conviction petition.

That summer, Calvin crossed paths with Emily Bolton, an English intern who came to Angola to help conduct a legal seminar for the inmate counsels. She was working with a local capital defense office while pursuing her law degree at Tulane University. During the seminar, she led a discussion on litigating claims of prosecutorial misconduct, and Calvin explained the challenges of obtaining evidence needed to support them.

"The first opportunity we have to show the courts that the state withheld evidence from us is precisely the moment we lose any right to counsel in post-conviction. We're on our own trying to locate and pay for our records," he said.

After the seminar, Emily asked Calvin if he could provide more details in writing.

"It is many years before a guy can save up enough here to purchase the records he needs," he wrote in a letter. "By that time, he is faced with every procedural bar in existence."

The next time Emily came to the prison, she called Calvin out for a legal visit.

"I'm trying to figure out if there's a way I can help," she said. "Tell me about some of the cases you're working on."

Calvin shared Dwight LaBran's story.

"This guy is innocent," he said. "But we need the police and the DA files associated with the prosecution witness—who goes by an alias—to prove it."

"What happens when you request his files from the police department?"

"They ignore us. We had to get Dwight's mom to go to the courthouse to pull files herself—that's how we found out the witness was using a fake name. In my own case, it took me a decade and more than a dozen court filings just to get things that I was entitled to under the Public Records Act. Never mind things that would require investigation, like a witness's criminal history. We spend years trying to get guys their records up here. More often than not, we're unsuccessful."

Emily was nearing the completion of her degree and planned to practice in Louisiana. "I want to start helping you find records," she said.

Calvin didn't hide his excitement. "We will take all the help you can give."

Emily secured a fellowship to work on cases of wrongful conviction among people serving life without parole in Louisiana. The inmate counsels helped her identify worthy cases, beginning with Dwight LaBran's.

Emily began investigating, requesting files. What she found quickly blew the case apart: not only did the state's star witness have outstanding warrants for his arrest when he testified, but those warrants disappeared after Dwight was convicted, suggesting the witness had been cut a deal.

Emily presented the undisclosed evidence to the trial court, and this time, the judge had no choice but to overturn Dwight's conviction. Knowing they couldn't successfully retry him, the state dismissed all charges, and in December 2001, Dwight went home. Emily, Calvin, and the inmate counsels celebrated his release as Innocence Project New Orleans's first exoneration.

EMILY KNEW CALVIN NEEDED AN INVESTIGATOR FOR HIS CASE, BUT when she offered her help, he declined.

He had recently received a decision on his habeas application. Despite hoping to supplement his petition with new facts before the court ruled, there hadn't been time, and his petition was denied. This rejection, more than any before, felt like a betrayal. The hope that federal courts would intervene on a state prisoner's behalf still ran deep, even in Calvin.

For now, getting an investigation done in his case would be no help. His task was to win a certificate of appealability from the Fifth Circuit; otherwise, he'd be out of court altogether. His case was on a knife's edge.

He knew he'd been extremely fortunate to win a COA for Big Dugger, especially as a pro se petitioner. What were the chances he could do it again? This was precisely the kind of crossroads he'd advised his students to watch out for: the moment to invest in a lawyer.

Over the past year, Calvin had developed a pen-pal friendship with a woman named Betsy. Laurie introduced them after Betsy saw a documentary about Angola and wanted to help those wrongfully convicted. She and Calvin started corresponding and forged a bond.

Now Betsy and her husband, Bill, were among his most steadfast supporters.

Soon after Calvin learned of his federal court denial, Betsy announced that she was traveling from New Hampshire to meet him face-to-face.

He decided not to share the news of his defeat, wanting their first meeting to be a happy one.

They sat in the visiting shed sharing food, chatting about their families and books they were reading, and for a moment, Calvin was able to set aside his worries. He would wait until she returned home to tell her about the court denial. When their visit was ending, though, he did make one request.

"Would you contact a lawyer for me?"

Betsy examined the scrap of paper where Calvin had written down a name and phone number.

"Of course, Calvin. Anything I can do to help."

"I want Chris Aberle to represent me and I have the money to pay his fees. It's very important that he knows that I'm the one offering to pay him—not you. Otherwise, he might think I'm scamming you."

Betsy turned over the paper and took out a pen. "I understand. Tell me exactly what I should say."

Betsy called Chris the following week, and he agreed to help— first with filing the COA, and, if they were successful, with Calvin's appeal to the Fifth Circuit. Calvin was elated. As far as the COA was concerned, a lawyer of Chris's experience could give him a fifty-fifty shot.

Chris filed the COA in early 2001. When he mailed an update in the spring, his letter contained wonderful news: The Fifth Circuit had agreed to review Calvin's case. The court determined that his legal issues were serious enough to warrant further review. He had made it through the gatekeeper.

The court set a briefing deadline and scheduled oral arguments for October.

Chris appeared before the court without Calvin, since defendants weren't entitled to attend oral arguments. After the hearing, Laurie sent Calvin an encouraging note reporting that the judges had asked thoughtful questions and appeared to know the record. "It was a tough panel, but I thought it went well."

While Chris was cautiously optimistic, he remained guarded. "I can tell you one thing: I didn't lose the oral argument. But we could very well lose the case."

In January 2002, the Fifth Circuit issued its decision.

Calvin took the ruling to the Camp F law library, hoping to read it in solitude. He had barely opened the envelope when the outcome was made clear. At the bottom of the last page, the word he dreaded stared back at him: "Affirmed."

He took a deep breath and held it, absorbing the thud of disappointment before he could read the court's reasoning.

In 1963, the US Supreme Court ruled in *Brady v. Maryland* that the state's failure to disclose exculpatory evidence violated a defendant's due process rights under the Fourteenth Amendment. Under *Brady*, courts had to determine on appeal whether withheld evidence was material to the verdict, possibly warranting a new trial.

"Given the evidence presented to the jury of Duncan's guilt, we do not find his alleged *Brady* violations undermine confidence in the outcome of his trial," the Fifth Circuit wrote. It also denied Calvin's *Cage* claim, deferring to Judge Parker's prior ruling.

Calvin set the opinion aside. The emotional roller coaster of initially winning the COA, only to face this defeat, was almost too much to bear. A wave of nausea forced his head to his knees.

He tried to steady his mind by focusing on the next task, but he was running out of road.

Unless the Supreme Court granted cert—an outcome in around 2 percent of cases each year—his legal options were exhausted. He would need new exculpatory evidence to file another post-conviction petition. Only one person could help him now.

2002

As Calvin had feared, the US Supreme Court declined to hear his case, marking the bitter end of a twenty-year-long fight in the courts.

Emily Bolton, now managing a growing staff and an expanding roster of cases at Innocence Project New Orleans (IPNO), came to see him at the prison.

Tugging at the sleeves of his sweatshirt, Calvin tried to ward off the chill in the cinder-block room. He'd lost weight from stress, and the cold seeped into his bones.

"Looks like I'm back to square one," he said wryly.

Emily hesitated as though on the verge of saying something.

Calvin could tell she was worried, and he knew why. That morning, he'd glimpsed his reflection in the side mirror of a guard's truck. The toll of not eating or sleeping had left its mark on his features; he looked gaunt and unlike himself. Despair was clawing at his heels.

"I know it must be very difficult to imagine starting over," she murmured.

He gave a brusque nod. This wasn't a time to let feelings in—he had to focus on making a plan.

"The thing I want before any other investigation is done in my case is for someone to find the girl that testified at my trial," he said. "It's my highest priority. I don't think that was Kristie Emberling. The statements she gave police and the testimony of the girl on the stand were totally different."

Did he sound paranoid? Perhaps, but that wasn't his concern.

"We'll certainly ask her about that when we find her," Emily said.

"I don't want any other aspect of my case investigated before we get to the bottom of the eyewitness testimony."

Emily nodded. "I'll find her, Calvin."

IT SEEMED AS THOUGH NO ONE WAS LEAVING ANGOLA THESE DAYS. The steady stream that began in the early 1990s with the *Lofton* and *Desdunes* decisions had trickled to nothing following Article 930.8 and AEDPA. Given the rising number of people sentenced to life without parole, and because Angola was where they were housed, it was rare to see anyone walk out of the prison's front gate.

Elderly men filled the hospital beds. The Human Relations Club, one of the prison clubs, had joined forces with a New Orleans social worker and the warden to establish a hospice program. Now middle-aged men were volunteering to nurse their elders through the stages of dying, knowing they were likely to face the same fate if the laws didn't change. The prison cemetery, Point Lookout, had five or six burials a week, also managed by incarcerated volunteers who led graveside services to lay each man to rest. The first cemetery had reached capacity, so the administration had established a second one across the road, and it was beginning to fill up, too.

Despite this bleak reality, in the early 2000s, some of Angola's most prominent leaders finally found their way through the eye of the needle.

The first was Norris Henderson, who had always maintained his innocence. In 2003, he was released on probation thanks to a provision in the 1977 law, in effect at the time of the crime, that allowed the judge to grant release for good behavior.

That same year, Checo Yancy, who had won a rare commutation of sentence from the governor in 1995, was released on parole under the same 20/45 law he had helped the Angola Special Civics Project push years earlier.

Finally, in 2005, with Calvin's assistance, Wilbert Rideau, the editor in chief of *The Angolite*, went home after forty-four years in prison. A decade earlier, his partner, Linda, had discovered that his grand jury pool had been handpicked to exclude Black people. Together, Calvin and Wilbert researched the equal protection case law, meeting three times a week to develop their claim. Wilbert's pro bono attorney presented their work and Linda's research to the federal courts in a habeas petition—fortunately, before AEDPA was enacted, or he might never have won relief. In 2000, the US Fifth Circuit Court of Appeals agreed that Wilbert's conviction was unconstitutional and vacated it. More than four years later, a jury at a new trial found him guilty of the lesser offense of manslaughter, and he was immediately released.

To see Wilbert, Norris, and Checo all go home lifted the spirits of those who looked up to them, including Calvin. Though their departure brought a profound sense of loss, it also brought a measure of hope. Still, no such good fortune had reached those in Julian Parker's section of court, and Calvin feared they would be the last to win any kind of relief, if they ever did.

He received a packet of photographs from Alvin, who had finished his term at the halfway house. He was renovating a blighted house he'd bought at a tax sale while still incarcerated.

You see how much weight I lost working seven days a week? Alvin wrote on the back of one of the photographs.

> I miss you, Calvin.
>
> Physically I'm free, but emotionally, I'm basically still living as if I'm confined. Eating with a spoon, cutting my own hair, working every day, and missing everyone I care about and love as true friends.
>
> Tell everyone hello. Melvin "Eyes" Smith, "GeGe," "Geggy," "George Miller" aka Shorty, Leo Jackson, Jeffery Lewis, "Big Snokes," Calvin Donaldson, Lil Chicken "Toca," "Big Chicken," "Joker," Warren "The Baby" Holmes, Joe Washington. And all the other brothers whom I fail to mention. Much love, always thought of and always missed.

Before long, Norris and Checo were making appearances in the photographs of friends like Alvin at barbecues, christenings, and funerals. Calvin was grateful for the window into their lives as free men, but in a penitentiary of thousands, he'd never felt more alone.

EARLY IN 2004, MAMIE VISITED CALVIN FOR THE FIRST TIME IN A decade.

Sitting face-to-face in the visiting shed, they shared a quiet moment, relieved to finally see each other again.

Mamie looked weary, and Calvin immediately felt guilty that she had made the long journey.

They chatted for a few minutes before her eyes locked on his. Something was troubling her.

"What's wrong?" he asked.

"It's about Lil' Calvin."

Lil' Calvin was Mamie's eldest son, named after his uncle. At sixteen, he was serving time in a juvenile institution for robbery. It pained Calvin to think his nephew had grown up without a father figure, knowing he would have filled that role if he could have. He longed to be there for Lil' Calvin, as Uncle Trim had been there for him. Instead, he was stuck in here.

"He's in Tallulah," said Mamie, her voice wavering. "And I want to get him out. But he don't want to come home."

Tallulah had been under federal investigation for years following reports of guard-on-child beatings, sexual assaults, and other deplorable conditions. Advocates and families were trying to get the government to close it down.

"He won't be any safer in New Orleans," Calvin replied stiffly. "He's living a better life in there than on the street."

"Calvin, you know what goes on at Tallulah," Mamie whispered, tears springing to her eyes. "Terrible things."

He tried a more sympathetic tone. "I know. But if he gets out and goes back home, the kids that were young when he went to the institution will be grown now. They will've taken his place. They'll see him as a threat."

Mamie pulled a tissue from her pocket, unwilling to meet his eye.

"Don't make the mistake that Brunetta made with me. If she had never intervened to convince my judge to let me out of the juvenile institution, I would have been in custody when they tried to accuse me of this crime," he continued. "Lil' Calvin knows how hard it is on the street. All we can do is pray that by the time he gets out, he has matured enough to navigate all this stuff. I'm tellin' you, Mamie, however hard it is, just leave him be."

"He's my *baby*." She glowered. "Don't tell me to leave him there!"

"Well, I can only tell you what I know from experience," he snapped.

She stood and headed to the exit. Calvin remained in his seat, stubbornly watching her leave.

They didn't speak for months. Then one day, a corrections officer told Calvin to call his aunt.

When Gail picked up, he could hear the anguish in her voice. Lil' Calvin had been murdered.

He'd been granted early release after Tallulah was ordered to close, returning to New Orleans on a Wednesday. The next day, he found a job. Then on Friday, a fourteen-year-old boy gunned him down in the street. He died instantly.

Gail visited Calvin soon after the funeral. In a photograph, he saw his nephew lying in a blond wood coffin, his skin ashen against the bright colors of the football jersey he was buried in.

Gail explained that the DA's office had put Mamie into witness protection because she had given information to police about the boy who murdered her son. They moved her and her remaining three children to a quiet suburb on the edge of the city, and she'd taken a job with a local catering company. Gail said Lil' Calvin's death had sent Mamie into a catatonic state. She didn't laugh anymore, or smile, or even seem to notice things going on around her. She was going through the motions, buried by grief.

Calvin wished he could be there to comfort his sister. As he left the visit with Gail, he wondered how many boys like Lil' Calvin were growing up under the same impossible conditions he and his friends had faced three decades earlier. He thought of Tommy Cage, once on death row and now serving life, who had been taken to Canal Street by his older brothers to pickpocket at the age of nine. What kind of society was this, that left its children with only two destinies: Angola or an early grave?

EMILY AND CALVIN WERE CONVINCED THAT THE DISTRICT ATTOR-ney's office had not turned over all the evidence in Calvin's file. When Emily first requested access, the custodian of records claimed it was missing. On her second attempt, they provided only the appellate file, stating they couldn't find his trial file.

From the scant documentation they did share, Emily discovered a valuable paper: the record from the physical lineup the police conducted with Kristie Emberling three months after Calvin was extradited from Oregon.

The notes indicated that Kristie had identified Calvin from behind a one-way mirror. The accompanying chart highlighted a clear deviation from proper procedure: instead of assembling a lineup with individuals who bore a resemblance to Calvin, the police had chosen people who looked distinctly different—their ages ranged from nineteen to twenty-eight, their heights from five foot six to five foot ten, and their weights from 118 to 185 pounds. In fact, it was a combined lineup, where suspects from two or more unrelated crimes were viewed simultaneously—a disavowed practice that the defense lawyers had objected to. The chart recorded Calvin's height as five foot nine and weight as 164 pounds, far from the "fat guy" Kristie had described after the crime.

While Emily pressed the DA's office to see more of Calvin's file, she expanded her search for records to Oregon. She sent an investigator to Clackamas County to unearth files from Calvin's arrest. At the sheriff's office, they found a staggering piece of new evidence: contemporaneous reports made by the Oregon deputies following their interrogation of Calvin.

Eager to share the discovery, Emily brought copies to the prison for Calvin to review.

"Peterson told the jury that he and Lieutenant Reed didn't know any facts about the crime at the time they questioned you," she said. "They claimed that you told them things only the killer could have known, right? But look here."

She pointed to a paragraph.

"Reed writes that he told you during that first meeting at the Job Corps that the victim in the case had been shot, and that he was accompanied by a woman who saw it happen. He also told you that the victim died following an attempted robbery and a scuffle. How did he know that if Detective Demma didn't tell him? Which means Demma was lying, too."

Calvin read the papers closely. Reed's notes indeed showed that they had been sharing facts about the crime—including the gender of the eyewitness—that Detective Peterson later claimed not to have known.

"So you think Demma included a summary of the crime when he faxed over the warrant for my arrest?" Calvin asked.

"Yes, and that's not all. Look at Reed's notes recording his conversation with you about your teeth."

Calvin read aloud.

"At this time, I informed him that one of the main reasons that she was able to identify him was because of his two gold teeth. . . . I asked him how long he had had the two gold front teeth. Duncan stated that he'd had them for at least two years."

"Kristie Emberling never mentioned any gold teeth," said Emily. "At trial, she specifically said the shooter *didn't* have gold teeth. So why would you have admitted to Reed that you had gold crowns at the time of the crime if he'd just told you that the witness used your teeth to identify you?"

"Because I was answering truthfully."

"Exactly. You did have gold crowns, and the person Kristie described to the police did not. The detectives didn't know that; they were probably just improvising during the interrogation to scare you into confessing."

Calvin read it over again. "This is good."

"We've got enough evidence here to file a new post-conviction application," said Emily.

Calvin shook his head. "I want to find Kristie first."

CALVIN WAITED PATIENTLY FOR THE INVESTIGATION TO BE COM-pleted in his case. In the meantime, he began to correspond with his

daughter, Ayana. She was in the midst of major life transitions—
graduating from high school and enlisting in the navy—and, to his
delight, seemed eager to reconnect. Her letters arrived suddenly and
came often: sweet, meandering notes about her day that veered
abruptly into questions about the past.

> Right now I'm in this class that will help me get a good job
> when I get out of the navy. If I pass this, I will be certified
> in basic computer skills. I know a lot of the stuff in this class
> already because I work with it on a daily basis. . . .
>
> Did you see me before you were arrested? My mama said
> that you went to jail right before I was born. What did you
> say when you first laid eyes on me? How did you feel?

Calvin received the letters enthusiastically, though he didn't always know how to respond to his daughter. It made sense that as
Ayana grew older, she wanted answers from him. He recognized her
longing, recalling his own desire to talk to his father when he was
sixteen. In one letter, she asked if Calvin had loved her right from the
beginning; in another, if he'd missed her as much as she'd missed
him. Calvin was grateful for these opportunities to tell his daughter
what she meant to him, but he wondered if he could give her all she
needed. He still longed for his own mother, and even at forty, nothing could satisfy the questions that lingered at his core.

In many ways, Ayana's upbringing mirrored Calvin's own. Her
mother, who joined her on the military base, had been permanently
diminished by years of battling substance abuse. And he—her father—
had spent Ayana's entire life behind bars. She had essentially grown
up as an orphan, tasked with raising her younger siblings. Regard-

less of how independent she might become, Calvin knew the longing for a parent never ceased.

Yet as long as Ayana was in the navy, he could rest assured that at least one part of the cycle had been broken. Against all odds, and with no thanks to her parents, she had found her way out of the New Orleans life.

IN OVER A DECADE WORKING ON DEATH ROW, CALVIN HAD WITNESSED the state carry out executions with painful frequency. Between 1991 and 2002, eight men—all of whom he counted as friends—were taken from their cells and transported to the "death house" at Camp F, where they were killed by lethal injection. Only those living and working near the death chamber could fully grasp the haunting and surreal nature of these state killings: the decades-long friendships they tore apart, the terror and grief they instilled in the men waiting their turn. To the rest of Louisiana, the executions were hidden from view, reported out from behind Angola's walls in brief newspaper articles.

One of these men, John Brown, was executed in 1997. John had become a close friend of Calvin's, and his sudden death left Calvin grieving and bewildered. Calvin had been sure that once the federal courts learned of John's traumatic childhood—marked by extreme abuse and a crippling drug addiction, beginning with an overdose at age eleven—they would intervene and stop his execution. But with the passage of AEDPA, Brown's appeals were sped up, and the federal courts didn't intervene. The system's callousness left Calvin rattled.

From that point on, he meticulously tracked the filing deadlines of every man on death row, acutely aware of how quickly their cases could move.

One day, while reading the Baton Rouge newspaper, he came across an article about a recent court hearing during which a young man on the row had an outburst at his attorneys.

Concerned, Calvin stopped by his cell to see what had gone wrong.

"My attorneys are doggin' me out," the young man said.

It wasn't unusual for the men on death row to get frustrated with their lawyers, since capital litigation was long and grinding by nature. Part of Calvin's job was to act as an intermediary and help them understand why their attorneys did the things they did.

"Which court are you in?" he asked, thinking it might help to explain the stages of litigation.

"Federal court."

Calvin startled. "Federal court? Aren't you still in state post-conviction?"

The young man shrugged. "I was in federal court for my last hearing."

Calvin's mind jolted with alarm.

"Call Nick Trenticosta," he said, referring to the death penalty attorney who, years earlier, had alerted the inmate counsels to AEDPA's passage. "Tell Nick you're in federal court, and you and your attorneys are not communicating. I'll help you file a motion."

Calvin prepared a motion to appoint new counsel and followed up daily until Trenticosta took over the case.

As it turned out, Calvin's concerns were justified. By the time Trenticosta stepped in, the district attorney had already moved for an execution date. The young man's new legal team managed to avert the threat of execution, and after the state courts refused to hear crucial evidence of his intellectual disability, the federal courts eventually ruled that he was indeed intellectually disabled and ordered his removal from death row. Years later, at a legal seminar, Trenticosta told Calvin that his quick thinking had helped save the young man's life. But far from comforting Calvin, it disturbed him to realize how easily the courts might have rubber-stamped an unlawful execution.

It wasn't long before he discovered another man on the row facing a similar predicament.

Juan Smith had been convicted in two separate cases for murders that occurred within a month of each other. In one case, he was sentenced to life without parole; in the other, he received the death penalty. During his death penalty trial, the state used his previous murder conviction to argue that he should be executed. In post-conviction, Juan was assigned lawyers for his capital case, but he wasn't entitled to an attorney for his noncapital case. When Calvin noticed an impending deadline to file a post-conviction application in the noncapital case, he tried to alert Juan's capital defense attorneys, but they didn't respond. As time passed, Calvin grew increasingly concerned. The outcomes of the two cases were intertwined, yet Juan's lawyers were on the verge of missing the opportunity to challenge his initial conviction.

As the post-conviction deadline neared, Calvin tried to obtain Juan's police reports, suspecting inconsistencies in a key eyewitness's testimony. Something about the man's statements in the trial transcripts seemed off. But the police department and district attorney's office demanded payments neither he nor Juan could afford.

With no alternatives left, Calvin drafted a post-conviction petition alleging that the state had withheld favorable evidence, even though he had no proof. Given the long history of constitutional violations in the Orleans Parish DA's office, the claim was plausible. Calvin hoped that, by preserving it now, future investigations might substantiate it.

A week before the filing deadline, Calvin filled out a draw slip for $3.85, the cost to mail Juan's petition to the clerk of court. He kept a copy in his lockerbox as insurance, in case Juan ever needed proof that it was mailed on time.

Years later, a newly appointed defense team delved into Juan's noncapital case and uncovered statements that indeed contradicted witness testimony central to the trial. One eyewitness, who initially told police he was too scared to look at his attackers—a statement never disclosed to the defense—later identified Juan, which was crucial evidence used to convict him. When Juan's legal team presented this new statement to the US Supreme Court, the court issued a scathing judgment, reprimanding the Orleans Parish DA's office for once again concealing exculpatory evidence. Juan's case was sent back for a new trial, and eventually he was removed from death row. Despite his relief, Calvin once again paled at a system so flawed that it took an inmate counsel to catch a vital deadline—one that might have barred a gross prosecutorial misconduct claim from ever being heard in court.

WHEN CALVIN SPOTTED EMILY'S NAME ON THE CALLOUT SHEET ONE morning, he knew it was about Kristie Emberling.

In the visiting room, Emily slid a piece of paper across the table. "I found her," she said.

Calvin stared at the handwritten statement, at once hungry and terrified to read it.

Emily didn't keep him in suspense. "It was Kristie Emberling who testified at your trial. She stands by her identification. But she told me a lot of helpful things that went on in the case."

Calvin's eyes dropped to Kristie's signature at the bottom.

"How can that be?"

"She obviously still feels guilty for making David leave the house that night; you can tell it weighs on her. And of course, she was able to get away and he wasn't."

Calvin shook his head. Emily spoke faster.

"Calvin, we see this a lot in wrongful conviction cases. Survivors feel guilty, even though it's not at all their fault, and the one thing they can do to honor the person they love is to help the police catch the perpetrator. Police often reinforce this narrative by telling them that the best way to help solve the crime is to get the identification right. It creates an artificial drive toward certainty. Being unsure can feel like a failure."

Calvin wasn't able to absorb what Emily was saying. He pulled the statement closer to read it for himself. The words on the page appeared jumbled. His cheeks flushed.

"I know you need time to digest this," Emily said. "But I want to point a few things out. All the hallmarks of a false identification are present. Kristie told me that she described the shooter's face to the police as being like the Creature from the Black Lagoon with 'big lips' and 'slanted, ugly, beady eyes.' This was a scared fifteen-year-old girl making a cross-racial identification based on a five-year-old mugshot of you from when you were fourteen. And she was making it seven months after the crime, after seeing multiple photo arrays.

For god's sake, she's comparing the shooter to a monster from a scary movie."

"But she thinks it's me," said Calvin pointedly.

"We don't need her to retract her identification to win your case," Emily insisted. "No ID expert is going to look at this and say it's even close to a reliable identification. Kristie told me that when you were arrested, she wanted to see you in person—to see your height and weight—before she could be sure. Why would she say that if she was certain when she signed the back of your photo? She admitted that the first time she saw you in person was on television when you arrived at the airport from Oregon and they made you do the perp walk for the cameras. The fact is, Kristie didn't firm up her ID until a year after the crime when she saw you in handcuffs."

Calvin's stomach was tied in knots. He didn't know what to say.

"How about I leave this with you, and you can call me in a day or two once you've had some time to look it over?"

He let out a breath. "I'm sorry, Emily. I just—I was sure it wasn't her. Before my trial, I didn't believe that anyone had made an identification. I thought Demma and the prosecutors were making it up. I never could figure out why the eyewitness put the shooter in winter clothes, even though the crime happened in August. After I saw that little girl crying on the stand, I just kept thinking, 'Damn, how can she be saying I'm the person? I know I'm not the person.' So I came up with the only explanation that made sense—that the police had found somebody to pretend to be her."

Emily looked at him with compassion.

"So much can happen to a person's memory after a traumatic event," she reiterated. "Kristie was vulnerable in a lot of ways; she was a child. But she also desperately wanted the police to solve this crime.

So there was pressure in both directions. The police needed to give her an answer, and she needed to give them an ID. She called me yesterday—"

"Kristie?"

"Yes. She was calling because she didn't want me to come back to her house to get an affidavit. She insisted she was sure about you, as though she'd been thinking about it after our visit. I wouldn't be surprised if she's still playing it over in her mind all these years later."

"Well, that wraps it," he said. "She's not going to change her story."

"No. But I don't think we need her to."

Calvin walked Emily back to the gate.

He knew how hard she had worked over the past year to track Kristie down, but he couldn't hide his disappointment. For years, the courts had relied on Kristie's testimony to uphold his conviction, and there was no reason to think that would change now.

As he watched Emily leave the A-Building, a wave of dread brought *To Kill a Mockingbird* to mind. Few weapons could be wielded more powerfully in the legal system than the word of a white woman.

Kristie Emberling's could bury him.

EMILY KEPT PULLING THREADS.

First, she tracked down Mack Ferrick and Bob Hartsuyker from Timber Lake, now retired, and obtained their statements. Both men, especially Hartsuyker, were horrified to learn that Calvin was still behind bars.

Hartsuyker's statement read:

> I have very strong feelings about what I witnessed those many years ago, both at Timber Lake Job Corps, and in New Orleans. I witnessed the arrest of Calvin in the office of Mack Ferrick. The police officers tried to press him hard on the facts, and kept asking him questions even after he had said that he did not want to talk to them. . . . He kept saying that they had the wrong person.
>
> The public defender told me that the arresting officers were claiming that Calvin had made an inculpatory statement when they arrested him. This was and is a lie. He did not tell the police anything that indicated that he knew that the witness was a woman, or that the victim was male and both were white.
>
> I was called to testify. I remember that the prosecutor objected to some of the questions posed by the public defender and the judge was also cutting me off. I would have said more if they had let me.
>
> I was present in the courtroom when the jury gave their verdict . . . I was so angered by the process, I swore never to set foot in New Orleans again.
>
> All Calvin received from the legal system was injustice. That injustice has haunted me all these years.

Calvin was moved by the men's enduring confidence, remembering the letters they had sent long ago, promising to hold his place at Timber Lake.

Emily also found an important transcript from Calvin's evidentiary hearing in 1997. At the hearing, Judge Parker admitted that he'd been an assistant district attorney assigned to Judge Shea's courtroom at the time of Calvin's trial. He acknowledged that he might have touched the case, though he didn't remember it.

If a judge had any past involvement in the prosecution of a case, the law required that he recuse himself and refer the case to another judge.

"We ought to consider filing a motion to recuse Judge Parker at the same time that we file your post-conviction petition," Emily suggested in a May 2004 visit.

Calvin agreed. "There were a lot of people at the DA's office who touched my case without their name being on the paper."

When he rose to leave at the end of their meeting, he noticed Emily hesitating.

"Calvin, before I go . . . there's something else I wanted to talk to you about," she said.

He sat back down, bracing himself.

Emily explained that she was returning to England. After many years away, it was time for her to go home. She hoped he'd understand.

He assured her that he did, though a quiet sadness settled over him. No one stayed for long; people leaving was just a fact of life.

"David Park will continue working on your case," she said.

Calvin was glad to hear this, having known David since he started in the office as an intern.

"Well, I appreciate everything you've done for me," he said. "You're smart to leave this crazy place."

"It's been an honor, Calvin. None of what we've accomplished—

bringing people home, IPNO—would have been possible without you and the inmate counsels."

He smiled bravely.

IN THE FIRST WEEK OF AUGUST, CALVIN'S LEGAL TEAM FILED A MOTION to recuse Judge Parker. Typically, upon receiving such a motion, a judge would transfer the case to another section of court for an impartial hearing.

Not Julian Parker. He set a hearing in his own court, where he vehemently dismissed the motion as "cockamamie."

"I don't remember what my supervisor told me to do twenty years ago, man!" Parker barked at Calvin's attorneys from the bench.

"But that's the point, Judge—"

"And where were you twenty years ago? What grade were you in?"

David Park balked. This was the side of Judge Parker he didn't want to be on.

"Elementary school, Judge."

"What grade?"

David shook his head. "I can't even figure it out."

"But you know about my supervisor's *Brady* practices twenty years ago and what he might have told me? I'm trying really hard to be patient with you so that I don't say something inappropriate. I don't remember what happened twenty years ago. And when you bring me the transcript that says I handled the case, I will be more than happy to recuse myself. But all this malarkey about appearances of impropriety is not going to cut the mustard."

After the hearing, Emily phoned Calvin to relay the events. The judge begrudgingly transferred the case to another section, and a hearing would be held in two weeks.

The judge's tirade was a sure sign that he had taken the motion personally.

God help me if this motion gets denied, Calvin thought.

EMILY CAME TO THE PRISON TO SAY GOODBYE. CALVIN'S HEART SANK as he watched her enter the A-Building for the last time. She had brought David Park with her, and the three of them settled in an empty visiting room to talk.

Calvin shook David's hand. "Thanks for taking over my case," he said.

"Here's a copy of your post." Emily pulled a pile of papers from her briefcase.

Calvin flipped through the stack like he was shuffling a deck of cards. It was ninety pages long.

"There's nothing in here we haven't gone over," she said. "But I think you'll be pleased when you see it all in one place."

Calvin turned to the procedural history at the front of the petition. Emily had listed every pleading he had filed since 1986. It filled five legal-sized pages.

He flipped to a section titled *Calvin Duncan has diligently striven to vindicate himself over the last 20 years but has been denied access to the courts and the documentation he needed.*

"My case has driven me crazy," he chuckled, before reading from the pleading aloud.

"The efforts that Mr. Duncan made, given his education levels and the constraints of prison life, are remarkable and are a compelling illustration of the difficulties facing prisoners who must represent themselves in post-conviction proceedings. . . . It is amazing that in the face of all these refusals, that Mr. Duncan kept trying, but he did, and it is his persistence in his efforts to prove his innocence that brings him before this court today."

Calvin set the papers back down.

"I like that," he told his attorneys. "The courts need to know what it's like for us in here, trying to keep our cases alive on our own."

"We included it to preempt any talk of due diligence from the state," David explained, "to show them that you have done everything in your power to present your claims to the courts as quickly and fully as possible."

They rose from the table. Calvin carefully tucked the mass of papers under one arm before Emily walked over to give him a hug. She handed him an address where he could write to her in England.

"We're going to get you out of here, Calvin," she said. "I am always here for you. If there's anything you need, please get in touch."

"Travel safe and let me know once you get there," Calvin told her. "I'll miss you, Emily."

He hung by the gate to watch her leave.

AS EMILY EXPECTED, THE HEARING ON THE MOTION TO RECUSE WAS delayed until early 2005.

While Calvin was waiting, he endured another difficult departure: Mrs. Rabalais announced that she was leaving Legal Programs.

Though she was in her seventies, her decision came suddenly and without explanation, and Calvin sensed that it wasn't of her choosing. Politics often played a role in staffing appointments at the penitentiary, and Calvin had a hunch that some larger forces were at play in Mrs. Rabalais's ouster, though she was professional to a fault and would never say a word out of turn. She would continue living on B-Line and become a part-time historian for the Angola museum, which lay just beyond the prison's front gate.

The inmate counsels threw a retirement party for her in the Main Prison law library, exchanging stories from her thirty-five years of service. The counsels shared chips and soda at wooden tables and foldout desks, a lone typewriter still sitting by the computers against the wall. Calvin recounted how, fifteen years earlier, he had bet Mrs. Rabalais that he could get a man named Henry Montrell out of prison. He thanked her for everything she had done for the program over the years; most of all, for standing up for the counsels when they believed in something.

There were battles he'd been able to wage only because he could always count on Mrs. Rabalais to have his back. He knew he wouldn't approach his work with the same fearlessness once she was gone.

IN FEBRUARY 2005, CALVIN ARRIVED AT TULANE AND BROAD FOR THE hearing on his motion to recuse. He was taken aback by the number of supporters waiting for him. His aunt Gail had organized a troop of family members to be there, including her own children. Alvin Abbott, along with Tyrone Smith—another friend from Angola—sat beside them. Alvin shot Calvin a toothy smile and he lifted a shackled hand in salute.

His gaze shifted to the last two people in the row: Mamie and her son Dwayne. Calvin hadn't seen his sister since before Lil' Calvin's death. She smiled, but her joy faded quickly, tension tightening her jaw. Calvin imagined how he must look through her eyes: the brother she had lost at barely eighteen, now a forty-one-year-old man, balding and in shackles. As he settled at the counsel table, he turned and offered her a reassuring smile. She lifted her hand in a tentative wave.

David Park rose to present the defense's argument. He outlined Judge Parker's role at the district attorney's office, explaining that Parker had worked under Glynn Alexander, a supervisor in Judge Shea's section who had prosecuted Calvin's case. David emphasized that it was standard practice for junior attorneys to assist their supervisors with all major felony cases in their section.

In rebuttal, the prosecutor insisted there was no definitive evidence that Parker ever worked on Calvin's case.

The judge asked no questions; her only remarks were to thank the attorneys for their presentations and to set a date for a ruling.

Calvin left the court hopeful. The judge's attentive and patient demeanor, so different from Julian Parker's, gave him a sense that he might have a chance.

Not long after he returned to Angola, Calvin received a letter from Mamie. The neatness of the handwriting made him suspect it wasn't hers, and he guessed that she had dictated her message to one of her daughters, the way he used to pay guys with good handwriting to pen his legal briefs in the parish jail.

Dear Calvin,

I was so happy to see you. You bring joy to my soul.

You look the same. I really miss you. I wish I could see you more often. You are the closest person in my life.

I hope you do good the next time you go to court. I will have this address for a while. I know you was thankful for the support. I wrote you a letter but I miss placed them when we were moving. I can't wait to you come home. I love you and I think about you every day.

Love always, my loving brother.

Gail had told Calvin that his sister was still struggling with depression. Lil' Calvin's murder had left her permanently altered. As he had so many times over the years, Calvin wished he could be out there to support her. The pain of their separation ached. He folded the letter and slipped it back into the envelope, trying his best to push it from his mind.

IN AUGUST 2005, HURRICANE KATRINA HIT THE GULF COAST.

While the hurricane was still approaching, the population at Angola was ordered to haul and pile sandbags to shore up the levees surrounding the prison. Men worked around the clock for days on end. Once the storm hit, the Mississippi River rose high against the levees. Mercifully, it never breached them.

Family members and friends began calling the prison to tell their loved ones that they were evacuating, shattering any sense of security. Down in New Orleans, the levees had broken, and the city was flooding. Though Calvin didn't hear from Mamie, he felt certain she would be okay—she never stayed in town when hurricanes came. Fortunately, Ayana was stationed at a military base in another state.

In the days that followed, Camp F's residents were moved to the Main Prison gymnasium to make space for women coming from the New Orleans jail. Angola took in over two thousand people from flood-affected detention facilities around the state. From the plasma building to the mail room, every available structure was converted into a makeshift dormitory.

The population clung to news broadcasts, hoping to learn what had happened to their families. Televisions blared day and night in cramped dayrooms, filled with images of New Orleanians waiting on bridges and outside the convention center in blistering heat. They were waiting for buses that never came, suffering without adequate food or water.

Long after the floodwaters receded and residents returned to rebuild the city, the courts remained closed. The New Orleans jail lost track of the detainees they were responsible for, having abandoned them to be rescued by the state. Hundreds of incarcerated people, whether arrested for assault or public urination, were lost in the system for months or longer.

Prior to the storm, Calvin received the discouraging news that the trial court had denied his motion to recuse Judge Parker. Although his lawyers had taken the issue to the state appellate court, their appeal only resulted in the original ruling being upheld. Shortly before the storm hit, they filed a writ with the Louisiana Supreme Court. Calvin remained hopeful that, upon reopening, the court would agree to hear his case. He had no idea how long that might take.

WHILE WORKING ON THE OFFICE COMPUTER AT DEATH ROW ONE LONG weekend, Calvin noticed something peculiar. He was using Westlaw, a legal database, to do research when he saw that additional features were suddenly available. He knew Westlaw offered newspaper archive searches and "people-finder" services for law firms and universities, but the inmate counsels weren't allowed access to those for security reasons.

The administration was renegotiating its contract with Westlaw, and only two months ago, Calvin had attended a meeting with a company representative to explain that the inmate counsels needed access to more of its content. Perhaps these new features were the result of those negotiations, he reasoned.

Whatever the explanation, an entire world of information was now at his fingertips, and excitement stirred as he thought about what to look up first.

His mind went immediately to his mother.

He still wasn't sure whether Tiny Duncan had died of breast cancer. He had always imagined another scenario: a young single mother, overwhelmed by raising four children, desperate to escape an abusive partner, leaving town one day and never coming back.

He pulled his chair closer to the computer and opened the News tab. Unsure if he even knew his mother's real name, he typed Mary Ann Duncan into the search bar.

No results.

He tried a few variations, but no obituaries that resembled his mother appeared.

Turning his attention to his estranged grandmother, Georgia Shriver, he hoped her obituary might offer some clues. Calvin had heard that when his mother passed away, she had been living in Georgia's home. He also knew his grandmother had lived on Feliciana Street because he had been named in a lawsuit after her surviving family failed to pay property taxes on her house. In fact, it was that lawsuit that first inspired Alvin Abbott to learn how to buy properties at tax sales.

Calvin found his grandmother's obituary on Westlaw, but to his dismay, it shed no light on his mother's fate.

He soon realized he wasn't the only inmate counsel who discovered Westlaw's expanded access that weekend.

By the time the company notified the prison that it had unlocked the extra features in error, the inmate counsels had made 741 searches. Prison officials promptly put Calvin and the other inmate counsels in lockdown while the matter was investigated.

The administration's main concern was whether the counsels were running searches on victims of crime or personnel who worked in the prison. Once Angola's investigators confirmed that Calvin had done neither, they downgraded his charge to a minor disciplinary infraction. He pleaded not guilty, knowing his conduct had not violated any posted prison policies, but was found guilty anyway. He received no sanctions.

After spending nearly three weeks in the cells, Calvin was returned to Camp F and restored to his Class A trusty status, his job as an inmate counsel intact. It was his first write-up since 1986.

IT TOOK THE LOUISIANA SUPREME COURT SIX MONTHS TO REOPEN after Hurricane Katrina, and in March 2006, Calvin finally received a response to his writ.

It was another denial. The recusal effort was over. His only path out of Angola led through the doors of Julian Parker's courtroom.

Gripped with dread, Calvin called his legal team. Wouldn't Judge Parker hold the recusal motion against him? He might even deny Calvin's post-conviction application out of spite.

His lawyers suggested letting things lie dormant for a while, hoping time would cool tensions with the judge.

Part 4

All human wisdom is contained in these
two words, "Wait and Hope."

EDMOND DANTÈS,
THE COUNT OF MONTE CRISTO

2007

A year and a half passed before a date was set for Calvin to return to court.

In the meantime, his legal team sought to recruit an attorney to help them regain their footing in Judge Parker's courtroom. They approached Glen Woods, a former prosecutor who had spent sixteen years at the Orleans Parish DA's office and prosecuted several high-profile murder cases. Woods said he wanted to meet Calvin before making any decisions—and he wanted to do it alone.

On the day that Woods came to Angola, the summer heat was stifling. The visiting room felt like a tinderbox, ready to ignite.

Sitting across from the former prosecutor, Calvin wiped beads of sweat from his hairline with a washcloth. Woods, on the other hand, looked suave in a casual blazer, a Havana hat perched on his head. Just like Al Capone, Calvin thought.

"I'm here on account of some old acquaintances who said I need to check you out," Woods said frankly. "That's the only reason I came today."

"I'm familiar with your work," Calvin replied. "In fact, I've been working on one of your old cases."

"Oh yeah? Which one is that?"

"Jerome Robinson."

"I remember that case." Woods gave a knowing smile. "I prosecuted that case."

He held Calvin's eye.

"My attitude when it comes to people who commit crimes is one of zero tolerance. And let me tell you something: I sent a lot of people to the penitentiary. I enjoyed my job." He shrugged. "But your lawyers sent more people here than I did."

Calvin didn't disagree. The prosecution wouldn't have succeeded so easily at his trial if his own lawyers had been better equipped.

"My philosophy is like this," Woods continued. "You know in baseball how you get three strikes?"

"Yes, sir."

"Well, I only take one swing, and I give it my all. These friends of yours told me I needed to come see you, so I've come to look you in the eye and see if you're telling the truth."

"I'd be glad to tell you the truth," Calvin said.

"Then shoot."

Woods sat back and crossed his arms.

Calvin started from the beginning, recounting his arrest on Mount Hood and his alibi on the night of the murder. He described the inconsistencies in the eyewitness statements, the prosecutors' notes acknowledging serious flaws in the case, and the recently surfaced report from Lieutenant Reed, which showed that the Oregon deputies had fed him details they later presented as proof of his guilty knowledge.

"Reed was under investigation by the FBI when he interrogated me," Calvin added.

He then described Detective Demma's role, including the apparent falsehoods he had told at trial.

Woods chimed in, "Detective Demma—that's my friend."

Calvin swallowed, worried he'd said too much.

"You're not wrong," Woods said.

Calvin flushed with relief. It seemed Demma's tactics were an open secret.

Emboldened, he asked, "So, are you gonna take that swing for me?"

Woods extended his hand. "I will. Parker and I go way back to our days in the DA's office, but your judge is his own man. I'll do what I can, but I can't promise you anything."

MUCH OF PARKER'S ANTAGONISM MELTED WHEN HE SAW HIS OLD colleague seated at the defense table. As Woods filed requests for subpoenas to obtain records concerning Calvin's arrest, the FBI's investigation of Lieutenant Reed, and the NOPD's homicide file, Parker listened passively and signed them without objection.

The subpoenas returned a windfall of new exculpatory evidence.

The Oregon sheriff's file included an Orleans Parish affidavit for a warrant of arrest that included a summary of the crime—further proof that Demma provided the victim's race and gender to the sheriff's deputies prior to Calvin's interrogation, and lied about it to the jury.

The FBI files detailed Reed's felony conviction for wiretapping the phone of a Clackamas County commissioner, and the lies he told during the investigation. They also implicated Detective Peterson, who was complicit in the crime. Peterson was present when Reed planned the wiretap and later attempted to conceal it—during the same period the two arrested and interrogated Calvin. Reed took the blame for the scheme, and charges against Peterson were eventually dropped, enabling him to testify at Calvin's trial without the jury knowing he had ever been arrested.

In addition, Calvin's lawyers discovered that several of the New Orleans police officers involved in his investigation were tainted by misconduct. The NOPD detective who arrived at the scene of David Yeager's murder and conducted early witness interviews later faced disciplinary proceedings for untruthfulness and filing false or inaccurate witness reports. The crime scene technician was reprimanded more than once for failing to properly collect evidence at crime scenes and was eventually dismissed from the NOPD for lying to the Public Integrity Bureau and falsifying statistics.

The subpoenas also unearthed Detective Demma's complete homicide file. Calvin had tried to obtain the file as early as 1992, and between 2003 and 2007, IPNO attempted to access it no fewer than six times. The evidence they uncovered through the judge's subpoena finally proved that Demma had misrepresented the truth.

Soon after the crime, Demma had written up a summary of facts that departed significantly from the version of events he would later recount to Calvin's jury. The summary described a struggle between the perpetrator and the victim, whereas he told the jury the shooting was calculated, "execution-style." Demma also testified that he "had no idea" if the Crimestoppers tipster sought the thousand-dollar reward, despite noting in his file that the tipster expressed interest in it. Demma's file contained mugshots of men—presumably suspects—of wildly different appearances: a young neighbor of Kristie's, an alternate suspect named Henry Duncan who was interviewed the day after the crime, two bearded white males, an Asian or Hispanic male, and an unknown Black man with facial hair and a distinctive haircut—none of whom resembled Calvin. The fact that police had investigated a Henry Duncan could explain why an anonymous tipster seeking a reward might use the name Duncan when calling Crimestoppers.

Armed with this wealth of new information, Calvin's team, which now included Park, Woods, and IPNO's executive director, Emily Maw, filed an amendment to his application for post-conviction relief, confident they would receive an evidentiary hearing.

THE DISTRICT ATTORNEY'S OFFICE FAILED TO MEET ITS DEADLINE to answer Calvin's application. When Parker asked the prosecutor in his section about the holdup, he demurred, saying it was up to the appellate division to respond. The judge ordered the state to answer Calvin's petition for a second, then a third, time.

More weeks came and went, and more deadlines passed. At a status hearing in October, Woods raised a formal objection: it was only fair that the judge bar the state from raising procedural objections to Calvin's petition, given they had missed so many deadlines of their own.

Judge Parker listened but made no ruling.

Another deadline passed; Woods tried again.

"On August thirteenth, 2008, Mr. Duncan filed an amendment to his supplemental application. Your Honor gave the state until

October ninth to answer," he told the judge at a status conference. "Then, October twelfth. We came in on the fifteenth, again complaining about them not filing an answer. You gave them another continuance. In total, Your Honor, you gave them over one hundred sixty days' worth of continuances just to file an answer."

Judge Parker turned to the prosecution. "Are you ready to make your argument in opposition?"

The assistant district attorney, a man named Bair, delivered his usual refrain.

"Judge, I haven't had a chance to review the record. Donna Andrieu from the appellate division is actually the attorney handling the case."

Parker flinched. "Mr. Bair, if it's a case on the Section G docket, someone has to be here to handle it. I told you on day one and I have told every senior that's worked in this section for the last eleven years: there's no such thing as Donna Andrieu's case, John Bair's case, Julian Parker's case. Every case belongs to the State of Louisiana."

The prosecutor drew back defensively. "Yes, sir. I'm just not omnipotent."

Parker took the posture of an indignant father, crossing his arms and leaning over the bench.

"People want to know, *why doesn't Judge Parker know how to do his docket?* Well, I've got a race car that is missing one wheel. You have to put your wheel on the car, Mr. Bair! We're coming to the point where the district attorney has just completely ignored my orders. And then today again I hear, *I don't know what's going on.* If this was the only case where I'm hearing the same things over and over, I'd say, let's give it another shot. But I have to agree with the petitioners in this case that even if Ms. Andrieu were here, the deadlines have long since passed. They don't play this nice down there at civil court when they're dealing with insurance companies and big plaintiff lawyers. Since I've walked in your shoes, I may give you more leeway than I really ought to."

He signed a paper in thick Sharpie and handed it to his clerk.

"So, with that, the motion in limine to bar the state from making procedural objections is hereby granted."

When Calvin received word of the order, a weight lifted. His most urgent fear was put to rest. No procedural bars meant that no matter what happened in state court, his claims were protected for federal review.

ON JANUARY 7, WOODS WAS STRUCK BY A BOUT OF THE FLU. DAVID Park appeared in court for the status conference, as did the chief of appeals, Donna Andrieu. She had finally produced an answer to Calvin's post-conviction application. David set it aside to read after the hearing.

"Just a few housekeeping matters, Judge," he began. "We received some documents from the NOPD last time we were in court, and more since then. But some of the information is unexplained. For instance, there is a photo array that nobody is identified in. We don't know what it is or who they are."

"Well, I think the custodian of records for the police department has only the obligation to turn the material over, not to explain it to you," Parker snapped.

He clearly wasn't going to offer David the same courtesies he had extended to Glen Woods.

"Correct," David replied cautiously. "But they should give us the documents in the order laid out by the subpoena—it's very important to this case."

"How old is this case?" asked Parker.

Donna Andrieu pounced. "Mr. Duncan was convicted in 1985, Your Honor. In regard to the subpoena of NOPD records, Mr. Park is alleging newly discovered evidence. The police report has been in existence since 1985. They've had several years to—"

"Y'all are talking about two different things," Parker cut her off.

"Correct," said David. He glanced at Donna Andrieu. What was she up to?

"Wait, wait a minute." The judge was suddenly incredulous. "Let me just put this in the record. In 1985, counsel for Mr. Duncan knew that the Oregon police officer, whatever he or she was supposed to be, did testify. They knew that. In 1985, they knew it."

"Your honor—"

"No, no! Don't interrupt me. They knew it in 1995, and they knew it in 2005. So, how is the fact that this supposed investigating officer didn't testify newly discovered evidence?"

"They didn't have the reports." David tried to explain. "They didn't have the knowledge that he was the actual lead investigator."

"Who didn't have knowledge?"

IPNO's director, Emily Maw, stood up from her seat. "I think, Judge, we're talking about a question of fact and whether this is a material issue. This could be resolved at an evidentiary hearing rather than us standing here discussing it. Maybe we could schedule a hearing on the case."

"That's fine with me."

"Your Honor," said Andrieu, "the state would object to a hearing."

Parker gave a sharp sigh. "Let me rule on the procedural objections first, and then we can move on, okay?"

The defense team didn't hide their frustration as they recounted the day's events to Calvin. Despite being absent from the case for nearly a year, Donna Andrieu had quickly regained the upper hand. She was trying to unsettle the judge's ruling barring the state from making procedural objections—and it was working.

WHEN THE TWO SIDES RECONVENED ON FEBRUARY 28, WOODS CAME out swinging.

"We had no knowledge of what the Oregon authorities had or possessed until Your Honor issued subpoenas. That's how we started getting all this information. I don't understand why we are here, then, for a ruling on a procedural objection, when the state had one month, two months, three months, four months, five months to file any procedural objections."

"Let me give you the answer," Judge Parker interrupted. "I can give you an answer to that right now."

"Sure."

"Because they are lazy and disorganized."

Parker hurled the insult with a raised eyebrow. Donna Andrieu stiffened.

"In other words, Mr. Woods, I don't think it was any sinister intent on behalf of the DA's office. But in my experience, that has been the hallmark of the post-Connick DA's office. Continuances, postponements, slothfulness, laziness, no attention to deadlines. Okay?"

"Your Honor, I'm a Connick protégé as well as you are. When

Your Honor gives somebody five chances to respond and they don't . . ."

"Just because it's set for a ruling doesn't mean I'm going to rule in the state's favor," Parker insisted.

"Should you rule in our favor, Your Honor, can we set a date for a merits hearing?" Woods asked.

"I need to hear from the state first."

"Very well, I'll tender."

Andrieu shot to her feet.

"I would like to address comments that were made by Your Honor and Mr. Woods with regard to the state because they are reflections of me personally," she said, seething. "I just want the record to reflect that I am not lazy and sloth-like. I have several post-conviction relief applications that I respond to, in every section of court, and I have a mandate that I and my staff adhere to: that we don't file motions to continue."

"What?" Parker looked ready to launch out of his seat and onto the courtroom floor. "How can you sit there . . ."

"My staff—"

". . . with a straight face—"

"Your Honor, my staff does not—"

"*How on earth can you sit there with a straight face and tell a whopper like that?*"

Andrieu paused. "When this case came to my division, we handled it."

"All right, all right. Let's cut to the chase." Parker turned to the defense. "Mr. Woods—"

"The chase is—" Andrieu cut in.

"If you interrupt me again—*if you interrupt me again*—you are going to be in trouble. Prove to me right now that Mr. Woods is not accurate when he says you've had five months!"

But Andrieu wouldn't be cowed. She reiterated that the information in question was not newly discovered.

"Lower your voice!" Parker chastised her.

"I'm sorry. Mr. Duncan raised on his direct appeal an issue with regard to that police report. The fact that this court—several years later—subpoenaed it doesn't mean that the record wasn't known to counsel before that. It is simply not newly discovered."

"That's what this case all boils down to." Parker's tone softened. "930.8, paragraph A. Not how many times a witness identified somebody. Not what Bruce Whittaker argued at trial. What's relevant is this: Did the petitioner prove, or the state admit, the facts upon which the claim is predicated were not known to the petitioner or his attorney?"

"Your Honor," Woods tried.

"In other words, Mr. Woods, no matter how many deadlines the state has missed, the court has to follow the letter of the law."

"Can I . . . ?"

"I'm listening."

"I can prove that, based upon discovery, that until we got a chance to look at that police report, we would have no way of knowing that there was exculpatory material in it. Those police reports from another jurisdiction were not subject to discovery by the defense. The State of Louisiana failed to comply with the mandate of *Brady v. Maryland* and turn over exculpatory evidence in this case. Your Honor has already said that the state waives procedural objections, and I'm sure you were aware of 930.8 when you said that. So, now it's time to get to the substantive merits of the case and decide whether there were such blatant *Brady* violations as to warrant a new trial. Thank you."

"Let me review the record overnight and we'll come back here tomorrow so I can rule. I need time to read through all this," said the judge.

THE HEARING THE FOLLOWING MORNING NEVER HAPPENED. JUDGE Parker was busy with another matter and rescheduled his ruling for two months later.

On the afternoon of March 6, Calvin received an instruction to call Emily Maw.

He clutched the phone to his ear, hoping they had at least secured an evidentiary hearing.

"Calvin." Emily was matter-of-fact. "Court just finished. I've just gotten back to the office."

"How was it?"

"Parker denied the petition, I'm afraid. But his reasoning was riddled with errors, including the failure to exercise due diligence."

Hearing this tempered Calvin's disappointment. The court couldn't rely on due diligence to deny his *Brady* claims; that argument was based on an old case the Louisiana Supreme Court had since overruled. Besides, Parker had already barred the state from raising procedural objections. The appellate court would surely reverse him.

Calvin shared this reasoning with Emily, and she agreed they had plenty to work with on appeal. She promised to send him the transcript as soon as it was available.

Several days later, the transcript of the hearing arrived in the mail. Calvin picked up the packet from the front office and took it to the Camp F law library, where he settled at a desk to read.

The hearing unfolded as he expected—until the final page.

When he saw Judge Parker's reasons for denying his petition, a passage from the Book of Job came to mind:

What I feared has come upon me; what I dreaded has happened to me.

His heart pounded as he read on.

"The first time the defendant's lawyer talked to me about this case, he told me that he knew about these police reports, but I let you go out and subpoena them anyway," Parker told Woods. "Whoever represented the man at the trial level could have done all these things long before 2002, which is, I think, when you filed the original application."

"2004," Woods corrected him.

"2004. Therefore, for the reasons I've cited today, the application for post-conviction relief and any supplements filed thereto, thereafter, is hereby denied—and I note your objection and you can take as long as you'd like to seek appellate review. Y'all have a good day."

Calvin stared at the page in disbelief.

Parker had made a factual finding on the record that Calvin's lawyers knew about the existence of Reed's report long before Calvin raised it as a *Brady* claim—an assertion that was wholly untrue. If the report wasn't considered "new," a terrible domino effect would ensue: Under AEDPA, the federal courts would count every day since Calvin's lawyers first discovered Reed's report against his one-year clock to file a habeas petition. Now it would be considered untimely, meaning the federal courts wouldn't even examine whether the state suppressed the report or whether Calvin deserved a new trial. Instead, the *Brady* claim based on Reed's report would be procedurally barred.

Calvin stood up from his desk. The ground beneath him lost its pull. He steadied himself on a chair as his anger gave way to panic.

He heard Job again: *What I feared has come upon me . . .*

As he moved slowly toward the door, the law library blurred around him. He needed to get to the dorm and lie down.

Outside the Education Building, Calvin noticed a group of men huddled at a table behind Dorm One. They were familiar faces: Sweet Tooth, Ribbet, Big Dugger, John Brown, and others he had known well over the years. They waved him over, and he waved back, his dizziness starting to subside. Thrilled to see them after all this time, he made his way toward the table.

But as he drew closer, the peculiarity of the scene came into focus.

All of these men are dead, he realized.

Yet there they were, still smiling, oblivious to his confusion.

I must be dead, he thought.

Far from scaring him, the revelation flooded Calvin with warmth. He could finally let go of his struggles and spend his days with his friends.

"How y'all doin'?" he started to say, but when he opened his mouth, the men vanished.

The table was empty again.

Calvin stood frozen, trying to comprehend what was happening.

Maybe he was coming undone.

He resumed his shuffle toward the dormitory, now desperate to lie down.

He woke the next morning still gripped by panic, shame creeping in. What would his students say when they found out the expert on procedural bars had been procedurally barred?

Thoughts tormented him in a singular, relentless voice.

How could you let this happen? You weren't even in the courtroom when Parker lit your case on fire. And your lawyers let it burn. You should never have handed your case over like that. You let this happen.

By the time he spoke to Emily, he'd worked himself into a frenzy.

"If you knew they were talking about the wrong police report, why didn't anyone say anything? The judge made a factual finding that Reed's report wasn't new under 930.8. Now I'm time barred. Not just in state court, but federal, too."

Emily tried to calm him. "Calvin, we knew Parker was making a mess of his ruling. There was no correcting him; it was better to let him make his own mistakes. We'll make sure the Fourth Circuit has the complete picture."

"But now I'm relying on the appellate court to overrule a trial judge's factual finding. What are the chances of that? I'm out of it now! I'm out of the game."

"Calvin, I know this isn't where we wanted to be. But Parker had made up his mind. It's hard to appreciate from the transcript alone the calculations we were having to make. I promise you, we will make crystal clear to the Fourth Circuit that Parker's factual finding was based on a blatant misreading of the evidence."

Calvin had been turned down by the state appellate court too many times to believe their arguments would prevail. He hung up the phone, still anxious.

In the weeks that followed, he scoured the record for anything that might pull him out of the hole he was in. He pored over Parker's denials and dissected his legal team's performance, festering in one's arrogance and the other's silences.

The more Calvin read through his case, the more convinced he became that his attorneys had mishandled key aspects. He worried they hadn't properly raised the issue of the arrest warrant that Detective Demma faxed to the Oregon deputies, failing to preserve it for appeal.

"That is not gonna suffice," he told them during a legal visit. "I may not know how to read or write, but I know how to properly raise a claim under the procedural bar rules, and I'm telling you, a footnote in a reply won't cut it."

Even small mistakes could cost him his freedom. Wouldn't it be better to make his own decisions if he was the one who had to live with the consequences? He wanted to part ways with his legal team and go it alone.

You knew better than to leave your case in the hands of other people. You know not to trust nobody. You can only count on yourself.

Back in the dormitory, he searched his case yet again. If only he could find a new issue to work with, an angle to find his way in. His greatest skill as an inmate counsel had always been spotting legal issues others didn't see. But now, his mind wasn't working properly; there was a block he couldn't shift.

He returned his files to his lockerbox, defeated, and lay back on his cot.

They might as well put me in a pine box and bury me at Point Lookout, he thought. I'm as good as dead.

2009

Calvin was working on the case of a friend named Charles Conway when he noticed familiar handwriting in Conway's file. It was the same handwriting Calvin had seen in the prosecution's old notes from before his trial, where an assistant district attorney suggested the state offer him a plea. The note had concluded that it would be "very difficult to get a conviction" based on the evidence they had against him.

Calvin learned from Conway that the handwriting belonged to the defense attorney representing him in post-conviction. The attorney had worked as a prosecutor in the Orleans Parish DA's office at the time Calvin was indicted.

Calvin alerted Emily, and IPNO collected an affidavit from the former prosecutor. In it, he explained that he'd written the note to his supervisor after hearing Kristie Emberling's and Detective Demma's testimonies before the grand jury. He felt the disparities in their accounts were too inconsistent for the state to rely on at trial.

Calvin's legal team included the affidavit in their writ to the Fourth Circuit. In addition, they pointed out thirty-two factual inaccuracies that Judge Parker had relied on to dismiss Calvin's postconviction application, asking the court to send the case back for an evidentiary hearing.

CALVIN HAD BEEN LOSING WEIGHT FOR MONTHS NOW AND WAS getting very little sleep. He was still reading his case obsessively, searching for potential legal claims he might have overlooked.

He wrote despondent letters to Emily Bolton in England, telling her he missed her the way he had missed his mother as a child.

"Stop reading your case, Calvin. It's making you depressed," she counseled. "Just put it down and wait for the Fourth Circuit to rule."

But when the court's decision finally came, it was the death knell Calvin had feared. The appellate court denied his writ.

His lawyers would petition the Louisiana Supreme Court, but there was little reason to think it would rule differently.

Calvin spiraled, feeling himself slipping into a nether space, detached from the people around him and his work as an inmate counsel. The fog he'd endured in years past now felt suffocating.

He decided that his only recourse was to challenge Judge Parker directly. He filed complaints with the Judiciary Commission of Louisiana and the US Department of Justice, arguing that Parker had committed serious malfeasance by failing to recuse himself from Calvin's case and others like it.

He also filed a pro se writ with the Louisiana Supreme Court, in addition to the one already submitted by IPNO. He knew what was happening wasn't their fault, but he was determined to present his own arguments and take charge of his case.

One morning, he was called to the A-Building for a legal visit. When he arrived, he saw that his entire legal team—attorneys and investigators—had come to the prison to see him. They implored him to hang on, their voices filled with concern. For their sake, he reassured them he would keep fighting, but he couldn't put faith in his own words. The worry on their faces struck fear into his heart. He knew he was in trouble. The God of Hope was leaving him.

The days were filled with uncertainty and half-dreaming. Calvin found his mind wandering into old memories from the past, rooms and places he didn't want to go.

He saw Aunt Nema throwing chicken on the vinyl floor of the kitchen, yelling, "Here, dogs! Here, dogs!" while Mamie wailed for their mother.

And the brown boots on the feet of a murdered man he once watched being pulled from the forest behind Almonaster Avenue by police, swamp water pouring from the bullet holes in his chest.

The memories were accompanied by an old sense of foreboding— tremors of a coming disaster. The voice in his head was relentless.

Ain't nobody comin'. Ain't no rescue comin'. You don't have the pleasure of depending on other people. Not your lawyers. Not your family. Nobody. This is how it's always been. It's how it's always gonna be. You're always gonna be on your own.

The Clouet Street curse had followed him to Oregon and then dragged him all the way here, a cosmic debt he could never repay. Uncle Trim had always said there was no escape. Perhaps he was better off making peace with it. Wasn't this where his life had always been headed?

Angola . . . When I was one, one, one . . .

His mind drifted back to the faces of his dead friends behind the dormitory. There was a reason they were urging him to join them— they knew he'd find rest where they were.

He had always believed that if he helped others, God would meet him halfway. But what if God didn't show up? What if the law he'd devoted himself to learning and teaching all these years turned out to be the very thing that killed him?

He had waited on God long enough.

THE NEXT TIME CALVIN MADE HIS ROUNDS, HE STOPPED AT THE CELL of an old friend on CCR. Years before, the man had poured battery acid on the tops of his feet as a protest against working in the fields. His scars were still bright red. Calvin shuddered at the sight.

He had seen people kill themselves many ways in prison. Suicide was more frequent and more public there than in the free world.

The longer he considered the possibility, the more his mind hardened around it. If battery acid could do that to your feet, what could it do to your heart?

Calvin began to make a plan.

In the days that followed, he bought a pack of AA batteries and a pack of cigarettes from the commissary. Then he found an acquaintance who shot heroin and traded the cigarettes for a syringe. He wrapped the syringe and the batteries in a cloth and tucked them away in his lockerbox.

He considered doing it at night in the dormitory, but his cot didn't offer any privacy. It would be safer to do it in his office at the law library after the callouts had left for the evening.

Once the plan was set, he experienced a profound sense of calm. His fatigue lifted, and he threw himself back into his work, enjoying playful banter with the guys on his rounds.

When the day came, he made his final rounds at CCR and tidied his belongings in the dormitory before returning to Camp F for chow. He paid no attention to the men at the table across from him or the stewed turkey on his plate. He wasn't worried about the people he was leaving behind. His thoughts were with the friends he would soon meet again.

When he finished his meal, Calvin returned to the dormitory to assemble the syringe. Then he hid it inside a legal writing book and walked to his office, placing the book on a shelf.

Once the callouts and the other inmate counsels had left for the evening, Calvin pulled the book down and opened it to the back where the syringe lay. He stared for a moment, then reached for it— just as a guard called his name.

"Duncan, there's mail for you."

Heat rushed through him as he hurried to return the book to the shelf. He made his way to the front office, gave his name to the woman at the counter, and watched as she checked his letter for contraband.

"Legal mail," she said, handing it to him.

He recognized Emily Maw's handwriting on the envelope.

Back in his office, Calvin sat down at his desk and opened the letter. It was only a few lines long.

Calvin, I know how difficult things are right now. But I promise they will change. We're all at the office working around the clock on your case. We're doing everything we can to win, and we will. I need you to hang on for me. We're going to get through this, but you must hang on.

A raw ache swelled in his throat.

All his life, he had longed for someone to fight for him, and now he had an entire team of lawyers and investigators dedicated to his freedom. The thought of leaving them this way—of crushing them—was unbearable. He struggled to suppress the rising panic in his chest as he tried to organize his thoughts. He needed a moment to breathe.

A student from his law class had asked for help with a child custody dispute, but Calvin had been too distracted by his case to make any progress. He decided to pull together some research to help the student along while he digested Emily's note.

As he made his way to the court reporters, he glanced over the shelves. He knew the name and location of nearly every book in the law library. How many hours had he spent here, studying and working on cases? His very first motion had been a request to possess a single book. Now, twenty years since Mrs. Rabalais hired him, he was the longest-serving inmate counsel in the prison. He had lived his life among these books. He knew them better than his family.

He found the court reporter he was looking for and marked a citation on a scrap of paper. Then he searched for another. Before long, he was absorbed in the task.

It was after midnight when he finally returned to his dorm.

Too tired to change his clothes, he collapsed onto his cot.

The low rasp of old-timers chatting in the dayroom helped ease him toward sleep.

I've been through hell all my life and made it this far, he thought. Why not at least see where I end up?

He drifted off then, finding the first deep rest he'd had in months.

Back in the Education Building, tucked inside a book, the syringe lay undisturbed in an old piece of cloth.

IN AN EFFORT TO LIFT HIS SPIRITS, CALVIN'S ATTORNEYS ARRANGED regular visits to the prison. Ora, an intern from Michigan, began coming, and he soon looked forward to their meetings. Her father was a rabbi, and she shared Calvin's interest in Scripture. They discussed stories and figures that inspired him, like Esther, who risked her life to defend her people. Calvin shared how Mwalimu had once urged him to act boldly at the mental health unit, much like Mordecai had urged Esther.

"What can I send you as a gift for Christmas?" she asked in a letter that December.

Calvin had one request.

"Could you ask if an elder of your synagogue would say the kind of prayer for me that a father says while touching the head of his son? I'm told that if a father blesses his son in prayer, then everything the father has blessed the son with comes true in the life of the son. My father never got to bless me, and I'm quite sure his father never blessed him. My father once did time in this same penitentiary that I'm in. I hope that the curse that was on him—and now on me—will be the last curse to follow my family."

Ora's response was humbling.

"I passed your request on to my father," she wrote. "And he gave you this blessing:

Y'varekh'kha ADONAI v'yishmerekha. Ya'er ADONAI panav eleikha vichunekka. Yissa ADONAI panav eleikha v'yasem l'kha shalom.

May God bless you and keep you. May God cause the divine light to shine upon you and be gracious to you. May God turn his face toward you, and grant you peace.

As Calvin read the rabbi's words, they flowed over him like water, seeping into the cracks of his despair and loosening its grip.

He sent Ora a reply. "Please, tell your father I said thank you."

2010

On a Friday afternoon in January 2010, Calvin received a message to call his lawyers. He waited impatiently to the sound of a New Orleans jazz tune while the receptionist put him through.

"Calvin?" Emily asked hurriedly.

"Yes, they said you put in a call—"

"Calvin, we won! The Louisiana Supreme Court is remanding your case for an evidentiary hearing."

"What?"

"The court reversed Judge Parker's ruling that your petition was untimely filed under 930.8."

He pressed the phone to his ear, trying to hear above the noise in the dorm.

"They reversed Parker?"

"Yes, and it's a terrific ruling, Calvin," said Emily. "Here, let me read it to you:

"The district court's judgment denying relator's post-conviction application as time barred under art. 930.8(A) is vacated, and the district court is directed to hold an evidentiary hearing only as it relates to relator's recent discovery of a police report authored by Lieutenant Roy Reed and the alleged suppression by the state of evidence relating to possible criminal activity of witness, Detective Loren Peterson. Unless the state establishes that events not under its control have prejudiced its ability to 'respond to, negate, or rebut' the newly discovered evidence . . . the district court is instructed to consider whether the State's failure to disclose the material undermines confidence in the outcome of the trial in violation of *Brady v. Maryland* and its progeny. In addition, although relator apparently failed to raise this issue in the district court in conjunction with his application, and 'the general rule is that appellate courts will not consider issues raised for the first time,' in the interest of judicial economy, the district court is also instructed to determine whether an arrest warrant, signed by Detective Demma of the New Orleans Police Department, which listed the race and gender of the victim, constitutes newly discovered evidence which requires consideration on the merits 'as facts . . . not known to the petitioner or his attorney under 930.8.' In all other respects, relator's application is denied."

Calvin listened in stunned silence. It was a perfect ruling. Even the arrest warrant, which the court acknowledged wasn't properly raised, was getting the green light.

"So, they have to consider the arrest warrant, Peterson's FBI investigation, and Reed's report?" he clarified.

"Yes," said Emily. "And this time, Parker must rule on the merits."

"This is amazing! Emily, this is . . ."

She finished his sentence. "This is how we're going to get you home."

WHEN THE PARTIES RECONVENED IN APRIL, JUDGE PARKER AND Donna Andrieu were recalcitrant.

"Those three pieces of evidence sent back by the Louisiana Supreme Court are not newly discovered," Andrieu insisted.

"For someone to come along thirty years later and say 'we didn't have these things,' and I'm supposed to believe that, and I'm also supposed to believe that in thirty years nobody bothered to take a look for these things, which were in the public record at all times pertinent hereto—that's one of the difficulties I have with this situation," Parker agreed. "There's been absolutely no credible evidence whatsoever that that police report and arrest warrant were not turned over by the police."

Calvin's lawyers said little, waiting to see if Parker would at least hold an evidentiary hearing. At last, he set a date for May.

"He's setting it up to ignore the Louisiana Supreme Court," Calvin told Emily.

"I think we ought to talk to Donna Andrieu and see if she will come to the table on this," Emily suggested. "We need to back off Parker for a while. Perhaps we can convince the DA's office that this evidence is newly discovered, and get them to stipulate to that in court."

"All right," Calvin agreed. "Let's see what she says."

CALVIN RETURNED TO HIS LAW CLASS THAT WEEKEND, GRATEFUL FOR the distraction. The class remained the highlight of his job, anchoring all his other work. It served as a training ground for new inmate counsels, dissected and explained new laws and court cases affecting the population, and coordinated efforts to file motions on emerging legal issues. These days, Calvin relied on his students as much as they relied on him. Some, like Buff and AC, were now seasoned inmate counsels. If he ever did get out of Angola, he knew they would carry on the work in his place.

One Saturday, Calvin was coming through the A-Building at the Main Prison after teaching class when a friend named Pernell Brown emerged from the hallway.

Pernell and his partner, Keisha, had just been married in a nearby conference room, one of twenty weddings at Angola that year.

"Calvin, hey!" Keisha cried.

"Congratulations." Calvin hurried over to hug them.

"How you been, baby?" she asked. Pernell stood beside her, his face aglow.

"Oh, I'm doin' all right." He was a bad liar. The prospect of Judge Parker finding yet another way to crush him kept him in a constant state of anxiety.

Keisha seemed to sense his troubles.

"Listen, you keep your head up," she said. "You 'bout to come home."

Calvin looked at her, puzzled. "What do you know about me coming home?"

He'd never once spoken to Pernell about his case.

Keisha's eyes flashed. "I see things in the future. And I'm tellin' you, Calvin, you about to come home."

WEEKS LATER, CALVIN RECEIVED WORD FROM A LIEUTENANT TO CALL his lawyers.

"Calvin, I just got off the phone with Donna Andrieu," said Emily. "The DA is offering you a deal."

Adrenaline spiked in his veins. "A deal?"

"They want to know if you would be willing to take an *Alford* plea to time served."

Calvin didn't hesitate. "Take it!" he shouted into the phone. "Take it! Take it! Damn, what happened?"

Hearing the excitement in his voice, Emily broke into a laugh. "At first I thought our most recent pleading convinced them. When I saw Donna Andrieu, she offered to stipulate that Reed's report was newly discovered evidence. She agreed that the Oregon sheriffs were crooks. But that's not where the plea came from. Apparently, the district attorney's first assistant called the prison to ask about your record. He discovered that you've only had three write-ups in all your time at Angola. Legal Programs and the wardens spoke very highly of you. He thinks you deserve to get out."

Calvin clung to the phone, barely believing the turn of events.

"You should be really proud of yourself," said Emily. "It's because of the person you are and the work you've done that they're willing to do this, Calvin."

THE STATE OFFERED A DEAL OF TWENTY-ONE YEARS FOR MAN-slaughter and forty-nine years for attempted armed robbery, which would allow Calvin to be released immediately, based on the law at the time of his conviction. The DA also agreed to let him take an *Alford* plea, a special plea agreement where the defendant didn't admit guilt but acknowledged that pleading guilty was in their best interest.

At this stage, pleading guilty to a crime he didn't commit was the least of Calvin's concerns.

Calvin wasn't supposed to talk about the deal with anyone outside his legal team, but he couldn't help sharing the news with one person.

"I'm so happy for you!" Mrs. Rabalais cried when he found her at the museum. "You are going to do so well on the outside. What are your plans?"

He told her he hoped to work at one of the public interest law offices in New Orleans as a paralegal.

"Do you have any advice for when I get into the workplace?" he asked.

Mrs. Rabalais thought for a second. "Two things. Don't get in romantic relationships with coworkers. And always dress professionally. I don't *ever* want to see you wearing a short-sleeved shirt under a sports jacket."

DESPITE THE PROMISING NEWS, SEVERAL SETBACKS DELAYED CALVIN from going to court. First, he was brought down from Angola for a status hearing, only to learn that the judge was out sick.

Later that week, when Calvin's attorneys requested a video conference, the judge's clerk told Emily she couldn't find the key to the filing cabinet holding Calvin's file. With the judge heading on vacation, court wouldn't resume until January.

"You ever get the feeling that someone's avoiding you?" Calvin joked.

"I'm so sorry that you have to spend another Christmas up there," said Emily. "I hoped we could get you home sooner than this."

The following morning, Emily and Donna Andrieu made one last attempt to get Calvin on the judge's docket, but when the judge failed to appear, Calvin was again returned to Angola.

When he arrived back at Camp F, a visitor was waiting. It was Tyrone Smith, his friend who had left the penitentiary in the early 1990s.

"I came to see if I can help you with anything when you get out," Tyrone said.

Calvin thought for a moment. "Mostly just advice. What should I expect out there?"

Tyrone shook his head. "The world has changed. You're no match for it, man. Be careful who you spend your time with. Even if they're family or old friends from the neighborhood, you gotta be careful not to end up in a bad situation."

Calvin considered this for a moment. "Well, that's how I survived this crazy place for twenty-eight years."

They laughed.

"What about something you need?" Tyrone asked.

Calvin pointed to the owllike frames perched on his nose. "A new pair of eyeglasses."

Tyrone said he would deposit sixty dollars into Calvin's account. Calvin gripped his hand and pulled him in for a quick hug.

"Good luck, brah," said Tyrone as they parted. "I'll see you on the other side."

IN MID-DECEMBER, EMILY PUT IN A CALL FOR CALVIN.

"Donna Andrieu got you on Parker's docket tomorrow. She heard that the judge was coming in to get some last-minute housekeeping out of the way before he leaves for vacation, and she cornered his clerk. Things have certainly gotten strange around here," Emily said with a laugh. "The DA is practically forcing you onto the docket. The judge won't know we're coming until he gets to court. I don't think he can avoid us this time."

The next morning, just before nine, Parker emerged from his chambers to take the bench. Calvin was already seated in the jury box off to one side. He hoped Parker wouldn't notice him.

Once the docket cleared for the day, Calvin was brought to sit beside Emily at the counsel table.

When the clerk called his case, Donna Andrieu pummeled her way in like a boxer who had heard the bell.

"Your Honor, the state is prepared to make a joint stipulation today that there is newly discovered evidence in this case. In light of that new evidence, including evidence that indicates the Oregon authorities withheld and distorted certain information, the state has offered Mr. Duncan an *Alford* plea to time served. Mr. Duncan, through counsel, has indicated that he would accept this plea. We are ready to move forward, Your Honor."

Parker stared at her. "You want me to put in an *Alford* plea on a first-degree murder charge?"

"Yes, Your Honor."

He leaned over the bench. "You want me to do anything of the sort, you need your boss to come in here and ask for it. I'm not even considering it before I see Mr. Leon Cannizzaro in my courtroom."

Donna Andrieu shot the judge a withering look before charging down the aisle. Emily followed her out.

A wooden clock with gold-plated numbers ticked on the wall behind the bench. Calvin watched its hands move, his own clenched tightly in his lap.

9:20.

9:30.

Each time the courtroom doors swung open, he hoped he would see the DA walk through.

9:40.

He heard a male voice in the hallway. Finally, the district attorney, Leon Cannizzaro, appeared at the door.

Cannizzaro followed Donna Andrieu into the jury room to talk privately. Emily sat in a row nearby, eyes locked on the papers in her lap.

The doors opened again. This time, it was Laurie White. She had recently been elected judge in another section of the courthouse.

Calvin greeted her with a grateful smile.

"Emily told me what's going on in here. How are you holding up?" she asked.

"I'm okay."

She turned to the bench and strode past the minute clerk toward the judge's chambers. Seeing her coming, Parker left the courtroom to receive her privately.

Calvin heard Donna Andrieu call Emily's name. He half turned to watch their movements in his periphery. He didn't know what was being negotiated, only that each second that passed made it less likely that he'd be able to take the plea before Parker left town.

Moments later, Laurie White emerged from the judge's chambers. She gave Calvin a quick nod on her way back down the aisle.

Emily mouthed a thank-you as Laurie left the room. Then she took a seat by Calvin, eyes ablaze.

"The DA doesn't want to offer the *Alford* plea," she said. "I don't know what changed."

Calvin rubbed his forehead. "Is he still offering me a plea to time served?"

Emily nodded.

"Then I'll take it. *Alford* or no *Alford*, I want to leave through those doors."

"Okay, I'll let them know."

She left to find Andrieu.

When Judge Parker reappeared, the DA approached the bench and spoke with him for several minutes before exiting the courtroom.

Emily returned to Calvin with a plea waiver form. He read it over. He would be sentenced to forty-nine years, with the understanding that, under the laws in effect at the time of his arrest, he would receive a 50 percent reduction for good behavior and be immediately released.

He was close now. He could feel it.

Donna Andrieu took her place at the prosecution table, joint stipulation in hand.

"All right." Parker was suddenly passive. "I've spoken to Mr. Cannizzaro. I understand that a plea of guilty is going to be entered by the defendant pursuant to a written plea agreement."

"Yes, Your Honor," said Andrieu.

Emily motioned for Calvin to stand. He pushed himself up in his shackles, heart pounding.

The clerk asked him to raise his right hand.

"I will tell the whole truth and nothing but the truth," he repeated.

Parker handed the papers back to the clerk and rose from his seat. "I'll be back in a minute."

He left for his chambers again. Emily and Calvin waited on tenterhooks, too afraid to move.

Donna Andrieu finished preparing the bill of information, which would be filed with the plea agreement to close the case.

The minute clerk shuffled through a stack of papers, then turned to look through a pile of files on Judge Parker's desk.

When the judge returned to the bench, she addressed him in a whisper.

"The court cannot locate the case file at this time," Parker announced to the room. "Now, I'm supposed to be leaving here for my vacation, and the time for dealing with this matter has come and gone."

"But Your Honor, we've got to finish this case," Andrieu pleaded.

"I don't give a hoot about this case," he replied sharply. "And I'm adjourning this matter until January."

With that, he left.

"Unbelievable." Emily exhaled wearily.

Donna Andrieu slapped the bill of information down on the tabletop, her face stiff with fury.

Corrections officers approached to escort Calvin back to the prison van.

"We're going to do whatever it takes to get you on the first docket of the New Year," Emily promised. "This is absolutely wretched, Calvin. And over the holidays, too . . ."

"I'll be all right," he assured her.

He headed toward the door, flanked by security. In truth, he didn't feel all right at all.

"YOU CAN SEE THE END OF THE TUNNEL NOW," EMILY WROTE HIM IN the days leading up to Christmas. "Just keep looking at it and don't give up. You have achieved this yourself, and you must pause to give yourself credit for where you've got to. . . . Stay strong, stay focused and DO NOT GET A WRITE UP while we're waiting!"

Staying strong was easier said than done. Calvin agonized over what might go wrong between now and January. If Judge Parker was determined to derail the plea agreement, he would find a way.

Calvin spent his days immersed in movies and music, trying to escape his own thoughts.

One evening, the familiar melody of his favorite Louis Armstrong song came over the radio. Reclining on his cot, headphones blocking out the noise of the dorm, he let the music wash over him.

Louis Armstrong's music was more than a passing comfort; like Calvin's favorite novels, it had been an enduring source of hope. Armstrong, too, had discovered his calling in an unlikely place—the New Orleans Colored Waifs Home for Boys—where, at age eleven, he was introduced to the cornet. Though Armstrong lived in a time marked by poverty, war, and racial segregation, Calvin admired that he chose to sing of beauty.

I see skies of blue, and clouds of white
The bright blessed day, the dark sacred night

And I think to myself
What a wonderful world . . .

Closing his eyes, Calvin contemplated how far he had come and how close he was to the finish. Emily was right—he needed only to hold on. As the song lingered on its final note, he thought of Ora's father's blessing. Perhaps the day was coming when he would finally be free.

CALVIN AND HIS LEGAL TEAM RETURNED TO COURT ON JANUARY 7, 2011.

Judge Parker's face hardened when he saw Emily and Donna Andrieu waiting, but his voice contained none of its usual acidity.

"When this case was last before the court, I had the opportunity to discuss this with District Attorney Cannizzaro, who recommended a plea bargain as a resolution, and I will abide by his request."

The minute clerk rose from her chair to swear Calvin in.

"Before I can accept your plea, I must be convinced that you understand your rights," Parker said.

It was the first time the judge had ever addressed Calvin directly. All he could think of were the tongue-lashings Parker gave anyone who didn't address him as "sir." Even the smallest slip could throw the plea into jeopardy.

"First, you have a right to trial by judge or jury, but when you enter this plea of guilty, you waive that right. Do you understand that?"

"Yes, sir."

"You are presumed innocent until the district attorney proves you're guilty beyond a reasonable doubt; but when you enter this plea of guilty, you waive that right. Do you understand that?"

"Yes, sir."

"Have you been forced, coerced, or threatened to enter this plea?"

"No, sir."

Calvin responded to each question with absolute focus, a tight-rope walker within reach of the ledge.

"Do you understand all of the possible legal consequences of pleading guilty and wish to plead guilty at this time because you are, in fact, guilty of the offense or offenses in the bill of information as amended?"

"Yes, sir."

It was the only time he would ever lie under oath.

"This plea is accepted by the court as having been knowingly and voluntarily made. Does counsel waive all sentencing delays?" Parker asked.

"Yes, Your Honor," Emily replied.

"All right. As to count one, I sentence you to serve twenty-one years at hard labor in the custody of the Louisiana Department of Corrections . . ."

A tumble of memories, like shooting ribbons of light, suddenly flooded the space behind Calvin's eyes. He remembered Uncle Trim making him eggs in the moonlit kitchen on Clouet Street, Mamie waving him off to the West Coast in his cousin's car, the mountains towering outside his dormitory window at Timber Lake, and the wildflowers lining the dirt road the day the police took him away. He recalled the desks in the back of the Main Prison law library, where he strategized cases and campaigns with Checo and Norris, and the yard at Camp F, where he walked with Alvin to discuss the law. He thought of Laurie White's first visit in the A-Building, and Emily Bolton's final goodbye at the gate.

In the eye of this horrific storm, he had stumbled upon immeasurable goodness: the bright blessed day, the dark sacred night.

"I sentence you to serve forty-nine years in the custody of the Louisiana Department of Corrections, to run concurrently with the sentence in count one and with full credit for time you have already served."

Relief flooded Emily's face, letting Calvin know that it was done. He let out a shallow breath.

"If there's nothing else?" Parker asked Donna Andrieu.

The prosecutor shook her head.

"Good." Parker planted the plea document face down on his desk and turned to his minute clerk. "This case is now closed."

THE TRANSPORT VAN CAME TO A STOP AT THE PRISON'S FRONT GATE. Calvin opened the door and stepped out, gripping a yellow envelope containing his discharge papers and a ten-dollar check from the State of Louisiana. A chorus of cheers reached his ears, and he saw his legal team waiting eagerly for him on the other side of the exit.

He took a step in their direction, only to realize that something was amiss. He looked down to find the sole of his shoe detaching from the upper. His lawyer shoes, stored in his lockerbox for twenty-five years for this day, had succumbed to dry rot.

Giggling at the absurdity, he pressed on, the sole slapping loudly against the pavement. Only when it pulled away completely did he relent and take the shoe off.

Straightening up, he paused, taking in the sight of the forested road ahead and the huddle of faces waiting to receive him. Then he limped, finally, into the free world, clutching the crumbling shoe in his hand.

Part 5

—⊣|⊢—

And the mists had all solemnly risen now,
and the world lay spread before me.

PIP,
GREAT EXPECTATIONS

2011

The world beyond Angola's barbed-wire fences and watchtowers
was both familiar and new to Calvin. New Orleans's rhythm, its
sights and sounds, were echoes of a past he had lived, but the opportunities it now presented were profoundly different.

His friends welcomed him as a long-awaited brother, and he was
in awe of how seamlessly they had carried their passions from prison
into their lives outside. Alvin owned multiple properties and was renovating them one by one. Tyrone was pastoring a community church
that welcomed people returning from prison. Norris was running
Voice of the Experienced (VOTE), an extension of the Angola Special Civics Project, securing voting rights for formerly incarcerated
Louisianans, while Checo led its Baton Rouge chapter. Wilbert was
publishing a book. When they asked Calvin about his plans, no one
was surprised by his answer: he intended to do legal work.

His relationships in the legal community immediately earned

him two job offers. Tracy, a lawyer who had worked on Calvin's case when she was an intern at IPNO, provided him a mother-in-law unit beside her Uptown home, rent-free, for a year. The unit's proximity to Tulane University was a happy benefit. Just three days after his release, Calvin enrolled in a bachelor's degree program in legal studies.

One afternoon at Tulane Law School, Calvin was walking the halls with Katherine Mattes, the lawyer he'd befriended at Angola, who had since become a law professor. She paused to introduce him to someone coming from the other direction.

Calvin immediately recognized Todd Stamps, who pulled him into a bear hug, his square glasses bouncing on his nose. "Man, it must've been thirty years!"

Noticing Katherine's confusion, Todd recounted the story of Calvin's long-ago visit to the law library.

"No one else wanted to help them because they were prisoners. I was the only one willing to load the books." His mouth twitched upward as he turned back to Calvin. "I remember you kept talking about McDonald's. You couldn't wait to eat a Big Mac."

Katherine explained that Calvin was an expert in post-conviction law and was helping teach a class for her students.

"I want you to come and meet my sons sometime, man," said Todd. "They need to see that things like this are possible."

DAYS AFTER CALVIN BEGAN HIS UNIVERSITY CAREER, HE ALSO JOINED the law office where I worked, which handled appeals for people on Louisiana's death row. Our offices were across the hall from each other, and even in passing, I could see how happy he was to be helping his old friends again from his new post. I had moved to Louisiana only two years earlier, and while I knew Calvin was a legend in the criminal defense community, it wasn't until we began taking daily walks that I learned snippets of his story.

The first time we visited a coffee shop down the street, Calvin glanced at the blackboard crowded with menu items and turned to me with a shrug. "I read in Wilbert's book that when you come home from prison, not to make any decisions you don't have to. So I'm gonna let you order me something—I don't care what it is."

I asked Calvin about his plans. He said he was forty-eight with the mind of a nineteen-year-old, and his life was just beginning. Though we saw the city through different eyes, I related to his tales of unexpected joys and unwelcome horrors as he slowly rediscovered New Orleans. He said Angola had left him at rock bottom, and he felt like Pip in *Great Expectations*, working his way out of the mist.

Another day, he pointed out a hotel on Poydras Street where he'd worked as a teenager, showing me the side door where he'd sneaked in people living on the street to spend the night in unoccupied rooms. His manager nearly fired him upon finding out, but, at the last minute, decided to turn a blind eye. I found myself wondering what had driven Calvin, at just seventeen, to risk his job for the sake of others. What early sense of justice had made him willing to defy the rules to help those in need?

Our jobs required regular trips to Shreveport, a small city in the northwest corner of the state, and over the next two years, we fell into a rhythm of conversations about Calvin's life, building a friendship on the road. Eventually, we agreed that his journey as an inmate counsel would make a compelling book. Once we decided to document his story in earnest, he would come by my house in the afternoons, and we would turn on the voice recorder and get to work.

The more I learned through our interviews, the more I saw that Calvin being wrongfully convicted—grotesque and unimaginable as it was—was in some ways the most ordinary aspect of his experience. New Orleans had the highest rate of wrongful convictions in the nation, with nearly all the victims being Black men who, like Calvin, grew up poor. Countless others had been arrested and convicted under circumstances that rendered the justice system a farce. How Calvin was able to survive, and respond to, his circumstances made his story remarkable. "The most brilliant legal mind in Angola" is how Wilbert, who spent forty-four years in prison, described him in his memoir, *In the Place of Justice*. From Angola's law library, Calvin helped launch historic class-action lawsuits, shepherded legal cases to the US Supreme Court, and gave scores of people a path to freedom—all while fighting for his own chance to go home.

And now that he was free, there was still more he wanted to accomplish.

ON WEEKENDS, CALVIN DEDICATED HIS TIME TO REBUILDING A blighted double-shotgun house, a generous gift from Alvin. His vision was to occupy the longer side while providing a home on the shorter side for friends returning from prison.

The first time Alvin had taken Calvin to see the house on Feliciana Street, Calvin had balked. Abandoned for three decades and flooded by Hurricane Katrina, it was covered in vines, and an addition on the back had slumped onto the ground. Calvin didn't think it needed a renovation—it needed to be torn down. Over time, how-ever, Alvin convinced him that the original foundation was strong, and the historic character of the house, which was more than a hun-dred years old, was worth preserving. Like so much of the city, it was easily dismissed, but to underestimate it would be a mistake. So Cal-vin began gutting the house on weekends, writing letters to non-profit housing organizations to share his story and solicit help. One organization, Common Ground, responded with enthusiasm and began sending teams of volunteers to work on the house for free.

NOT LONG AFTER COMING HOME, CALVIN RODE ALVIN'S BICYCLE through the Seventh Ward, drawn to the site where David Yeager had been murdered. He felt compelled to see if it matched the image he'd carried in his mind for so many years.

He rode past Kristie Emberling's old house first, now dilapi-dated and abandoned; then he passed the neighboring house where three brothers had reported seeing the couple walk by on their way to the bus stop.

At the intersection of North Roman and Esplanade, Calvin hopped off his bike. The bus stop was still there, and the city bus still followed the same route to Tastee Donuts, the late-night diner farther up Esplanade Avenue where Kristie and David had planned to eat.

Calvin found the low brick wall where the couple had waited for the bus. Behind it stood a colonial-style home with arched windows, a wide front porch, and brick columns framing the entrance. Terra-cotta tiles lined the sloping roof, reminiscent of a Spanish mission. The house, likely grand in its day, now appeared run-down and de-void of life.

A wave of sadness rolled through Calvin as he ran his hand over the wall. David Yeager's death had shaped Kristie Emberling's life just as it had shaped his. For thirty years, Kristie had lived with the trauma of that night and the sense that it was up to her to secure justice for her boyfriend. She'd clung to Calvin's conviction the way he'd clung to Mount Hood. They'd both been forced to survive a tragedy of someone else's making.

CALVIN PRESSED FORWARD. WITHIN EIGHTEEN MONTHS OF HIS RElease, he secured a prestigious national fellowship to develop a program providing people in prison with updated legal materials and expanding access to the courts in post-conviction proceedings. He secured legal representation for some of the clients he'd left behind at Angola and cofounded a reentry organization in New Orleans for people returning home.

Some tasks, however, took more time. Reestablishing connections with his family was a complex endeavor, and one that Calvin couldn't rush.

He was grateful to have made it home in time to see Aunt Gail before she passed away. Her children said she had been holding on only for him, and she died within weeks of his release.

Once, when we were walking near the office, a woman with long braids and a youthful face beamed as she called out Calvin's name. It was clear they hadn't seen each other in a long while, so I walked ahead to give them privacy. When Calvin caught up with me, he explained that the woman was his younger half sister, Janie. He hadn't seen her since the summer in Pearl River when he was sixteen, though she had written to him during his incarceration. Janie was living the New Orleans life, he said, slipping his wallet back into his pocket. He was uncertain when, or even if, he would see her again.

Nearly a year of freedom passed before he visited Mamie. Calvin was apprehensive about spending time at her house, especially since the Clouet Street cousins had become a fixture in her life. She had spent her childhood longing for a family, and after his incarceration, he knew their cousins were all she had; still, he had no desire to be around them. More important, he wasn't sure how to bridge the gulf that existed between him and his sister after so many years apart.

He brought Mamie to his house after it was gutted, excited to show her his progress.

"One of two things is gonna happen," he assured her with a laugh. "Either this house is gonna stand, or it's gonna fall. And if it fall, know that I am under the rubble."

His sister looked, tight-lipped, at the stripped lath and plaster walls and the holes in the floor, and though he knew she was only worried for him, her hesitation stung. Prison had shown him the depths of his resolve, yet she had no way of knowing what he was capable of.

Then, in 2014, Mamie was diagnosed with breast cancer.

By the time she went to the doctor, the disease was already advanced. When she showed Calvin the edge of her breast, the skin was black as ebony.

The first round of chemotherapy worked well enough for her to return home for a few months, but then the cancer came back with a vengeance.

Calvin began visiting her each morning before work. He was the only one at the hospital who could maneuver her into a comfortable position, wedging a wooden chair between her back and the hospital bed. He sat by her from six until nine, then walked to the office, never mentioning to his coworkers that his sister was ill.

One morning toward the end, Calvin stood in the doorway to Mamie's room, watching the thin cotton blanket rise and fall with each shallow breath. She was fading away. He remembered what it was like to watch Weasel disappear, and his stomach churned with a familiar dread.

A few nights earlier, before the nurses upped her morphine, Mamie had cried out for their mother in her sleep. The anguished sound had cut Calvin in two.

Seeing her now, and thinking of the struggles she had endured, he felt grateful that, at least this time, he could be there for her.

Sensing him at the door, Mamie roused.

"All I seem to do these days is sleep," she said self-consciously, wiping the corner of her mouth.

Calvin took a seat in a red leather recliner by her bed, relieved to spend time with her while she was lucid. "What do they have planned for you today?"

"Nothing. They say there's no sense in putting me through more chemo."

After a pause, he said, "I paid your electric bill."

"I hate that I can't work." Mamie adjusted her position against the pillow. "I'm sick of sitting here doing nothing. I wish they'd let me go."

Calvin chuckled. They were still so alike, he and his sister. She let almost anyone depend on her, though she relied on no one.

After coming home, Calvin realized how much his family had shielded him from his sister's suffering through the years. Her first love and the father of her children had been addicted to drugs, and she'd mostly had to raise her kids alone. Her eldest boy was murdered, and her younger son was serving a ten-year sentence for robbery. It saddened Calvin that the Clouet Street curse had followed Mamie, too.

"How's the food?" he asked.

She scrunched up her nose. "God, what I wouldn't give for some real chicken."

"How about some grits?" He reached for the white paper bag he'd brought from the cafeteria downstairs.

Mamie pulled the lid off the Styrofoam container inside and dove in hungrily. When she was finished, remnants of the white paste crusted her top lip. Calvin wiped them away.

"Remember how I used to have to chase those boys away from you when we was kids?" he said.

Her eyes flashed with amusement as she took a sip of water through a straw.

"Even up at the penitentiary, they'd tell me, 'I remember your sister,'" he teased. "And they were smart enough to remember me, too."

At the mention of the prison, Mamie's expression changed.

"I worry about my boy in there," she said softly. "I don't want a funeral, Calvin, but there needs to be one so Dwayne'll be allowed to come and see me. Just make sure it's only you and the kids, all right?"

It was the first time she had spoken of her wishes.

Calvin nodded. "I'll take care of it."

"I can't pay for the service; I wish I had somethin' to help you with it."

"I got it, Mamie. I got everything. I promise."

She looked down at the floor, and he was reminded of the jail visit long ago when Aunt Gail had made her confess she was pregnant. She had avoided his gaze that day, too.

"Calvin, I'm sorry I wasn't there for you all those years," she murmured. "There wasn't a day you weren't on my mind."

He reached for her hand.

"After I lost Lil' Calvin, having both of you gone . . ." She fell silent.

Calvin listened to the hum of the fluorescent lights in the hallway.

Like Aunt Gail before her, Mamie had become the family matriarch—Mama Mamie to the neighborhood kids. He understood why she had worked so hard to build a family of her own, but it pained him that she'd never had anyone to share it with.

"I always wanted to get free so I could be out here to help you with everything," he said finally. "Whenever people ask me, 'You got any siblings?' I always say, 'I got a sister: Mamie.'"

"Me too, Calvin." Mamie met his eye. "You the only person I ever had in this world."

IN 2015, MY HUSBAND, BIDISH, AND I TRAVELED WITH CALVIN TO Oregon.

Calvin had first mentioned wanting to return to Mount Hood within weeks of coming home. But life had kept him busy, and he didn't seem to mind, assured that there was a season for everything.

We flew to Portland, rented a car, and followed a map to the hand-carved sign for Timber Lake Job Corps. Thirty years later, the campus was still in operation.

A current student, Matthew, gave us a tour of the grounds. We walked past the dormitories on a forested path, tracing one side of the small, unnamed lake. Matthew pointed out the workshop where Calvin would have once learned welding. The campus seemed virtually unchanged.

Calvin spotted a mother duck shepherding five fluffy chicks from one edge of the lake to the other.

"They told us if we ever broke one of their eggs, we'd be in big trouble." He laughed. "They didn't play when it came to those ducks."

Calvin turned to Matthew to ask about his future plans. He said he intended to continue his education at a nearby community college. "Me too," said Calvin happily, as though they might have been contemporaries. "I'm getting my bachelor's degree."

Back in the parking lot, we watched Matthew return up the hill with our visitor passes. Calvin paused at the car door, tucking his hands into his khakis. His oval glasses caught the sun as he surveyed the grounds a final time.

"You can't imagine what it was like for a boy from the 'hood to see this place. After all those years of dreaming about it, I can't tell you how it feels to see it again."

We set off back down the mountain, our bodies swaying with the curves in the road. Halfway down, Calvin opened his window.

"I can hear the river!"

We pulled over and he jumped out, chasing the sound. Bidish and I hurried to keep up.

Looking ahead, I saw nineteen-year-old Calvin's fearless form scaling the fallen trees and jagged rocks. After years believing, like Moses, he might die before seeing the promised land, it was as if something in him was splitting open.

He hopped up onto a large boulder at the river's edge and looked out over the Clackamas River, water roaring at his feet. This was the spot where he and the other boys had played their game, seeing who could stay underwater the longest in the river's frigid temperatures.

"We used to dangle wire in here," Calvin called over his shoulder. "Never caught a thing. I think it's kind of sad that I never learned how to fish. That's something fathers teach their sons."

Bidish and I stepped forward to find our own rocks, the three of us watching the current.

A hawk appeared above the tree line, its feathers an intricate weave of tans and browns. It hung still in the air, searching for prey, then swooped beneath the trees, out of sight.

Calvin knelt down and dipped his hands in the river, feeling the water move between his fingers. Standing back up, he wiped his hands dry on his pants before turning to us.

"When I caught sight of these mountains, I said, 'We haven't been living right.' I didn't know life until I knew this place. And then, it was all snatched away."

I noticed his smile falter, and it struck me that most of Calvin's joyful moments were accompanied by loss. One loss in particular couldn't have been far from his mind today. Mamie had only recently passed.

"I needed to do this," he said quietly. "I really did."

TWO DAYS AFTER HIS RETURN TO NEW ORLEANS FROM OREGON, Calvin and his friends celebrated the renovation of his house with a ribbon-cutting ceremony.

Later that week, he went to get coffee with Alvin.

"I go by the house nearly every day to stand on those hardwood floors and just take it in," he said.

"What you mean you 'go by it every day'?" Alvin jolted upright in his chair. "You ain't livin' in it?"

Realizing his confession, Calvin searched for an explanation. "I like it where I am at Common Ground. I got my own room downstairs with everything I need. And I like talking to the volunteers that come through there to work on houses. They tell me stories about places they're from and places they've been, and I tell 'em about Angola."

Alvin cocked his head to one side, then erupted in a belly laugh.

"We so messed up in the head, man," he said, still laughing. "I mean, really. We are *messed up*. You think you're fine, then somethin' happen an' you realize you as messed up as those crazy dudes we used to help in Camp J." Alvin's smile faded. "Once or twice since I came home, I'm talkin' about years after I got out, I'd be walking down the street and realize I got tears streaming down my face. I don't know why." He shook his head. "How crazy is that?"

Calvin let out a long breath. Everyone kept telling him how well he was doing since coming home, but even now, even with the house finished, anxiety followed him like a shadow. It was a relief to know that his best friend understood.

Calvin's new home was only blocks from where his mother had lived right before she died. After finally tracking down Tiny's obituary, he learned that she had, in fact, passed away from cancer. It brought him some closure to know that she hadn't abandoned him and Mamie, but it would take time for the truth to settle in his bones, if it ever did.

He developed an evening ritual of cycling past the empty lot where his grandmother Georgia Shriver's house once stood, as though he might find his mother there. One night, feeling an impulse to speak with Tiny, he sat on a slab of concrete from the old house and began talking. His words flowed with rare candor—about his work, his romantic relationships, and the task of learning to live on the outside again. He returned night after night, sometimes sharing about his day, other times sitting quietly, just enjoying the peace in her presence.

CALVIN CALLED ME SOON AFTER THE RIBBON CUTTING ON THE HOUSE. He had just visited his daughter and grandson and expressed gratitude that so many threads in his life were finally coming together.

Ayana, now a homeowner, was navigating life as a single mother. Her journey wasn't without complications, but her son remained her North Star, and she was determined to build a happy life for him.

Calvin couldn't say they had a typical father-daughter relationship, nor did he expect one after thirty years of separation. Ayana had no use for a father this late in life, but as long as she knew he was there for her, he was content to be her friend. He was glad he could be there for his grandson, too.

So far, Calvin had chosen to keep his dating relationships casual. Whenever he sensed a woman's desire for interdependence, he would take his leave, unwilling to relinquish any autonomy. Recently, however, he had met a woman he not only liked but admired—someone who valued her independence as much as he did. He was feeling optimistic that this connection would last.

Partway through our conversation, he said abruptly, "I can't stop thinking about our time at Mount Hood." Then there was silence, as if he was deciding how to explain something.

"When the Oregon police took me away, I thought I would come right back, but that's not what happened. Everything I was convinced would happen back then turned out to be totally wrong. So over time, it was like, maybe I'd been wrong about Oregon, too.

"See, when you're in hell for that long, shut away from the outside world, you start to imagine things. Guys rely on fantasies to survive. I started to think that maybe I couldn't trust my own memories. That I'd dreamed Oregon up to cope with my situation."

Calvin told me what he'd learned from Viktor Frankl, that when a man loses hope, he loses his hold on life itself.

"When you're in a situation like that, you have to tie your hope to something external," he explained. "Your family. Where you come from. Your future. For me, my hope was Mount Hood. That was the place I first felt free. I had experienced so much trauma when I was a kid, and then I finally escaped all that when I got out there. But once I was in prison, I started to think maybe Oregon was just my fantasy.

"When I saw that river, I knew I'd been right this whole time." His voice was filled with relief. "Everything was just the way I remembered it.

"Now, I am really free."

CALVIN HASN'T STOPPED ADVOCATING AGAINST INJUSTICE. SOON AFTER his release, he partnered with Louisiana lawyer Ben Cohen to challenge nonunanimous jury verdicts at the US Supreme Court. For over two decades as an inmate counsel, Calvin had argued that Louisiana's system of split jury verdicts was unconstitutional. Now free, he was well positioned to help identify cases for Cohen to bring to the nation's highest court. After twenty-two petitions were denied, their twenty-third succeeded. The Supreme Court declared in *Ramos v. Louisiana* that nonunanimous jury verdicts were indeed unconstitutional, stripping the two states that still relied on them—Louisiana and, coincidentally, Oregon—of the ability to rely on them any longer.

That same year, 2020, Calvin was accepted into law school. His first choice, Lewis & Clark School of Law in Portland, Oregon, was eager to offer him a place.

During his first semester, in a civil procedure class, his professor assigned a 1992 case about the conditions endured by people laboring in the fields at Angola prison. When the class gathered to discuss it, Calvin informed the professor—and the room of astonished faces—that he had served time at Angola and was one of the inmate counsel substitutes who brought that very lawsuit to the courts.

In 2021, Calvin was officially cleared of any involvement in the murder of David Yeager, whose death remains unsolved. Calvin's case was added to the National Registry of Exonerations, one of forty-six from Orleans Parish since 1993.

At age sixty, he graduated from law school.

Today, he lives in New Orleans, still working to ensure that people incarcerated in Louisiana's prisons and jails have meaningful access to the courts.

Acknowledgments

We wish to express our deep gratitude to the individuals we've had the honor to work with at the Louisiana State Penitentiary—some of whom remain incarcerated, some who have returned home, and some who are no longer with us. Your stories and experiences are not only woven throughout these pages but have profoundly shaped this book. A special thank-you to Alvin Abbott, Checo Yancey, Everett Offray, and Louis Gibson for your insights and contributions. We are also grateful to the past and present staff of *The Angolite*, including longtime editor in chief Wilbert Rideau. *The Angolite* has been an extraordinary resource for documenting, and often predicting, the story of mass incarceration in America, offering a prophetic view of what our society stands to lose when we throw away the keys.

Calvin wishes to acknowledge those who advocated for him over the years: Mrs. Dora Rabalais, for giving me the opportunity; Laurie

White, for stepping in when there was no one else to help and for believing in my innocence; and my legal team from Innocence Project New Orleans, without whom I might still not be free. To the many individuals who played a role in Calvin's release but could not be named in the story, we honor your immense contributions here: Richard Davis, Peter Levert, Rob McDuff, Tracy Pratt, Keely Sawyer, Neal Walker, and Shannon Wight.

We are enormously grateful to Ginny Smith Younce, our editor, who long believed in this story and helped us uncover its beating heart, as well as to Caroline Sydney for her keen insights and steady guidance. Working with such a wise and generous team has been a privilege—we have learned so much from you. Our thanks extend to everyone at Penguin Press and Penguin Random House who graciously lent their time and expertise, including Susan VanHecke, Randee Marullo, Yuki Hirose, Stephanie Ross, Liz Calamari, Melanie Koch, Matt Boyd, Danielle Plafsky, and Ximena Gonzalez. We are particularly indebted to Ann Godoff and Scott Moyers, whose vision and commitment have left a lasting impact on this project and on us personally.

To Anna Stein, our intrepid guide, who made this journey so rewarding—and fun—we still can't believe how lucky we were to land in your orbit. Thank you for your tremendous wisdom and dedication. Thank you as well to Karolina Sutton, Brooke Ehrlich, Julie Flanagan, Blythe Zadrozny, and the team at CAA for your support.

We deeply appreciate those who shared their expertise and guidance, especially David Groff, whose involvement marked a turning point in the life of the book, and to Michael Admirand, Lillie Eyrich, Rachel Shur, Joanie Williams, and Andy Young. Our thanks also go to those who shared the gifts of beauty and respite along the way,

Acknowledgments

including Upper House and the Hambidge Center for Creative Arts and Sciences.

To our family members, friends, and coworkers who offered feedback on our pages, covered for us in our absences, and cheered us on at the finish line—thank you for your wisdom, friendship, and encouragement. You have supported us in more ways than you know.

Finally, we wish to extend a special thank-you to Rose Vines, Bora Reed, Adam Haslett, and, above all, Bidish Sarma. Though words fall short, please know how profoundly grateful we are for all you've done.

Bibliography

BOOKS

Bergner, Daniel. *God of the Rodeo: The Quest for Redemption in Louisiana's An- gola Prison*. New York: Crown, 1998.

Carleton, Mark T. *Politics and Punishment: The History of the Louisiana State Penal System*. Baton Rouge: Louisiana State University Press, 1971.

Hillyer, Reiko. *A Wall Is Just a Wall: The Permeability of the Prison in the Twentieth-Century United States*. Durham, NC: Duke University Press, 2024.

Howard, Robert. *The Other Side of the Coin: The Spiritual Life of a Black Man*. Self-published, 2008.

Prejean, Helen. *Dead Man Walking: An Eyewitness Account of the Death Pen- alty in the United States*. New York: Vintage, 1993.

Rideau, Wilbert. *In the Place of Justice: A Story of Punishment and Deliver- ance*. New York: Knopf, 2010.

Stevenson, Bryan. *Just Mercy: A Story of Justice and Redemption*. New York: Spiegel & Grau, 2014.

Vogel, Brenda. *The Prison Library Primer: A Program for the Twenty-First Century.* Lanham, MD: Scarecrow, 2009.

Woodfox, Albert. *Solitary: Unbroken by Four Decades in Solitary Confinement: My Story of Transformation and Hope.* New York: Grove, 2019.

Woodward, Bob, and Scott Armstrong. *The Brethren: Inside the Supreme Court.* New York: Simon & Schuster, 1979.

ARTICLES

From *The Angolite*, the prison newsmagazine of Louisiana State Penitentiary:

"The Forgotten Men," May–June 1980.

"Life: No Rhyme, No Reason," September–October 1982.

"The Revolution: Taking On the Courts," July–August 1988.

"The Lonesome Valley," March–April 1990.

"Legal Spectrum: The Cage Decision," January–February 1991.

"The October Assault," November–December 1991.

"The Meaning of Life," June–July 1995.

"Legal Spectrum: The Great Writ," May–June 1996.

"The Replacements," November–December 2008.

Kovarsky, Lee. "Original Habeas Redux." *Virginia Law Review* 97, no. 1 (2011): 61.

Pelot-Hobbs, Lydia. "Organizing for Freedom: The Angola Special Civics Project, 1987–1992." PhD diss., University of New Orleans, 2011. University of New Orleans Theses and Dissertations, Paper 349.

Rech, Nathalie. "Black Women's Domestic Labor at Angola (Louisiana State Penitentiary) During Jim Crow." *International Labor and Working-Class History* 101 (2022): 44–63.

Saifee, Seema T. "Decarceration's Inside Partners." *Fordham Law Review* 91, no. 1 (2022): 53–126.

Segura, Liliana. "The Untold Story of Bill Clinton's Other Crime Bill." *The Intercept*, May 4, 2016.

Stevenson, Bryan A. "The Politics of Fear and Death: Successive Problems in Capital Federal Habeas Corpus Cases." *New York University Law Review* 77, no. 3 (2002): 699–705.

Uhrig, Emily G. "A Case for a Constitutional Right to Counsel in Habeas Corpus." *Hastings Law Journal* 60 (2009): 541–604.

Uhrig, Emily G. "The Sacrifice of Unarmed Prisoners to Gladiators: The Post-AEDPA Access-to-the-Courts Demand for a Constitutional Right to Counsel in Federal Habeas Corpus." *University of Pennsylvania Journal of Constitutional Law* 14 (2012): 1219.

PROJECTS, REPORTS, AND COURT FILINGS

American Civil Liberties Union. *Abandoned and Abused: Orleans Parish Prisoners in the Wake of Hurricane Katrina.* August 2006.

Armstrong, Andrea. *The Impact of 300 Years of Jail Conditions.* The Data Center, March 2018.

Chrastil, Nick. "The Section G Project" (four-part series). *The Lens,* 2020. thelensnola.org/the-section-g-project.

Duncan v. Cain, Warden, Petition for Supervisory Writs Concerning the Trial Court's Order Denying Mr. Duncan's Post Conviction Relief Application on the Basis of the Time Bar Contained in La. C. Cr. P. art. 930.8(1), No. 2008-K722, Fourth Circuit Court of Appeals, Orleans Parish, Louisiana, 2008.

In Re: Duncan v. Cain, Warden, Petitioner's Application for Post-Conviction Relief, Section G, Docket No. 290-908, Criminal District Court, Orleans Parish, Louisiana, 2004.

Kaplan, Carol G. *Federal Review of State Prisoner Petitions: Habeas Corpus.* US Department of Justice, Bureau of Justice Statistics, March 1984.

King, Nancy J., Fred Cheesman, and Brian Ostrom. "Habeas Litigation in the U.S. District Courts." Vanderbilt Public Law Research Paper No. 07-21, National Institute of Justice Online, 2007.

Louisiana Advisory Committee to the US Commission on Civil Rights. *A*

Study of Adult Corrections in Louisiana. Washington, DC: US Government Printing Office, 1976.

Ryan, Joanne, and Stephanie L. Perrault. *Angola: Plantation to Penitentiary.* New Orleans: US Army Corps of Engineers, 2007.

State of Louisiana v. Calvin Duncan a/k/a Calvin Jones, trial transcripts, Section G, Docket No. 290-908, Criminal District Court, Orleans Parish, Louisiana, January 28–29, 1985.

The Visiting Room Project. "Archive." Loyola University New Orleans, 2022. visitingroomproject.org.

Index